The Product Life Cycle and International Trade

Contributors

F. Michael Adler
William H. Gruber
Seev Hirsch
Dileep Mehta
Sotirios G. Mousouris
Robert B. Stobaugh
Jose R. de la Torre, Jr.
Yoshihiro Tsurumi
Raymond Vernon
Louis T. Wells, Jr.

The Product Life Cycle and International Trade

Edited by
LOUIS T. WELLS, JR.
Associate Professor of Business Administration
Harvard University

Division of Research
Graduate School of Business Administration
Harvard University
Boston · 1972

Library of Congress Catalog Card No. 78–184791
ISBN 0–87584–095–7

Printed in the United States of America

Preface

In recent years the theory of international trade has seen some dramatic innovations. The innovations have come largely as a result of what has appeared to be the inability of traditional theory to explain what has been observed in the real world. In most fields of intellectual endeavors, when basic hypotheses are challenged as not being adequate to explain observations, a number of rival hypotheses result. The new hypotheses are generally not so intellectually satisfying as the traditional wisdom. They tend to be "partial" explanations. A long period elapses before a generally acceptable all-encompassing model reappears. In the meantime rival hypotheses are put to the test of empirical observation. Some are laid to rest. Some are found to be useful. In international trade theory a similar series of events has transpired. The traditional wisdom, classical and neoclassical trade theory, was found by many to be inadequate to explain satisfactorily the actual flows of goods from one nation to another. The predictable result was the generation of alternative hypotheses to explain the real world phenomena. One set of these hypotheses, generally called a "product life cycle model," has been found by a number of researchers to be useful in explaining flows of trade. Some of the tests of this model have been published; others have not previously been available. My purpose in putting together this book has been twofold: (1) to encourage the authors of the unpublished studies to make their findings available to a wider audience, and (2) to bring together in one volume the results of some of the important research.

As a guide to the reader, the first paper provides a brief history of the development of the product life cycle trade models. It gives a summary of the findings of the empirical research, reviews the contributions of the major writers in the field, and relates the product life cycle theory to some of the other recent propositions offered to explain international trade in manufactured goods. Part I presents empirical studies of trade in particular industries. Part II presents country studies of trade, starting with advanced countries and moving to less developed countries.

I am grateful to the publishers of the articles that have appeared before for permission to reprint them here. I must also thank the authors of the articles that were written for this volume. They were patient with my harangues and deadlines. I also appreciate the contribution of the Division of Research of the Harvard Graduate School of Business Administration, which financed the assembly of this book. Final responsibility for the contents of the papers, of course, rests with the authors and the editor.

All the authors represented in this book, except those of the article for which he is a co-author, were formerly students of Professor Raymond Vernon. This fact makes clear the tremendous importance of his contribution to the development of the ideas that are presented in this collection of studies.

Soldiers Field   Louis T. Wells, Jr.
Boston, Massachusetts
December 1971

Table of Contents

International Trade:
The Product Life Cycle Approach

LOUIS T. WELLS, JR.

International Trade:
The Product Life Cycle Approach

Introduction

Classical and neoclassical theories of international trade have served the discipline of economics well. From a rigorous set of assumptions, economists have been able to derive logically answers to a whole series of questions: What kinds of goods will a country export and import? What would be the gains from a policy of free trade versus a policy of restrictions on trade? And so on. The rigor of the models has made them useful as pedagogical devices.[1] They have also been used many times as tools of analysis to lead to recommendations for government policy. However, the inability of traditional theory to describe actual trade patterns has led a number of economists to exercise considerable caution in using the models for policy recommendations for business or government. The reticence is well stated by Harrod:

> It does appear that, in the present phase of static theory, its exponents can no longer derive from it confident recommendations for helping humanity. The first fresh flush of zeal has departed.[2]

The questioning attitude toward traditional theory owes much of its existence to the important study of U.S. trade published by Leontief in 1953.[3] Tracing through the linking industries in the U.S. input-output table, Leontief demonstrated that United States export industries were more labor-intensive than the industries which would replace American imports. This finding clearly contradicted traditional wisdom. The factor proportions theory (generally called the "Heckscher-Ohlin" theory[4]) claims that a country will export those products the production of which makes most use

3

of its abundant factors; it will import products which require relatively more of its scarce factors of production. Since the United States was thought to be well endowed with capital and poorly endowed with labor, relative to other countries, it should, according to a simple two-factor version of the factor proportion theory, export goods whose production processes were more capital-intensive than those of its imports.

Leontief's findings set the stage for a debate which was predictably long and complex. His methodology was attacked, but subsequent work tended to confirm the inadequacy of an unmodified version of the simple Heckscher-Ohlin theory to explain international trade patterns.[5] Some economists attempted to retain essentially the neoclassical model with only slight changes in assumptions.[6] These attempts were also not completely successful. Minor changes were not sufficient to add significantly to the theory's ability to explain actual trade in manufactures; major changes were so drastic as to destroy the universality and the closed logic of the traditional theory. However, some success was obtained by adding natural resources to capital and labor as factors of production,[7] and by recalculating the capital used in the manufacture of a product by taking into account the capital embodied in skilled labor.

Some of these departures from the Heckscher-Ohlin factor proportions concept laid part of the foundation for the product life cycle models of international trade. Leontief himself, for example, explained the seemingly paradoxical results of his study by claiming that U.S. labor was more productive than foreign labor. Important to several later hypotheses to explain U.S. export patterns is the role of skilled labor in export industries.

Other elements of the foundation were laid by the attempts of economists to explain the persistent "dollar shortage" in the world immediately after World War II.[8] These authors turned to the lag in technological innovation as an important factor in explaining international trade patterns. Product life cycle proponents were later to incorporate many concepts of these authors into their models.

Although many of the assumptions of the product life cycle

model go back to the changes in the classical assumptions made by economists in response to Leontief's findings and the "dollar shortage" problem, the total "model" was not generated until researchers were willing to let disappear a great deal of the elegance of traditional economic theory. Much of the pioneering work was done at business schools, by people whose allegiance was to practical problem solving rather than to an academic discipline. Probably the first complete description, which differed only in small details from later versions, was offered by Vernon in 1966.[9] Businessmen had generally ignored the traditional wisdom of trade theory, since they found it of little help in solving the problems they found. Researchers in business schools were interested in developing more useful tools for policy formulation—for the firm or for governments. Although the resultant "product life cycle model" was inelegant, compared to traditional theory, it did turn out to be helpful in explaining certain trade flows in manufactured goods. And this was sufficient for the purposes of business research. Recently, some economists who are more in the mainstream of the discipline have begun to accept many of the elements of the product life cycle theory and have made some progress in putting the pieces back together into a more rigorous statement.[10] But the attempts thus far to put the model into the framework of traditional economic theory still reduce the richness of the less rigorous statements.

The Product Life Cycle Trade Model

The Underlying Assumptions

The product life cycle explanations of international trade are based on assumptions that are sufficiently different from those of traditional trade theory that one is compelled to outline some of the major assumptions before the model can be presented. While the traditional theory is based on free availability of information and stable production functions, the product life cycle models are based on assumptions that the flow of information across national borders is restricted and that products undergo predictable changes in their production and marketing characteristics over time. The product life cycle model is also based on the assumptions that the production process is characterized by economies of scale,[11] that it changes over time, and that tastes differ in different countries (i.e., each product does not account for a fixed proportion of expenditure for buyers at different income levels, given a set of international prices).

That information does not flow freely across national boundaries leads to three important conclusions: (1) innovation of new products and processes, it is argued, is more likely to occur near a market where there is a strong demand for them than in a country with little demand; (2) a businessman is more likely to supply risk capital for the production of the new product if demand is likely to exist in his home market than if he has to turn to a foreign market; and (3) a producer located close to a market has a lower cost in transferring market knowledge into product design changes than one located far from the market.

Economists have long been concerned with the nature of the process of innovation. Economic literature has carried a debate on whether innovation is influenced by factor proportions.[12] Under the classical assumptions, the answer is that innovation is not biased by relative factor scarcity, since innovation occurs as long as the return is positive. However, if innovative skill is viewed as a scarce resource to be allocated where return is highest, one might expect innovation to be influenced by factor endowments. A country which is well endowed with capital relative to labor might be more likely to innovate items or processes which conserve on labor by substituting capital than would other countries. Or, more generally, with limited flow of information across borders, a country would be more likely to innovate products and processes for which it has a relatively strong demand. If the United States is the highest income country and is relatively capital abundant, its innovators would be most likely to come up with products which appeal particularly to high income consumers or products and processes which save on expensive labor. One would, then, expect the United States frequently to be the first to innovate and to produce new products that satisfy needs of high income consumers and which are labor saving. On the other hand, other countries might be earlier with the development and production of products that are more suited to their needs.

The generation of a commercial product is an imperfectly understood, complicated process. However, a few characteristics of the stages in the development can be described with some confidence. Behind any new product lie some very basic scientific principles which, typically, were reasonably well understood long before the actual commercial product appeared.[13] For example, the principles upon which photography is based were discovered by Leonardo da Vinci some 400 years before the first commercially successful cameras were made. The industrial electric motor lagged behind Faraday's principles by some 40 years. Workable radios lagged behind the developments of Maxwell and Hertz by 20 or 30 years. It is important to note that no western nation seems to have a monopoly, or a significant lead, in the knowledge of these basic scientific principles. University contacts, scientific journals, academic meetings, and so on, generally assure that knowledge of basic scientific principles spreads to most of the industrialized nations long before commercially successful products are generated based on the new principles.[14]

Even principles based on secret defense research are usually well known long before the appearance of commercial products based on them. Daniel Bell claims that modern defense research produces little in the way of civilian products.[15] The claim may not be completely accurate, but it does illustrate that the lag between the learning of scientific principles and the development of commercial items is likely to be long.

The steps that follow the discovery of basic principles are very different. The role of the entrepreneur becomes critical in the development of a commercial product. Although the pure scientists may work in a corner of the world fairly isolated from the grubby business of demand and profits, there is considerable evidence that product innovators and developers do not. At some point in the chain leading from scientific principles to a commercial product, costs begin to mount. These costs are for developments which are no longer of interest to the pure scientist or to his benefactors who are trying to push back the frontiers of scientific knowledge. At this point, the entrepreneur steps in. Someone whose motivation is profit must provide the funds for product development.

When the entrepreneur enters, potential demand plays a critical role. The businessman turns to the market with which he is familiar to make a forecast of likely profits. If he sees little demand for a product, he is unlikely to support further development. Some recent empirical studies tend to confirm that demand plays a very important role in the development of new products.[16] The old saying "necessity is the mother of invention" may have a lot more truth than economists had previously admitted. This old wisdom plays an important role in the product life cycle model.

The set of assumptions from which the model gains the "product life cycle" part of its name arises from the work of a number of economists and researchers in the field of marketing.[17] They have found it useful to consider changes in demand and production processes which occur as a product ages.

For a period after a new product is introduced, standards for comparing performance of various versions do not exist.[18] Many variations of a product are available.[19] For example, the early automotive enthusiast was offered a choice of internal combustion, steam, or electric power plants, cars with three or four wheels, and a selection among an almost endless combination of other technical features. During this early period of a product's development, most buyers are unable to compare prices of different versions directly. The price elasticity of demand facing a single producer is not as great as it will be later when the buyer can be turned to a competitor's product which is clearly cheaper than that of another firm. As the consumers' desires become well known through exploration of alternative product forms, standardization begins to take place.[20] Frequently, performance measures appear. As the customer is better able to compare prices of products from different firms, the individual firm is faced with an increasingly elastic demand curve.

The frequent design changes which occur early in the life of a product lead to short production runs. These runs require a greater input of labor, relative to capital, than will be needed later when specialized machinery and techniques can be used for mass assembly of a more stable product line. In addition to being more labor intensive than later in the product's life, manufacture initially requires a greater input of skilled labor. The manufacturing process is not broken down into simple tasks to the extent that it will be later in the product's life. Also, special skills are needed early for constructing pilot models, engineering changes in design, and manufacturing tools and dies, many of which, due to design changes, will be discarded before they are worn out.

The relative inelasticity of demand facing a firm, the inelasticity of total demand which leads to a "creaming" price strategy in some product lines, and the shorter production runs result in costs and prices that are higher early in the cycle than they will be later. Stobaugh has demonstrated in a product life cycle framework this fall in prices for petrochemicals.[21]

Many of the proponents of the product life cycle concept assume further that customers who purchase the product early in its life will have higher incomes than those who will buy it as it matures. Several studies in the field of marketing have examined this assumption for a wide range of products. Marketing literature usually refers to the early purchasers of a new product as "innovators." Innovators are generally found to be younger, more educated, higher in income, and higher in social status than other members of the community. These findings are summarized by Kasarjian and Robertson.[22] According to one study, 90 of the 112 published studies of innovators which mentioned income found a positive relationship.[23] Seven found a negative relationship, three a conditional relationship, and twelve no relationship. Similar importance was found for education, literacy, and level of living, which are, no doubt, highly correlated with income. Another study also found a relationship in a number of countries between income and acceptance of innovation in agriculture.[24]

The data in a number of these studies are somewhat unconvincing for two reasons. The income levels of early purchasers of a product are, in several cases, compared with income levels of the community. If the new products are such that later buyers will also be higher than average income consumers, then the data show nothing about the innovators compared with the later purchasers. And there might well be such a bias in the new products studied. Secondly, it has been shown for a number of products that price tends to fall over the product life cycle. If one were to use time-series data to eliminate the problem of comparable groups—comparing innovators to later purchasers of the same product—one could not be sure what increase in purchase on the part of lower income groups was due to an innovator-follower phenomenon and what was due to price reductions. For the purpose of the trade model, this difference is unimportant. For the businessman concerned with pricing of products, it may be very valuable to know the separate effects of income and price.

The important elements of the product life cycle can be summarized in tabular form:

Cycle Phase[25]

	Early	*Growth*	*Mature*
Demand Structure	Low price elasticity for aggregate demand and for individual firm. Nature of demand not well understood by firm.	Growing price elasticity for firm. Price competition begins.	Basis of competition is price or product differentiation through marketing techniques.
Production	Short runs, rapidly changing techniques dependent on skilled labor. Low capital intensity.	Mass production methods.	Long runs with stable techniques. Labor skills unimportant. Capital intensive.
Industry Structure	Small number of firms.	Large number of firms, but many casualties and mergers.	Number of firms declining.

The Model

Using assumptions similar to those just discussed, a number of writers offer an explanation of trade patterns in manufactured goods. The description that follows is somewhat of a composite version.

Most authors begin by arguing that the United States is more likely than other countries to initiate production of certain kinds of items—those that appeal to high income consumers or are labor saving. Innovation, remember, is more likely to occur near a particularly large market for the product. Even if innovation does not occur first in a large market, the first commercial production is likely to occur there. Businessmen are likely to provide risk capital for products whose markets they know. They are more likely to be familiar with their own home market than with those in other countries. Thus, an American is more likely to make a favorable projection of profits for products suitable to the U.S. market than would a European, who would see a smaller home market and know little about, for example, the American market.[26]

Why does manufacture take place in the United States instead of abroad? The American entrepreneur is faced with little pressure to reduce costs by using cheaper foreign labor, since overall demand and the demand facing the individual firm are relatively price-inelastic. The businessman does, however, have a great deal of pressure to maintain quick communication with the market, whose needs are not well known. He decides to manufacture close to the market at the early stage of the product's life so that he can translate market information into rapid product changes, and so that problems which arise from product changes can be communicated quickly to maintenance and sales personnel. Hirsch, in his pioneering work on the product life cycle and international trade, examined the problem of producing an unstandardized product far from the market.[27] He found that marketing requirements were critical in determining why optical crystals were produced in the United States, close to the market rather than in Israel, where scientific personnel are relatively cheaper.

Most authors extend the argument of U.S. advantage beyond

high income and labor saving products to a claim that the United States will lead in a majority of new products. Two reasons are offered. One follows from the assumption that new products appeal more to higher income customers initially than they will later. Thus, new products which might later have a market elsewhere will face a better chance of initial success in the United States. Another reason is that the majority of new products are products which are developed for high income buyers. I have argued elsewhere that the "technological gap" between the United States and Europe is noticed not so much because Europe does not innovate new products, but because the United States innovates those products which become important in Europe as incomes grow.[28]

But what are the implications for international trade? For a period, American producers are likely to have a virtual monopoly on the manufacture of new products which are introduced there. Some foreigners demand the new products and U.S. exports begin. Or, in the case of products which are introduced elsewhere due to local demands, exports begin from that country. (In the argument which follows it will be assumed that the product was introduced in the United States.) A potential manufacturer in another country may face a technological barrier to entry. Some fixed costs will be associated with acquiring or developing the production skills which the initial manufacturers have acquired. In addition, if the foreigner faces an information barrier with regard to export markets and begins production based only on his home market, he will, for a time, have higher production costs than the American manufacturers who are producing for a larger home demand.

A number of researchers have examined the competitiveness of U.S. exports of new products. Gruber, Mehta, and Vernon showed the U.S. export strength in industries which are associated with a high research effort.[29] And these industries, they argued, are the ones with a high rate of new product development. Hirsch demonstrated for the electronics industry that the United States export advantage was in the growth sectors of the industry.[30] Stobaugh demonstrated similar results for petrochemicals, after adjusting for "balancing trade" (see later).[31] I showed that U.S. exports have grown more rapidly in consumer durables that had a high income elasticity of demand than in those which were less income-elastic.[32] Hufbauer found that the advanced nations specialized in the export of differentiated products, if differentiation can be measured by the coefficient of variation in unit export values at a given point in time.[33] Consistent with these findings were those of Houthakker and Magee that the manufactured exports of the United States are less price-elastic than the imported manufactures.[34]

As foreign incomes grow, as lower income consumers abroad begin to buy the older product, and as prices begin to fall, U.S. exports increase. However, at some point, a market abroad is large enough that manufacture begins there. Either a local entrepreneur sees that he can undersell imports if he manufactures locally, or an American firm invests to preclude a local from taking the market that the American has been supplying by exporting. The length of time until foreign production begins is dependent on the economies of scale, tariffs, transportation cost, the income elasticity of demand for the product, and the income level and size of the foreign market. The time is shorter where economies of scale are reached at low volumes, tariffs and transportation costs are high, income elasticity of demand is low, and the income level and size of the foreign market are large.[35] I showed the effects of economies of scale and transportation costs on U.S. exports of consumer durables;[36] Stobaugh demonstrated for petrochemicals the effects of market size, investment climate, and the strength of the chemical industry in the country in determining when manufacture of a product was begun in a particular market.[37]

In what might be called the second phase of the cycle, when production has begun in a foreign market, American exports to that market cease to grow as rapidly as before; they may decline. However, U.S. exports continue to go to markets where production has not begun.

In the third phase of the cycle, U.S. exports to nonproducing countries begin to be displaced by exports from other nations. Major markets overseas reach sufficient size that manufacturers do not suffer from high costs associated with small scale. The capital costs for such firms may be no more than for firms in the United States—in fact, the producing unit may be a subsidiary of an

American parent. Faced with lower labor costs, but the same transportation and tariff charges, these firms take away markets in third
countries that were previously supplied from the United States.
Adler showed that U.S. exports found a less price-elastic market
in the advanced countries than in the less developed ones.[38] This
finding is consistent with the product life cycle idea that the
advanced countries will provide a relatively large market for the
recent American innovations. By the time the markets of the less
developed countries are important, the American products will face
competition from European manufacturers.

The role of these "middle countries" in the product life cycle
has been studied by Tsurumi, Mousouris, and Hirsch, who looked
at the trade patterns of Japan, Greece, and Israel.[39] These countries typically export products that are in earlier stages of the
product life cycle to countries which are less developed and products which are later in the cycle to more advanced countries. In
the case of exports down the ladder of development, the advantage
of the middle countries lies in economies of scale and technology
which are associated with their higher incomes. In exporting up
the ladder, they are taking advantage of their cheaper labor.

In the fourth phase, foreign production in some countries reaches
sufficient scale that costs are low enough to overcome the transportation and tariff protection which the American manufacturer
has. The United States becomes a net importer of the product.

A further phase has been hypothesized in which the less developed countries become exporters of the mature products.[40] In early
articles on the product life cycle, the authors were hard pressed
to find illustrations. The recent influx of standardized textile products and electronic components from the less developed countries
into the United States indicates the increasing importance of this
phase.

Little systematic work has been done to date to examine the
exports of manufactures from less developed countries. The work
of Lary is an exception.[41] He found that the nonresource based
manufactured exports were intensive in their use of unskilled labor.
Although his model was essentially that of factor proportions, he
does qualify the theory somewhat by recognizing the problems of

foreign market penetration for certain goods. Another study of manufactured exports from less developed countries is the work of de la Torre.[42] He applied the product life cycle concept to the manufactured exports of Mexico, Colombia, and Nicaragua. His results showed that these less developed countries did tend to export products which were late in the product life cycle. Where marketing techniques played an important role, the exports usually involved some participation by a foreign firm. Where marketing techniques were not critical, local firms could export without affiliation with multinational enterprises from the advanced nations.

The effect on U.S. trade of the movement of efficient production facilities from the United States to less developed countries is shown in the schematic presentation of Figure 1.

**Figure 1. A Schematic Presentation of the U.S.
Trade Position in the Product Life Cycle**

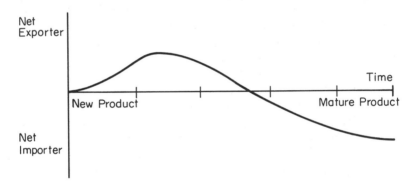

	Phase I	Phase II	Phase III	Phase IV	Phase V
	All production in U.S.	Production started in Europe	Europe exports to LDC's	Europe exports to U.S.	LDC's export to U.S.
	U.S. exports to many countries	U.S. exports mostly to LDC's	U.S. exports to LDC's displaced		

Modifications to the Basic Model

At least three refinements to the simple model have been introduced; they cover "pockets" of specialized production, "balancing" trade, and trade based on product differentiation by models.

I added a qualification to the model by examining products for which the income elasticity of demand is so high that no national market is large enough to support production at a level where scale economies lead to a significant fall in unit costs.[43] In this case, "pockets" of specialized production may arise near clusters of high income consumers in various countries. As incomes rise and lower income customers begin to buy the product, the item may move into the cycle hypothesized in the general model. Sailboats and high performance sports cars come immediately to mind. Both have been produced in small volumes, essentially by hand operation, in a number of countries. However, both products have recently been mass produced in the United States, as the market has become large enough to support assembly-line techniques. This addition to the model is based on the assumption that the producing firm faces a fairly flat cost curve over a range of low volume output. It does seem consistent with an intuitive evaluation of how goods are manufactured. A rapid drop in costs may occur as volume becomes large enough to support the introduction of special-purpose machines and processes, some of which may come in large, indivisible units. The spread of programmed machine tools and similar innovations may, however, change the nature of the cost curves for many items.

A second refinement was introduced by Stobaugh.[44] In his study of the applicability of the simple product life cycle theory to trade in petrochemicals, he noted that countries export "erratically" long after the simple model would predict that they would only import. Detailed study led to the conclusion that the trade was a balancing of capacity with demand. In the industry that he was studying, plant capacity comes in lumpy units. As a market grows, a new plant is occasionally installed which increases the total capacity above the demand in the country (the home demand is relatively price-inelastic). Exports would be offered at marginal cost until the capacity was needed for home demand. With oligopolistic multinational enterprise, exports and imports of the same product could be occurring at the same time. If there is a tacit agreement to hold market shares constant at home, one company might export its excess capacity while another company is importing from an overseas affiliate to make up for a temporary shortage of domestic capacity.

Another refinement helps to explain the fact that the United States exports and imports at the same time products of the same product category.[45] The explanation is based on the existence of different models of a product. The product life cycle model of international trade would predict that a country would have a comparative cost advantage in a version of a product for which home demand is strong relative to that in other countries. To test this hypothesis I compared prices of locally manufactured consumer durables for the United States, Germany, and Japan for different models. It was demonstrated that the United States has, relatively, the largest market for the "luxury" versions, Germany for the middle range, and Japan for "primitive" versions. Prices for various versions of the products of each country were compared. As hypothesized, the United States had a "comparative advantage" in the luxury versions, Germany in the middle range, and Japan in the simple models. Consistent with the refinement, America was found to be importing "primitive" versions of consumer durables while simultaneously exporting luxury versions.

This explanation of the existence simultaneously of exports and imports of the same product class helps in an understanding of some of the pricing strategies of firms that are engaged in international trade. A Canadian study of tractor prices in different countries showed a price pattern which was similar to that found in the study of consumer durables, with each country having comparatively lower prices in models most in demand in that market.[46] On the surface, this similarity can be of considerable surprise. The persistence of different price structures in different countries was easy to understand for consumer durables; international trade accounted for a small part of sales. Presumably the trade barriers

—tariff, freight, service facilities, etc.—were high enough that the domestic cost structure of each market remained as the essential determinant of prices. However, the persistence of such price differences in tractors was disturbing; the potential barriers of tariff and freight were demonstrated in the Canadian study to be low enough not to account for the price differences. The same multinational enterprises were selling the various models of tractors in the different markets. International trade was very important. If a multinational enterprise could reach economies of scale for a small tractor in the United Kingdom, one might expect the U.S. prices for the smaller tractor to reflect the British costs. The product life cycle model offers some help in understanding these price patterns.

A hypothesis which probably explains the phenomenon is that the multinational enterprises are acting as "discriminating oligopolists." They are pricing low where the price elasticity of demand facing the firm is high, and high where the price elasticity of demand is low. The question still remains as to why the firm faces price elasticities of demand which differ by model in the different countries. To explain this phenomenon, I return to economies of scale.

Assume for the moment that a new entrant to tractor production faces considerable barriers to entering the export market. The need for investment in advertising, sales facilities, service facilities, etc., makes this assumption plausible for such an industry. Assume further that economies of scale are important in tractor production (demonstrated in the Canadian report). A new entrant to the domestic market might find entry relatively easy for the line which has a large demand. He might need to capture only a small percentage of the home demand to have sufficiently long production runs. However, if he enters a line for which demand is relatively small, he may have to capture a very large percentage of demand to have sufficiently long runs. In fact, the total domestic market might be too small to reach low costs. Remember, though, that the multinational enterprises already produce for a large foreign demand. They are able to reach lower costs for such lines.

What does this mean for the pricing structure? The multinational enterprise faces the threat of new entrants in each market for the popular models in that country. It must price relatively low for that line. For less popular lines, it does not face as serious a threat from local competition. It can price as a "discriminating oligopolist" as long as another multinational enterprise does not try to underprice the firm. The concept of "keep out" price is applicable.[47]

Of course, the firm probably also faces an aggregate demand which differs in price elasticity by model. The less popular models may be less price-sensitive in total, since they may be used for special purposes for which the more popular models are not easily substitutable. Refrigerators provide an example. The small models coming into the United States have typically been used for camping equipment and vacation houses, where there is not room for large models. On the other hand, large American models have been popular in Europe in large houses of wealthy individuals who seemed to derive some status from their possession. Both classes of users probably provided a price-insensitive market.[48]

Thus, in an industry where the barriers to entry to international markets are high, where cooperation is practiced by the firms which are multinational, where economies of scale are important, and where arbitrage is difficult, one might expect to find prices in individual markets which are close to what the prices would have been without international trade. The reader who has tried to have an American dealer honor the warranty on a car bought outside the United States, not through an American dealer, may be aware of one of the techniques used to reduce arbitrage. Techniques include refusal of service for machines bought abroad and lack of parts stock for equipment which is not the "export model." Where these conditions are met, a country may be importing and exporting various models of a product, with a significant portion of the "gains from trade" accruing to the multinational firm.

A Comparison of the Product Life Cycle Model with Other Trade Theories

The Heckscher-Ohlin Model

The differences between the product life cycle trade model and traditional trade theory are manifold. A listing of the assumptions underlying the Heckscher-Ohlin model and the product life cycle concept reveals how basic these differences are[49] (see p. 20).

Heckscher-Ohlin	*Product Life Cycle*
1. Identical production functions in all countries for each commodity, or differences due only to a neutral efficiency differential.	1. Production function changes with time; early in the life of the product it is more labor- and skill-intensive than later.
2. Linear, homogeneous production functions with diminishing marginal productivity for each factor.	2. Increasing returns to scale.
3. Nonreversibility of factor intensities.	3. Reversibility not excluded. Some authors argue that reversal will not occur late in the cycle. Such authors assume essentially identical production functions in all countries in the late phase.
4. Identical consumption patterns in all countries at any given set of international prices, i.e., all commodities are consumed in the same proportions regardless of income level.	4. Consumption patterns differ by income levels. Some goods account for a higher proportion of consumption for countries at higher levels of income. Such products are called "high income" products.
5. Perfect markets, free trade, and no transportation costs.	5. The transmission of knowledge across international boundaries is assumed to have a cost. Inside a country, the transmission of knowledge between firm and market is assumed to have a cost. Trade barriers and transportation costs are allowed to exist.
6. International immobility of productive factors.	6. Capital is assumed by many authors to be at least partially mobile.
7. Qualitatively identical production factors.	7. No assumption.
8. Full employment, static.	8. No assumption on employment, dynamic.

In addition, the Heckscher-Ohlin theory is offered as an all-encompassing model. Product life cycle theories are offered only as explanations of trade in manufactures.

The predictions of actual trade patterns derived from the two approaches are, in some cases, diametrically opposed. The Heckscher-Ohlin approach leads to a prediction that U.S. exports will consist of goods which are more capital-intensive than U.S. imports. On the other hand, the product life cycle model predicts manufactured exports which are more labor-intensive than imports, since the United States generally exports more new products than other countries, and new products have more labor-intensive production processes than will the same products later in their development. Unless one is willing to postulate that products are becoming continuously more capital-intensive such that today's new products are more capital-intensive than yesterday's old products, it follows that U.S. exports will be more labor-intensive than imports. Thus, the product life cycle model does offer an explanation which is consistent with the findings of Leontief.

The Heckscher-Ohlin approach offers little help in predicting changes over time in trade patterns. The product life cycle model does give ways of describing the changes in patterns which have occurred and of predicting future patterns. A number of empirical tests reported in this book are dynamic.

On the other hand, the product life cycle model does not provide an explanation of trade in products other than "footloose" industrial goods. For trade in agricultural products, for example, one must usually return to a factor-proportions approach.[50]

Human Skills Models

Leontief himself explained his findings by suggesting that American labor was so much more productive than foreign labor that the United States is actually relatively well endowed with labor. This explanation was challenged by Kreinin who found that the higher cost of labor in America is not offset by its higher rate of productivity.[51]

The works of Kravis, Keesing, Waehrer, Kenen, and Yahr build a somewhat more complicated argument that "skill-endowments" are important determinants of trade patterns.[52] These studies are constructed on a framework which is similar to the neoclassical approach. Skilled labor is treated as a separate factor in a Heckscher-Ohlin type model, or the "embodied capital" in the training of skilled labor is taken as an addition to the capital embodied in the U.S. exports.

Kravis had demonstrated that the U.S. export industries were characteried by higher wages than import-competing industries.[53] Waehrer then showed that these wage differences reflected differences in skills.[54]

Keesing, in several studies, examines the skill levels in U.S. export industries.[55] He finds that the explanatory power of a factor endowment model is greatly improved if skilled labor is taken as a separate factor.

In the approach used by these authors, the model is essentially static. And the results are consistent with the predictions of the product life cycle model. For the United States, industries which are heavy users of skilled labor lead in exports. But we would expect these to be the industries generating the new products that the product life cycle model would predict to be candidates for export. Some of the authors offer suggestions for modification which would lead to dynamic models.[56] Keesing, for example, varies the Heckscher-Ohlin model slightly, allowing for some international factor movements. He further suggests the possibility of recognizing research and development as an additional factor in the model, with a lagged process of spread of innovation. The changes lead to something that is hardly distinguishable from the product life cycle model.

Demand Similarity Models

An important influence on the product life cycle model was the work of Linder.[57] He was instrumental in publicizing the idea that home market demand was an important determinant of what product lines would be manufactured in a country. Similar concepts have appeared in earlier writings, for example those of Frankel:

ts where foreign markets are large enough to provide opportu-
ties for large scale manufacture.

Recent extension of the work is providing a framework for view-
g the foreign investment decision. When additional factors such
size of the firm and elements of industry structure are intro-
uced, the model becomes a fairly powerful tool to explain patterns
f foreign investment.[67]

For government policy, the models are also already of value.
or example, they give useful clues as to what kinds of products
night be at the threshold of being exportable from less developed
countries. Policies aimed at standardized products with long production runs may be more likely to generate an increase in exports
han would policies that are directed simply at all labor-intensive
products.

For the advanced countries, the models offer food for thought
as to what the effects of the spread of multinational enterprises
might be. With the establishment of efficient information networks
among subsidiaries, the gap between introduction in the first market
and a second market might be diminishing. If this is happening,
the United States will have a shorter period of exports for new
products.

But the purpose of this article is not to explore all the policy
implications of the product life cycle. The few suggested above
indicate the potential of the models. And some of the articles in
this book delve deeper into the policy implications.

Useful as they are for policy purposes, the product life cycle
models are not yet fully satisfying for the theoretical economist.
Many parts of the models are not stated rigorously. The tests that
have been made are all very limited. They examine only parts of
the model and treat only a few products, a single industry, or the
trade of a single country. The attempts to add rigor and to place
the model into the language of neoclassical economics is well
under way. And indications are that many more empirical studies
will soon be available.[68] The model has proved to be useful.
No doubt many of its elements will remain in the next round of
refinements to theories that attempt to explain the flows of goods
in international trade.

[. . . a country] with a large internal market for low quality goods
is more likely to compete successfully in countries with a demand
for similar goods, than one whose internal markets are mainly in
goods of higher quality, because less adaptation of production
processes to export requirements will be needed in the former
case.[58]

Linder also emphasized the role of economies of scale in determining trade flows.

Perhaps Drèze's work should be included in the category of
demand similarity models.[59] He argues that Belgium's comparative
advantage lies in standardized, intermediate products. It is in these
products that Belgium has an internal demand sufficiently similar
to demand in other countries such that her manufacturers can
attain economies of scale.

The empirical validity of Linder's prediction that trade would
be most intense between countries with similar income levels and
least intense between countries with very different income levels
has not been settled.[60] However, the contribution has been very
important.

Technological Gap Models

The developers of the product life cycle theories owe still another debt to Kravis.[61] In the 1950s he, along with Balogh and
Williams, put forth a number of the ideas that were later to appear
in the product life cycle explanations.[62] These authors, and Posner,
Freeman, Douglass, and Hufbauer, are often credited with the
technological gap explanation of trade flows.

Kravis stressed the advantages to the innovating country which
came from the possession of the newest products as opposed to
advantages accruing from lower costs. The authors who stressed
a technological gap assumed that technology was not a free good
and that a time period would elapse before other countries obtained
the know-how. Kravis describes something similar to the product
life cycle, where the United States may eventually become an importer. Kravis himself offered only very weak statistical evidence
to support his hypothesis concerning the role of availability.

Posner built on these early works and introduced explicitly the concept of "imitation lag."[63] This concept was to be picked up later by Hufbauer and Freeman who tested these models statistically. Posner divided the lag into two components—the demand lag and the reaction lag. The demand lag arises from the fact that new foreign goods may not be regarded as perfect substitutes for domestic goods. The reaction lag is the time between the production of a new product abroad and the time when a potential producer in the local market views the foreigner as a likely competitor to whom he should react with local production. The difference between these two lags gives rise to the possibility of international trade. The earlier manufacturer might export the product to the country in which the demand lag is shorter than the reaction lag.

Freeman, who looked at the plastics industry in advanced countries, showed that location of production and per capita exports were a function not of factor costs but of technical progress in the country, measured by research expenditures, patents, and innovation.[64]

Hufbauer found that a country's share of world exports in synthetic materials could be explained by looking at "imitation lag" and market size.[65] Wage rates played little role. He placed countries in a "pecking order" by their imitation lag. New synthetics were found to be introduced rather consistently in countries at the top of the order and exported down the scale. As the technology spread, production moved down the scale, displacing exports of the top countries. These countries at the top, however, then developed new export products. Hufbauer was not very much concerned with why a country took a particular position on the "pecking order." It was clear, though, in his analysis that demand characteristics and market size had an important influence. Hufbauer admitted that he was unable to separate quantitatively the effects of the technological gap from scale economies. However, he did prove the usefulness of the technological lag concept in explaining trade patterns in at least one group of products, synthetic materials.

Douglass also used Kravis' "availability" concept and said that trade in the movie industry could be explained on the basis of product variation.[66] He argued that there was an "imitation lag"

similar to Hufbauer's technological gap. When a cou[...] a leader, perhaps due to a larger supply of techn[...] more research investment, or more favorable govern[...] and policies, that country would have a continuing[...] related innovations, because one innovation in a se[...] demand for improvements in related products. The[...] sessing the lead would, for a time, have an advantage[...] products containing new innovations. Douglass clain[...] United States gained an early lead in the movie indus[...] able to export successfully movies incorporating proc[...] tions, such as sound, color, and wide screen, which v[...] available in the rest of the world.

The empirical findings of the proponents of the te[...] gap models are consistent with the product life cycle[...] Missing from the gap models is an explanation as to v[...] countries will lead in specific technologies. The empiric[...] the gap proponents, however, provides important supp[...] usefulness of the product life cycle in explaining internat[...] in manufactures. The technological gap theories shou[...] looked on as models which compete with the product[...] concept; they are consistent with it.

Conclusion

The product life cycle and related trade models have[...] subject of a considerable number of empirical tests. Th[...] indicate that the models are useful for understanding tl[...] of manufactured goods across international borders.

For the businessman, the models already provide a fra[...] that can be of assistance in scanning for products that ar[...] candidates for export. Products that are relatively new, have[...] technological content, appeal to high income consumers,[...] labor saving are good prospects. Especially good candidat[...] those that are also characterized by increasing returns to scal[...] shipping costs, and low tariff rates abroad. On the other han[...] businessman can predict import competition for standardized[...]

[. . . a country] with a large internal market for low quality goods is more likely to compete successfully in countries with a demand for similar goods, than one whose internal markets are mainly in goods of higher quality, because less adaptation of production processes to export requirements will be needed in the former case.[58]

Linder also emphasized the role of economies of scale in determining trade flows.

Perhaps Drèze's work should be included in the category of demand similarity models.[59] He argues that Belgium's comparative advantage lies in standardized, intermediate products. It is in these products that Belgium has an internal demand sufficiently similar to demand in other countries such that her manufacturers can attain economies of scale.

The empirical validity of Linder's prediction that trade would be most intense between countries with similar income levels and least intense between countries with very different income levels has not been settled.[60] However, the contribution has been very important.

Technological Gap Models

The developers of the product life cycle theories owe still another debt to Kravis.[61] In the 1950s he, along with Balogh and Williams, put forth a number of the ideas that were later to appear in the product life cycle explanations.[62] These authors, and Posner, Freeman, Douglass, and Hufbauer, are often credited with the technological gap explanation of trade flows.

Kravis stressed the advantages to the innovating country which came from the possession of the newest products as opposed to advantages accruing from lower costs. The authors who stressed a technological gap assumed that technology was not a free good and that a time period would elapse before other countries obtained the know-how. Kravis describes something similar to the product life cycle, where the United States may eventually become an importer. Kravis himself offered only very weak statistical evidence to support his hypothesis concerning the role of availability.

Posner built on these early works and introduced explicitly the concept of "imitation lag."[63] This concept was to be picked up later by Hufbauer and Freeman who tested these models statistically. Posner divided the lag into two components—the demand lag and the reaction lag. The demand lag arises from the fact that new foreign goods may not be regarded as perfect substitutes for domestic goods. The reaction lag is the time between the production of a new product abroad and the time when a potential producer in the local market views the foreigner as a likely competitor to whom he should react with local production. The difference between these two lags gives rise to the possibility of international trade. The earlier manufacturer might export the product to the country in which the demand lag is shorter than the reaction lag.

Freeman, who looked at the plastics industry in advanced countries, showed that location of production and per capita exports were a function not of factor costs but of technical progress in the country, measured by research expenditures, patents, and innovation.[64]

Hufbauer found that a country's share of world exports in synthetic materials could be explained by looking at "imitation lag" and market size.[65] Wage rates played little role. He placed countries in a "pecking order" by their imitation lag. New synthetics were found to be introduced rather consistently in countries at the top of the order and exported down the scale. As the technology spread, production moved down the scale, displacing exports of the top countries. These countries at the top, however, then developed new export products. Hufbauer was not very much concerned with why a country took a particular position on the "pecking order." It was clear, though, in his analysis that demand characteristics and market size had an important influence. Hufbauer admitted that he was unable to separate quantitatively the effects of the technological gap from scale economies. However, he did prove the usefulness of the technological lag concept in explaining trade patterns in at least one group of products, synthetic materials.

Douglass also used Kravis' "availability" concept and said that trade in the movie industry could be explained on the basis of product variation.[66] He argued that there was an "imitation lag" similar to Hufbauer's technological gap. When a country was once a leader, perhaps due to a larger supply of technological skills, more research investment, or more favorable government attitudes and policies, that country would have a continuing advantage in related innovations, because one innovation in a sector creates a demand for improvements in related products. The country possessing the lead would, for a time, have an advantage in exporting products containing new innovations. Douglass claimed that the United States gained an early lead in the movie industry and was able to export successfully movies incorporating product innovations, such as sound, color, and wide screen, which were not yet available in the rest of the world.

The empirical findings of the proponents of the technological gap models are consistent with the product life cycle approach. Missing from the gap models is an explanation as to why certain countries will lead in specific technologies. The empirical work of the gap proponents, however, provides important support for the usefulness of the product life cycle in explaining international trade in manufactures. The technological gap theories should not be looked on as models which compete with the product life cycle concept; they are consistent with it.

Conclusion

The product life cycle and related trade models have been the subject of a considerable number of empirical tests. The results indicate that the models are useful for understanding the flows of manufactured goods across international borders.

For the businessman, the models already provide a framework that can be of assistance in scanning for products that are likely candidates for export. Products that are relatively new, have a high technological content, appeal to high income consumers, or are labor saving are good prospects. Especially good candidates are those that are also characterized by increasing returns to scale, low shipping costs, and low tariff rates abroad. On the other hand, the businessman can predict import competition for standardized products where foreign markets are large enough to provide opportunities for large scale manufacture.

Recent extension of the work is providing a framework for viewing the foreign investment decision. When additional factors such as size of the firm and elements of industry structure are introduced, the model becomes a fairly powerful tool to explain patterns of foreign investment.[67]

For government policy, the models are also already of value. For example, they give useful clues as to what kinds of products might be at the threshold of being exportable from less developed countries. Policies aimed at standardized products with long production runs may be more likely to generate an increase in exports than would policies that are directed simply at all labor-intensive products.

For the advanced countries, the models offer food for thought as to what the effects of the spread of multinational enterprises might be. With the establishment of efficient information networks among subsidiaries, the gap between introduction in the first market and a second market might be diminishing. If this is happening, the United States will have a shorter period of exports for new products.

But the purpose of this article is not to explore all the policy implications of the product life cycle. The few suggested above indicate the potential of the models. And some of the articles in this book delve deeper into the policy implications.

Useful as they are for policy purposes, the product life cycle models are not yet fully satisfying for the theoretical economist. Many parts of the models are not stated rigorously. The tests that have been made are all very limited. They examine only parts of the model and treat only a few products, a single industry, or the trade of a single country. The attempts to add rigor and to place the model into the language of neoclassical economics is well under way. And indications are that many more empirical studies will soon be available.[68] The model has proved to be useful. No doubt many of its elements will remain in the next round of refinements to theories that attempt to explain the flows of goods in international trade.

FOOTNOTES

1 For summaries of theories, see Gottfried Haberler, *A Survey of International Trade Theory* (Princeton: Princeton University, July 1961), International Finance Section, Revised Edition; John Chipman, "A Survey of the Theory of International Trade," *Econometrica*, Vol. 33, July and October 1965, Parts 1 and 2; Jagdish Bhagwati, "The Pure Theory of International Trade," *The Economic Journal*, Vol. 74, March 1964, pp. 1–84.

2 Roy Harrod (ed.), *International Trade Theory in a Developing World* (New York: St. Martin's Press, Inc., 1963), pp. 1–30.

3 Wassily Leontief, "Domestic Production and Foreign Trade: The American Capital Position Re-examined," *Proceedings of the American Philosophical Society*, Vol. 97, September 1953, pp. 332–349.

4 Although Heckscher and Ohlin proposed much more complex explanations for trade, the term "Heckscher-Ohlin" has come to be applied to a factor proportions model which considers only a small number of factors.

5 Leontief's work inspired a number of similar tests of trade patterns in other countries. Among these were:
  R. Bharadwaj, "Factors Proportions and the Structure of 'Indo-U.S. Trade," *Indian Economic Journal*, Vol. 10, October 1962, pp. 105–106; K. W. Roskamp, "Factor Proportions and Foreign Trade: The Case of West Germany," *Weltwertschaftliches Archiv*, Vol. 91, 1963, pp. 319–326; Masahiro Tatemoto and Chinichi Ichimura, "Factor Proportions and Foreign Trade: The Case of Japan," *Review of Economics and Statistics*, Vol. 41, November 1959, pp. 442–446; and Donald F. Wahl, "Capital and Labour Requirements for Canada's Foreign Trade," *Canadian Journal of Economic and Political Science*, Vol. 27, August 1961, pp. 349–358.
  Leontief redid his calculations using a different base year: see Wassily Leontief, "Factor Proportions and the Structure of American Trade: Further Theoretical and Empirical Analysis," *Review of Economics and Statistics*, Vol. 38, November 1956, pp. 386–407.

6 W. Max Corden, *Recent Developments in the Theory of International Trade* (Princeton: Princeton University, March 1965), International Finance Section, p. 28; Bhagwati, *op. cit.*, and Harrod, *op. cit.*, summarize this literature.

7 M. A. Diab, *The United States Capital Position and the Structure of Its Foreign Trade* (Amsterdam: North Holland, 1956); J. Vanek, *The Nat-*

ural Resource Content of United States Foreign Trade, 1870–1955 (Cambridge: The MIT Press, 1963); S. Naya, "Natural Resources, Factor Mix, and Factor Reversal in International Trade," *American Economic Review*, Vol. 57, May 1967, pp. 561–570. See also L. A. Weiser, "Changing Factor Requirements of United States Foreign Trade," *Review of Economics and Statistics*, Vol. 50, August 1968, pp. 356–360.

8 See Thomas Balogh, *The Dollar Crisis: Cause and Cure* (London: Oxford University Press, 1949), and John H. Williams, *Trade Not Aid: A Program for World Stability* (Cambridge: Harvard University Press, 1953).

9 Raymond Vernon, "International Investment and International Trade in the Product Cycle," *Quarterly Journal of Economics*, Vol. 80, May 1966, pp. 190–207. Many elements of the model appeared earlier in Raymond Vernon, "The Trade Expansion Act in Perspective," *Emerging Concepts in Marketing*, Proceedings of the American Marketing Association, December 1962, pp. 384–389.

10 A significant work in this regard is Harry Johnson, *Comparative Cost and Commercial Policy Theory for a Developing World Economy* (Stockholm: Almqvist & Wiksell, 1968). Many elements of the model are also in Richard Caves, "Foreign Investment, Trade and Industrial Growth," The Royer Lectures, University of California, Berkeley, December 1–2, 1969. See also Herbert G. Grubel, "The Theory of Intra-Industry Trade," in I. A. McDougall, et al. (ed.), *Studies in International Economics* (Amsterdam: North Holland, 1970), with a comment by W. Max Corden.

11 The importance of scale is evident in Hollis Chenery, "Patterns of Industrial Growth," *American Economic Review*, Vol. 55, September 1960, pp. 624–654, and in John Haldi and David Whitcomb, "Economies of Scale in Industrial Plants," *Journal of Political Economy*, Vol. 75, August 1967, pp. 373–385.

12 Much of the argument is summarized in Charles Kennedy, "Induced Bias in Innovation and the Theory of Distribution," *The Economic Journal*, Vol. 74, September 1964, pp. 541–547.

13 The distinction between science and the application of science is sharpened in Vannevar Bush, *Modern Arms and Free Men* (Cambridge: The MIT Press, 1968).

14 See also Herbert G. Grubel and Anthony D. Scott, "The International Flow of Human Capital," *American Economic Review*, Vol. 56, May 1966, pp. 268–274.

15 Daniel Bell, "The Post-Industrial Society," in Eli Ginzberg, *Technology and Social Change* (New York: Columbia University Press, 1964), p. 53.

16 A vast body of literature is developing around the causes of innovation. For a few sources, see Jacob Schmookler, *Invention and Economic Growth* (Cambridge: Harvard University Press, 1966), especially Chapters VI, VII, and XII; James R. Bright, *Research Development and*

Technological Innovation (Homewood: Richard D. Irwin, Inc., 1964) p. 61 ("Unlike fundamental scientific research, design is motivated by need rather than by curiosity"); Staffan Burenstam Linder, *An Essay on Trade and Transformation* (Stockholm: Almqvist & Wiksell, 1961), pp. 88–89; Levi Griliches and Jacob Schmookler, "Inventing and Maximizing," *American Economic Review*, Vol. 53, September 1963, pp. 725–729; Jacob Schmookler, "Economic Sources of Inventive Activity," *Journal of Economic History*, Vol. 22, March 1962, pp. 1–20; Charles F. Carter and Bruce R. Williams, *Industry and Technical Progress: Factors Governing the Speed of Application of Science* (London: Oxford University Press, 1957); J. Langrish, *Innovation in Industry: Some Results of the Queen's Award Study*, Research Report No. 15, Department of Liberal Studies in Science (Manchester: University of Manchester, September 1969); S. Meyers, *Technology Transfer and Industrial Innovation* (Washington: National Planning Association, 1967); Wolfgang P. Strassman, *Technological Change and Economic Development* (Ithaca: Cornell University Press, 1968); and for a summary of the earlier literature see Richard R. Nelson's "Introduction" to Universities—National Bureau Committee for Economic Research, *The Rate and Directions of Inventive Activity: Economic and Social Factors* (Princeton: Princeton University Press, 1962).

17 Some of the elements of the description appear in Simon Kuznets, "Retardation of Industrial Growth," *Journal of Economic and Business History*, Vol. 1, August 1929, pp. 534–560, reprinted in Simon Kuznets, *Economic Change* (New York: W. W. Norton and Company, 1953). Most of the concepts appeared in Joel Dean, "Pricing Policies for New Products," *Harvard Business Review*, Vol. 28, November 1950, pp. 45–53, and then in Theodore Levitt, "Exploit the Product Life Cycle," *Harvard Business Review*, Vol. 43, November 1965, pp. 81–94. See also Donald K. Clifford, Jr., "Managing the Product Life-Cycle," *European Business*, No. 22, July 1969, pp. 7–15; and William E. Cox, Jr., "Product Life Cycles as Marketing Models," *Journal of Business*, Vol. 40, October 1967, pp. 373–384. For a summary of empirical tests of the concept, the reader is referred to Rolando Polli and Victor Cook, "Validity of the Product Life Cycle," *The Journal of Business*, Vol. 42, October 1969, pp. 385–400.

18 See Polli and Cook, *op. cit.*, for approaches to the problem of defining a new product.

19 See, for example, Dean, *op. cit.*

20 For one description of this search for information on product design see R. A. Jenner, "An Information Version of Pure Competition," *The Economic Journal*, Vol. 76, December 1966, pp. 786–805. For other approaches, see Neil W. Chamberlain, *A General Theory of Economic Process* (New York: Harper, 1955) and Edward H. Chamberlain, "The

Product as an Economic Variable," *Quarterly Journal of Economics,* Vol. 67, February 1953, pp. 1–29.

21 Robert B. Stobaugh, "The Product Life Cycle, U.S. Exports and International Investment," unpublished doctoral dissertation, Harvard Business School, 1968, and Robert B. Stobaugh, "Systematic Biases in the Terms of Trade," *Review of Economics and Statistics,* Vol. 49, November 1967, pp. 617–619. He adds lowered costs due to "learning" as a contributing factor to the price decline. Some studies disagree with this proposition, but they are generally studies which treat new brands as new products. In these cases, prices do not necessarily fall as the brand ages.

22 Harold H. Karsarjian and Thomas Robertson, *Perspectives in Consumer Behavior* (New York: Scott, Foresman & Company, 1968).

23 James F. Engel, David T. Kollat, and Roger D. Blackwell, *Consumer Behavior* (New York: Holt, Rinehart and Winston, 1968), p. 563.

24 See E. M. Rogers, *Diffusion of Innovation* (New York: The Free Press of Glencoe, 1962) which also contains a useful bibliography of other studies on innovators.

25 This table draws heavily on Seev Hirsch, "The United States Electronics Industry in International Trade," reprinted in this book.

26 The argument, based on the assumption that information does not flow freely across national borders, is similar to the concept of "horizons" for decision making used by Charles P. Kindleberger, in *Foreign Trade and the National Economy* (New Haven: Yale University Press, 1962). Similar ideas emerge in Richard M. Cyert and James G. March, *Behavioral Theory of the Firm* (Englewood Cliffs: Prentice-Hall, 1963), and in the literature on "scanning," such as Francis J. Aguilar, *Scanning the Business Environment* (New York: The Macmillan Company, 1967). The results of experimental psychologists show that people tend to project less favorable results than would be "rational" when the information for projection is scanty. These findings are consistent with this argument.

27 Seev Hirsch, *Location of Industry and International Competitiveness* (Oxford: The Clarendon Press, 1967), originally a doctoral dissertation, Harvard Business School, 1965. See Seev Hirsch, "Technological Factors in the Composition and Direction of Israel's Industrial Exports," in Raymond Vernon (ed.), *The Technology Factor in International Trade* (New York: Columbia University Press, 1970), and Hirsch, "The United States Electronics Industry in International Trade."

28 Louis T. Wells, Jr., "Die Technologische Lücke und der Markt," *Europa Archiv,* No. 7, April 10, 1968.

29 William H. Gruber, Dileep Mehta, and Raymond Vernon, "The R&D Factor in International Trade and International Investment of United States Industries," reprinted in this book. See also William H. Gruber

and Raymond Vernon, "The Technology Factor in a World Matrix," in Vernon, *The Technology Factor in International Trade*, pp. 233–272.

30 Hirsch, "The United States Electronics Industry in International Trade."

31 Robert B. Stobaugh, "The Neotechnology Account of International Trade: The Case of Petrochemicals," included in this book.

32 Louis T. Wells, Jr., "Test of a Product Cycle Model of International Trade," reprinted in this book.

33 G. C. Hufbauer, "The Impact of National Characteristics and Technology on the Commodity Composition of Trade in Manufactured Goods," in Vernon, *The Technology Factor in International Trade*, pp. 145–231.

34 Hendrik S. Houthakker and Stephen P. Magee, "Income and Price Elasticities in World Trade," *Review of Economics and Statistics*, Vol. 51, May 1969, pp. 111–125.

35 For an indication that the time lag might be decreasing for Europe, see John H. Dunning, "European and U.S. Trade Patterns, U.S. Foreign Investment and the Technological Gap," International Economic Association Conference, University of Western Ontario, Toronto, August/September 1969.

36 Wells, "Test of a Product Cycle Model of International Trade."

37 Stobaugh, "The Product Life Cycle, U.S. Exports and International Investment."

38 F. Michael Adler, "The Relationship Between the Income and Price Elasticities of Demand for United States Exports," reprinted in this book.

39 Sotirios Mousouris, "Manufactured Products and Export Markets: Dichotomy of Markets for Greek Manufactures," included in this book. Yoshihiro Tsurumi, "R&D Factors and Exports of Manufactured Goods of Japan," included in this book. Hirsch, "Technological Factors in the Composition and Direction of Israel's Industrial Exports."

40 For a use of the product life cycle model to provide a description of the characteristics of products that would be suitable candidates for export from the less developed countries, see Raymond Vernon, "Problems and Prospects in the Export of Manufactured Goods, from the Less Developed Countries," U.N. Conference on Trade and Development, Geneva, March–June, 1964; Donald R. Sherk develops some of these ideas in "The New International Trade Models and Their Relevance for Developing Asia," *Malayan Economic Review*, Vol. 14, October, 1969, pp. 1–17.

41 Hal B. Lary, *Imports of Manufactures from Less Developed Countries* (New York: National Bureau of Economic Research, Columbia University Press, 1968).

42 Jose R. de la Torre, "Marketing Factors in Manufactured Exports from Developing Countries," included in this book.

43 Louis T. Wells, Jr., "Product Innovation and Directions of International Trade," unpublished doctoral dissertation, Harvard Business School, 1966, and "A Product Life Cycle for International Trade?" *Journal of Marketing*, Vol. 32, June 1968, pp. 1–6.

44 Stobaugh, "The Neotechnology Account of International Trade: The Case of Petrochemicals."

45 Wells, "Test of a Product Cycle Model of International Trade," and Mousouris, "Manufactured Products and Export Markets: Dichotomy of Markets for Greek Manufactures." For similar ideas, see Grubel, "The Theory of Intra-Industry Trade," Jacques Drèze, "Les exportations intra-C.E.E. en 1958 et la position belge," *Recherches Économiques de Louvain*, XXVIIᵉ année, 1961, extrait du N° 8, "Quelques réflexions sereines sur l'adaptation de l'Industrie Belge au Marché Commun Européen," *Comptes Rendus des Travaux de la Société Royale d'Economie Politique de Belgique*, N° 275, December 1960, and Linder, *op. cit.*

46 Royal Commission on Farm Machinery, *Special Report on Price of Tractors and Combines in Canada and Other Countries*, Toronto, December 1969.

47 See, for example, Donald Dewey, *The Theory of Imperfect Competition: A Radical Reconstruction* (New York: Columbia University Press, 1969).

48 See Wells, "Product Innovation and Directions of International Trade."

49 This list of assumptions for the Heckscher-Ohlin hypothesis comes primarily from Robert E. Baldwin, "Determinants of the Commodity Structure of U.S. Trade," Workshop of Economic Development and International Economics, Social Systems Research Institute, University of Wisconsin, Madison, October 1962, p. 2. Some changes have been made to make the list comparable to the assumptions of the product life cycle model. Economists have, of course, relaxed many of the assumptions of the Heckscher-Ohlin model to obtain variants of neoclassical theory. Few of the resultant models have been tested empirically. Ronald Findlay's "Factor Proportions and Comparative Advantage in the Long Run," *Journal of Political Economy*, Vol. 78, January/February 1970, pp. 27–34, provides an interesting example of a dynamic model and references to other attempts to change the static nature of the pure Heckscher-Ohlin approach.

50 For a study of trade in a number of raw materials which introduce concepts outside the Heckscher-Ohlin approach, see John E. Tilton, "Choice of Trading Partners: An Analysis of International Trade in Aluminum, Bauxite, Copper, Lead, Manganese, Tin, and Zinc," *Yale Economic Essays*, Vol. 6, Fall, 1966, pp. 419–474.

51 Mordechai Kreinin, "Comparative Labor Effectiveness and the Leontief Scarce-Factor Paradox," *American Economic Review*, Vol. 55, March 1965, pp. 131–139.

52 Donald B. Keesing, Peter B. Kenen, Helen Waehrer, and Merle I. Yahr,

contributors to Peter B. Kenen and Roger Lawrence, *The Open Economy: Essays on International Trade and Finance* (New York: Columbia University Press, 1968).

53 Irving Kravis, "Wages and Foreign Trade," *Review of Economics and Statistics*, Vol. 34, February 1956, pp. 14–30.

54 Helen Waehrer, "Wage Rates, Labor Skills, and United States Foreign Trade," in Kenen and Lawrence, *op. cit.*, pp. 19–39.

55 See, for example, Donald B. Keesing, "Labor Skills and the Structure of Trade in Manufactures," in Kenen and Lawrence, *op. cit.*, pp. 3–18, and "Labor Skills and International Trade: Evaluating Many Trade Flows with a Single Measuring Device," *Review of Economics and Statistics*, Vol. 47, August 1965, pp. 287–294.

56 See footnote by Keesing in Kenen and Lawrence, *op. cit.*, p. 7.

57 Linder, *op. cit.*

58 H. Frankel, "Industrialization of Agricultural Countries and the Possibilities of a New International Division of Labour," *Economic Journal*, Vol. 53, June–September 1943, pp. 188–201.

59 Drèze, *op. cit.*

60 See, for example, Gruber and Vernon, "The Technology Factor in a World Trade Matrix," whose findings tend not to support the Linder hypothesis. For a contrary finding, see Seev Hirsch, "Trade and Per Capita Income Differentials: An Empirical Test of Burenstam Linder's Theory," mimeograph, 1969.

61 Irving B. Kravis, "Availability and Other Influences on the Commodity Composition of Trade," *Journal of Political Economy*, Vol. 64, April 1956, pp. 143–155.

62 Williams, *Trade Not Aid: A Program for World Stability.*

63 Michael Posner, "International Trade and Technical Change," *Oxford Economic Papers*, Vol. 13, October 1961, pp. 323–341.

64 Christopher Freeman, "The Plastics Industry: A Comparative Study of Research and Innovation," *National Institute Economic Review*, Vol. 16, November 1963, pp. 22–62.

65 Gary Hufbauer, *Synthetic Materials and the Theory of International Trade* (Cambridge: Harvard University Press, 1966).

66 Gordon K. Douglass, "Product Variation and International Trade in Motion Pictures," unpublished doctoral dissertation, Massachusetts Institute of Technology, 1963. For a study of computers in a similar framework, see Alvin J. Harman, "Innovations, Technology and the Pure Theory of International Trade," unpublished doctoral dissertation, Massachusetts Institute of Technology, September 1968.

67 See Raymond Vernon, *Sovereignty at Bay: The Multinational Spread of U.S. Enterprises* (New York, Basic Books, 1971).

68 The correspondence that I have had with others indicates a wide interest in empirical tests of various aspects of the model.

PART I

INDUSTRY STUDIES

The United States Electronics Industry in International Trade

SEEV HIRSCH

(Reprinted by permission of *National Institute Economic Review*, No. 34, November 1965, and the author)

Seev Hirsch

Seev Hirsch is Associate Professor and Dean of the Leon Recanati Graduate School of Business Administration, Tel-Aviv University. He joined the school in 1965 after spending five years in the United States. He is a graduate of the Hebrew University, Jerusalem, and holds M.B.A. and D.B.A. degrees from Harvard University.

His publications include The Export Performance of Six Manufacturing Industries: A Comparative Study of Denmark, Holland and Israel *(New York, Praeger Special Studies, 1971), and* Location of Industry and International Competitiveness *(Oxford: The Clarendon Press, 1967).*

The United States Electronics Industry in International Trade

The Product Cycle View of International Competitiveness

This note* analyzes the recent experience of the United States electronics industry in terms of a "product cycle" view of international competitiveness. This view starts from the observed fact that, as a product passes from invention to maturity, the rate of growth of demand will vary; it will begin slowly, accelerate for a time, and then slow down again when the product becomes mature.[1] The proposition put forward here is that these phases of growth tend to be accompanied by changes in the relative importance of the various factors of production—skilled and unskilled labor, capital, and management ability. These changes—set out in abbreviated form in Table 1 and Chart 1—have implications for international competitiveness.

In the introductory phase of a product cycle, runs are short; units are frequently custom-made or manufactured in batches rather than by means of a continuous process. Product specifications are loose, and frequent changes are introduced in the technology. Because of this, manufacturers try to keep down their investment in fixed assets. Rather than install special purpose machinery, they tend to rely on subcontractors and independent

* This note was prepared by Mr. Seev Hirsch; it is taken from a doctoral dissertation on "The Location of Industry and International Competitiveness," presented at the Harvard Graduate School of Business Administration. The research was supported by the Harvard University Program on Technology and Society under a long-term grant from the International Business Machines Corporation.

Table 1. Characteristics of the Product Cycle

Characteristics	Cycle phase		
	Early	*Growth*	*Mature*
Technology	Short runs. Rapidly changing techniques. Dependence on external economies.	Mass production methods gradually introduced. Variations in techniques still frequent.	Long runs and stable technology. Few innovations of importance.
Capital intensity	Low.	High, due to high obsolescence rate.	High, due to large quantity of specialized equipment.
Industry structure	Entry is know-how determined. Numerous firms providing specialized services.	Growing number of firms. Many casualties and mergers. Growing vertical integration.	Financial resources critical for entry. Number of firms declining.
Critical human inputs	Scientific and engineering.	Management.	Unskilled and semi-skilled labor.
Demand structure	Sellers' market. Performance and price of substitutes determine buyers' expectations.	Individual producers face growing price elasticity. Intra-industry competition reduces prices. Product information spreading.	Buyers' market. Information easily available.

Chart 1. The Relative Importance of Various Factors in Different Phases of the Product Cycle

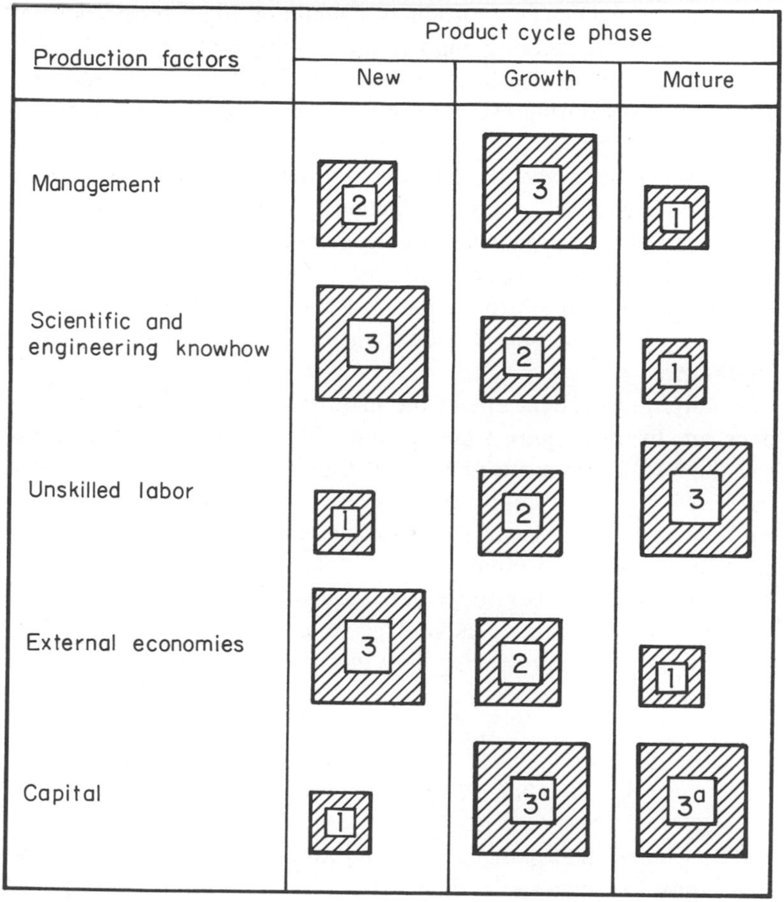

Production factors	Product cycle phase		
	New	Growth	Mature
Management	2	3	1
Scientific and engineering knowhow	3	2	1
Unskilled labor	1	2	3
External economies	3	2	1
Capital	1	3[a]	3[a]

The purpose of the blocks is simply to rank the importance of the different factors, at different stages of the product cycle. The relative areas of the rectangles are not intended to imply anything more precise than this.

[a] Considered to be of equal importance.

specialist firms to perform for them a large number of manufacturing operations. It is important, therefore, that production should
take place where "external economies" of this kind are easily
accessible. Further, new products contain a high proportion of
scientific and engineering inputs; the employment costs of engineers and scientists are likely to account for a higher proportion
of total outlays during the early phase than in any other phase of
the product cycle.

Products that survive the introductory stage next enter the growth
phase, during which mass production and mass distribution are
introduced. Production runs are lengthened and special purpose
machinery is used to reduce unit cost. The ratio of labor to capital
is reduced, and the production process becomes more capital-
intensive. In this phase management ability assumes critical
importance.

Finally, the product enters the mature stage. Product specifications are by now quite standardized; the sequence of operations
and their scale are more or less fixed, and the technology is fairly
stable. Management ability probably matters less in this phase, and
the relative importance of external economies and of scientific and
engineering inputs declines as well. The cost of unskilled labor
begins to matter rather more. Consequently countries which may
have had a comparative advantage in producing the item when
it was in its growth phase may lose that advantage when it becomes
a mature product.

The United States Electronics Industry

The United States electronics industry provides quite a good
case study for analysis in these terms. In the first place, it covers
a wide range of products, ranging from radios, now an old-
established product, through electronic computers, scarcely known
before 1950, to lasers, which have yet to make their commercial
impact. Electronic goods may therefore be found in all phases of
the product cycle.

Secondly, the volume of international trade is considerable, and the United States is a major trader. If her trade in electronics were insignificant, then random factors might be responsible for the apparent changes in trade trends. As it is, changes in these trends can legitimately be assumed to be the consequences of changes in the United States' competitive strength.

The "product cycle" view would suggest that the United States' competitive position would be strong in products which are in the growth phase; and that it might be becoming relatively less competitive in the more mature products, where unskilled labor costs begin to matter. The figures of output and trade appear to bear out these conclusions.

The output of the industry is commonly divided into six categories, which between them account for some 80 per cent of the industry: government and industrial electronics; special purpose electron tubes; components and accessories; consumer products; radio and television receiving tubes; and cathode ray picture tubes.[2] These groups will, it is true, include within them products in different phases of the product cycle; for example, color television—a growth product—is included with monochrome television. But, by and large, the first three groups—that is, government and industrial products, components and accessories, and special purpose tubes—appear to include products which are mainly in the growth phase; the products in the other three groups—consumer products, receiving tubes and cathode ray tubes—seem mostly to be in the mature phase. Certainly this is the conclusion derived from simply taking the rates of growth of value added in the various groups (Table 2); this is probably the best criterion to use, to decide whether the products in a group are in general still in the growth phase or not.[3] The product cycle view of competitiveness would lead us to expect to find that the United States electronics industry was strongly competitive in the three fast-growing groups, but that its competitive position was weakening in the other three.

This is in fact what the trade figures show, if we use changes in the trade balance as a criterion of competitiveness. This is the best available measure, rather than the ideal one; but there seem no very strong reasons for thinking that it would give the wrong

Table 2. United States Electronics Industry: Growth Rates
of Value Added, by Principal Industry Groups

Industry Groups	*Value added, $ million*		*Annual % changes (compound)*			
	1947	*1962*	*1947–62*	*1947–54*	*1954–58*	*1958–62*
Total industry	794	6,435	15.0	18.6	6.1	17.9
Growth sectors						
Government and industrial	137	3,013	22.9	27.8	14.2	23.4
Components and accessories	198	1,977	16.6	20.3	6.1	21.2
Special purpose tubes	18	273	19.9	28.8	11.9	13.2
Mature sectors						
Consumer products	365	869	6.0	10.0	−4.4	10.0
Receiving tubes	⎱ 76	239	⎱ 9.6	22.9	2.3	−4.3
Cathode ray tubes	⎰	63	⎰			−1.5

Source: *Views of the United States Electronics Industry:* Evidence presented before the United States Tariff Commission and the Trade Information Committee, March 1964, p. 15.

answer. It is true that in some instances imports might be prevented from coming in by high tariffs, in spite of price movements which were favorable to competing countries and unfavorable to the United States. But in this case the weakening in competitiveness should normally show up on the export side, and so still appear in the trade balance. These trade balance figures show (Table 3) that in all three growth sectors the trade balance improved between 1960 and 1963. In two of the three mature sectors, the trade balance worsened considerably; and it almost certainly did so as well in the third group, cathode ray tubes, for which import figures are not separately shown before October 1963. However, between 1960 and 1963 exports of cathode ray tubes halved. The pattern therefore seems to fit. The United States appears to be competitive in growth sectors; but in mature sectors its competitive power seems to have been waning.

If, for any product, imports and exports were large enough,

Table 3. United States Balance of Trade in Selected Electronic Product Groups, 1960-1963
(in millions of dollars)

Product Groups	1960	1961	1962	1963[a]	% Change, 1960–64
Growth products					
Government and industrial products					
Exports	202.9	249.9	336.9	338.7	67
Imports	13.2	17.4	38.0	41.4	214
Balance	189.7	232.5	298.9	297.3	57
Special purpose tubes					
Exports	21.6	22.0	24.1	25.9	20
Imports	2.4	3.8	3.4	4.5	88
Balance	19.2	18.2	20.7	21.4	11
Components and accessories					
Exports	89.6	113.1	137.6	161.4	80
Imports	32.5	41.5	65.7	60.1	85
Balance	57.2	71.6	71.9	101.3	77
Mature products[b]					
Consumer products					
Exports	58.2	72.0	74.9	75.7	30
Imports	80.0	98.1	134.2	159.4	99
Balance	−21.8	−26.1	−59.3	−83.7	−284
Receiving tubes					
Exports	14.4	16.4	13.8	12.4	−14
Imports	10.6	13.9	22.9	24.2	128
Balance	3.8	2.5	−9.1	−11.8	—
All electronic manuf.					
Exports	408.0	494.7	603.5	624.1	53
Imports	138.7	174.8	264.3	289.7	109
Balance	269.3	319.9	339.2	334.4	24

[a] Estimated on the basis of trade returns for the first 11 months of the year. [b] Exports of cathode ray tubes declined from $21.3 million in 1960 to an estimated $10.1 million in 1963. Import figures were not separately recorded before October 1963. It appears, however, that the United States had an export surplus; so it is virtually certain that the trade balance worsened over this period. SOURCE: *Views of the United States Electronics Industry*, Statistical Appendix, Table XVIII.

the slow rate of growth and the competitive weakening would be one-and-the-same phenomenon. It would consequently be quite improper to say that the competitive worsening occurred because the product was entering a mature phase of slow growth. It would rather be the other way round: that output was growing slowly because competitive power was weakening. However, with the United States electronics industry, imports and exports are too small a part of domestic demand for this to be so. For consumer products and receiving tubes—the two mature sectors for which separate trade figures are available—exports are only about 4% of total shipments. Further, even if there had been no imports, and the whole of home demand had been met from home output, the growth rates for these two product groups would still have been relatively slow (Table 4). The slow rate of growth—a characteristic of a mature product—and the competitive weakening appear to be two distinct phenomena.

Table 4. United States Output and Imports of Electronic
Consumer Products and Receiving Tubes
(in millions of dollars)

Mature Products	*1958*	*1960*	*1962*	*Annual % changes (compound) 1958–1962*
Consumer products				
Output	1,516	1,737	1,906	+5.9
Imports	17	80	134	
Output *plus* imports	1,533	1,817	2,040	+7.4
Receiving tubes				
Output	383	397	310	−5.2
Imports	5	11	23	
Output *plus* imports	388	408	333	−3.7

Source: *Views of the United States Electronics Industry*, Statistical Appendix, Tables V, VI, and XVI.

The Manufacturing Process

It is of some interest to see whether the two groups of electronic products—those in the growth phase and those in the mature phase—show the expected product cycle characteristics in other ways, as well as in international trade. We would expect the growth sectors to employ more skill-intensive methods; we would expect the mature sectors to be more capital-intensive now than they were when in the growth phase.

One would not expect to find that *every* product in the mature phase was produced in a more capital-intensive way than *any* product in the growth phase. The steel industry, for example, was probably more capital-intensive than the textile industry through all phases through which both industries passed. What the product cycle view suggests is that for any particular product the ratio of the capital stock to value added will be higher in the mature than in the growth phase. To demonstrate this, figures are needed of the capital employed throughout the life cycle of the same product. Figures of this kind are not normally available because it is often only at a fairly late stage in the growth phase that the product becomes sufficiently important to be separately distinguished in the statistics.

However, within the electronics industry—where there are basic similarities in the technology of the various industry groups—it is probably reasonable to expect to find, in general, that products in the mature sectors are produced in a more capital-intensive way than products in the growth sectors. This does in fact appear to be the case. The receiving tubes sector has been described in a recent survey as manufacturing "standardized sizes and types of tubes at competitive prices requiring large capital investment in plant and equipment."[4] The consumer product sector has been similarly described as manufacturing items which are "generally mass-produced, using automatic mechanized processes."[5] The processes commonly used in military and industrial equipment manufacturing are described by contrast "not as highly mechanized as electronic components and consumer produce plants . . . fabrication and assembly operations are difficult to mechanize because of the

Table 5. United States Electronics Industry: Proportions of Production and Nonproduction Workers, 1958-1962
(in thousands)

Industry Groups	1958	1962	Annual % change (compound)
Growth products			
Government and industrial			
Total employment, *of which*	129.5	282.6	*21.5*
Production workers	78.1	147.9	*17.3*
Nonproduction workers	51.4	134.7	*27.2*
% of nonproduction workers	39.7	47.7	
Special purpose tubes			
Total employment, *of which*	20.4	24.8	*5.0*
Production workers	14.5	15.2	*1.2*
Nonproduction workers	5.7	9.6	*13.9*
% of nonproduction workers	27.9	38.7	
Components and accessories			
Total employment, *of which*	132.2	237.9	*15.8*
Production workers	102.9	169.7	*13.3*
Nonproduction workers	29.4	68.2	*23.4*
% of nonproduction workers	22.2	28.7	
Mature products			
Consumer products			
Total employment, *of which*	66.5	82.9	*5.7*
Production workers	52.0	66.0	*6.1*
Nonproduction workers	14.5	16.9	*3.9*
% of nonproduction workers	21.8	20.4	
Receiving tubes			
Total employment, *of which*	36.9	26.6	*−7.9*
Production workers	30.9	21.4	*−8.8*
Nonproduction workers	6.0	5.2	*−3.5*
% of nonproduction workers	16.3	19.5	
Cathode ray tubes			
Total employment, *of which*	8.6	6.8	*−5.7*
Production workers	7.0	5.4	*−6.3*
Nonproduction workers	1.6	1.4	*−3.3*
% of nonproduction workers	18.6	20.6	

SOURCE: *Views of the United States Electronics Industry*, Statistical Appendix Tables I-VII, Census data.

relatively short production runs and frequent design changes."[6]

The expectations derived from the product cycle view are also borne out in comparisons of the skill intensity of the methods of production. We would expect the growth sectors to employ a higher proportion of skilled people than the mature sectors. This is what the employment situation in the industry shows. In all three growth sectors there is a much higher proportion of nonproduction workers than in any of the mature sectors (Table 5). Indeed in the government and industrial sector nearly half the employees are nonproduction workers as against only one-fifth in the consumer products and other mature sectors. Where this proportion is high, the input of scientific and engineering skill is high as well.[7]

Implications and Conclusions

The product cycle approach thus appears to fit the experience of the United States electronics industry reasonably well. This approach throws some light on the so-called "Leontief paradox." Professor Leontief published in 1953[8] an analysis of the capital intensity of United States export industries, as compared with that of "import-competing" industries. Since the United States has traditionally been regarded as a country abundantly endowed with capital, Leontief expected to find that the exporting industries had the higher capital intensity. Instead, he found the opposite: the capital stock per employee in import-competing industries was 30% higher than in the export industries. A similar contradiction of expectations was found for Japan. With capital relatively scarce and labor relatively cheap, one might have expected to find that Japanese export industries were less capital-intensive than the import-competing ones—whereas in fact it is the other way round.[9]

The product cycle approach helps to explain these apparent paradoxes. The growth products, in which the United States is likely to be most competitive, are not necessarily produced in a highly capital-intensive way; indeed their main characteristic— judging from the electronics industry—is their high skill content.

The mature products, in which Japan has considerable export success, tend to have high capital-output ratios; but their skill content—in the widest sense—is relatively low. It is in engineering and scientific skill and managerial ability, rather than in capital, that the United States has the greatest competitive advantage.

The product cycle view suggests that international competitiveness, for any one industry, is not likely to be constant over time. A country which has a strong competitive position now may well lose that position when the industry enters a new phase. The electronics industry illustrates this thesis. The superior competitive position which the United States had in certain electronic consumer goods in the early nineteen-fifties disappeared in less than a decade. The strong position which Japan and Hong Kong have gained in transistor radios and other electronic consumer goods is not wholly explained by low labor costs in these countries. Industrial electronic products have a higher labor content than radio sets (classing nonproduction workers as well as production workers as labor). In 1962 in the United States total labor costs made up two-thirds of value added for government and industrial electronic products, but less than half value added for consumer products.[10] Yet in this industrial field, because of the high skill and management requirements, there has been no challenge as yet to United States supremacy. Japan and Hong Kong can compete successfully with the United States in the production of electronic consumer goods not only because their labor costs are lower, but also because these are mature products, with stable technology, requiring relatively little engineering, scientific, and managerial skill.

By viewing their competitive potential as a dynamic process, manufacturers in the advanced countries might be able to anticipate the decline of their competitive strength in products which are approaching the mature phase of the cycle. Equally, government planners and industrial entrepreneurs in less developed countries might be able to identify products which are moving into the mature phase, whose technology is stable enough to be exportable to areas where engineers, scientists, managers, and skilled workers are scarce.

1 See, for example, S. Kuznets, *Economic Change*, Norton, 1953, p. 254; J. P. Jordan, Yale, "The Strategy of Nylon's Growth, Creative New Markets," *Modern Textiles Magazine*, February 1964; C. F. Rassweiler, "Product Strategy and Future Profits," *Research Review*, April 1961; A. Patton, "Top Management Stake in a Product's Life Cycle," T. L. Berg and A. Shuchman (ed.), *Product Strategy and Management*, Holt, Rinehart and Winston, Inc., 1963.

2 The Standard Industrial Classification numbers for the six groups are as follows: Government and industrial electronics—SIC 3662; Special purpose electron tubes—SIC 3673; Components and accessories—SIC 3679; Consumer products—SIC 3651; Radio and television receiving tubes—SIC 3671; Cathode ray picture tubes—SIC 3672.

3 These indices of the rise in value do not allow for price changes. However, the difference in growth rates between the three rapidly growing sectors and the rest is so marked, over the whole period 1947–62, that it would almost certainly show up in volume indices as well, if these were available. Corrections for price changes can be made to four of the sectors, for the period 1957–59 to 1962; the consequential changes in growth rates are not substantial. The main difference is that the output of special purpose tubes, which during this period rose a little faster than the output of consumer products when measured in value terms, rose a little more slowly when measured in volume terms:

	Price index 1962 1957–59 = 100	Annual % change (compound) in value added in:	
		value terms	volume terms
Special purpose tubes	103	+13.2	+12.5
Consumer products	88	+10.0	+13.5
Cathode ray tubes	102	−1.5	−1.9
Radio and receiving tubes	99	−4.3	−4.1

SOURCE: *Views of the United States Electronics Industry*: Evidence presented before the United States Tariff Commission and the Trade Information Committee, March 1964, Tables III, V, VI, and VII.

4 *Views of the United States Electronics Industry*, March 1964, p. 135.

5 U.S. Bureau of Labor Statistics, *Employment Outlook and Changing Occupational Structure in Electronic Manufacturing*, Government Printing Office, Washington, 1963, p. 5.

6 U.S. Business and Defense Services Administration, *The United States Industrial Outlook for 1963*, ER–63, Government Printing Office, Washington, 1963.

7 *Views of the United States Electronics Industry*, p. 12: "A high proportion of nonproduction workers is engaged in research and development."

8 W. Leontief, "Domestic Production and Foreign Trade: The American Capital Position Re-examined," *Proceedings of the American Philosophical Society*, 1953.

9 M. Tatemoto and S. Ichimura, "Factor Proportions and Foreign Trade, the Case of Japan," *Review of Economics and Statistics*, November 1959.

10 *Views of the United States Electronics Industry*, Tables II and V.

Test of a Product Cycle Model of International Trade: U.S. Exports of Consumer Variables

LOUIS T. WELLS, JR.

(Reprinted by permission of *Quarterly Journal of Economics*, Vol. LXXXIII, February 1969)

Louis T. Wells, Jr.

Louis Wells is Associate Professor at the Harvard University Graduate School of Business Administration. He is a graduate of Georgia Institute of Technology and holds the M.B.A. and D.B.A. degrees from Harvard University.

He authored, with John M. Stopford, Managing the Multinational Enterprise: Organization of the Firm and Ownership of the Subsidiary *(New York: Basic Books, 1972). He has published articles on international trade, concession agreements in developing countries, joint ventures, and organizational structure of the multinational enterprise.*

Test of a Product Cycle Model of International Trade: U.S. Exports of Consumer Durables

In the last few years there has been a flowering of theories which could be characterized as "cycle models" purporting to explain international trade in various manufactured goods. Hufbauer,[1] for example, attempts to explain trade in synthetic materials by the use of a technological gap concept, whereby the leading countries have an initial advantage which they lose after some time period to countries further down the "pecking order." Douglass[2] uses a very similar concept to explain U.S. exports of motion pictures. Hirsch[3] tries a more complex approach to trade based on the "product cycle" concept in marketing and is successful in describing U.S. exports in the electronics industry.

This article presents the results of an attempt to make a somewhat more rigorous test of a trade cycle model which is very similar to those proposed by Hirsch and by Vernon.[4] The study examined U.S. exports of consumer durables to see if certain patterns could be observed which the cycle model would predict.

A very abbreviated statement of the model follows with a summary of the argument used to support it. The reader with interest in a further elaboration of the underlying arguments is referred to Vernon[5] [and to the first article in this book].

The Cycle

The model claims that certain kinds of products go through a cycle which could be described in four stages: (1) the United

AUTHOR'S NOTE: Tables and figures presenting in detail the results of the tests outlined in this article are reproduced in the appendix. Part of this study was made possible by a grant from the Ford Foundation.

States is initially an exporter with a monopoly position, (2) foreign production begins to displace American exports in some markets, (3) foreign goods become competitive in third markets, further reducing American exports, (4) finally foreign goods are competitive in the United States. According to the model, the time period for the completion of the stages and the shape of the cycle will be determined by the appeal of the product to different income groups, the economies of scale available, and the importance of transportation and tariff costs.

The argument begins with an examination of what kinds of new products are likely to be introduced in the United States. The basic assumption underlying this part of the argument is that market stimulus is not equally available to all, but is strongest for those closest to the market. It is argued that the inventor is more likely to respond to demands with which he is most familiar, those of his own country. Similarly, an entrepreneur is more likely to make a favorable profit forecast for a new product if it satisfies demands with which he is well acquainted. American inventors and entrepreneurs have a special knowledge of a uniquely large high-income market. Thus, they are especially likely to develop and to initiate manufacture of products which satisfy wants connected with high incomes.

Not only is an American more likely to be the first manufacturer of new products which satisfy needs associated with high-income consumers, but he is also likely to locate his first plant in the United States. During the early stages of the product life cycle, ease of communication with consumers and specialized suppliers is likely to be more important than possible cost savings arising from using cheap foreign labor inputs. The highly differentiated nature of the product and the nature of first demands result in low price elasticity for the firm. Ability to meet the customers' as yet not well-specified needs is more important than having the lowest price.

At this point, American manufacturers have a monopoly position in the new product. Potential foreign consumers must order from the United States. American exports begin and continue to increase as foreign customers become aware of the product and as their incomes grow allowing them to purchase the item. Hence, one would expect to find increasing exports of high-income products.

But the model goes on to say that the United States will eventually experience a decline in competitiveness for these same products. Again much abbreviated, the argument is that production will begin overseas—instituted either by a foreigner or by an American investor—when the foreign market becomes large enough to support a plant capable of producing at an average cost lower than American marginal cost plus transportation and duties.[6] Note the variables that have appeared. The foreign market size is dependent on the income elasticity of demand for the product—if the product is "lower-income," foreign production should start sooner. But costs are a function of plant size in the cycle model. So economies of scale become important in determining the timing of the beginning of foreign production. Also, the timing is determined by the amount of tariffs and freight charges. Foreign production should start earlier if foreign tariffs and international transportation costs are high.

It is on these variables—income elasticity, economies of scale, and freight costs (no consistent pattern was found for tariffs on an individual product from country to country)—that this study will focus. But before an examination of the exact effect which each of these variables should have on American export performance, the description of the cycle will be completed.

Foreign production, initially in a relatively high-income foreign country, will at first be able to compete with American products only behind its own tariff walls. But as the market and plant size grow, more efficient production may take place and the foreign producer can compete with American plants in third markets. The decline in the rate of growth of United States exports of a particular product which started as foreign competition first began is continued. Eventually, lower labor costs abroad may allow the foreign manufacturer to compete successfully for a segment of the American market.

The early foreign producers, usually Western Europeans, may face a similar cycle of their own. Their exports to the lower-income countries may expand until the markets of the less-developed countries are large enough to support domestic production. When the markets are large enough—or duties high enough—local production begins in these lower-income countries. Moreover, these countries with even lower wage rates may, after a time, begin to compete in export markets. As Vernon[7] says, only shreds of evidence are available for this stage of the cycle. Cheap machine-made cloth from Taiwan and standard computer components from Argentina may portend this stage which could become more important.

Of course, this was an oversimplification of the argument underlying the model but it has been well stated elsewhere. The variables which determine the characteristics of the trade cycle stand out clearly—income elasticity of the product, economies of scale, tariffs, and transportation costs. The next part of the article will look in more detail at the effects the model would predict that each of these variables would have on American exports and then give the results of an examination of the data for consumer durables to see how well actual trade in these products conforms to the predictions.

High-Income Products

The model would predict that United States exports of high-income products would be growing compared with exports of low-income products.

Ideally, one needs as a measure of income appeal an expression which describes the income elasticity of demand. Moreover, the measure should be valid for all countries. Such a measure was, of course, not available for individual items such as were being studied. However, good data are available as to who buys consumer durables in the United States. The diversity of the American market provides a little support for the contention that a ranking of products by the United States elasticity might be similar to a ranking based on world data. The American data were compared with various foreign measures for those products for which data were available to see whether the American ranking appeared to be very different. The contention that United States figures show patterns similar to foreign data was demonstrated to be sufficiently valid.

The Starch Consumer Survey[8] provided a source from which two useful measures of the income nature of products could be calculated—(1) the income elasticity of ownership and (2) the percentage of households owning the durable ("saturation"). The income elasticity of demand was considered useful as it might be a fair substitute for world income elasticity of demand which would have been more appropriate. "Saturation" appeared to be useful as a means of comparing American ownership patterns with foreign patterns. The income elasticity of ownership and the saturation level were calculated for twenty products[9] from the 1961 Starch data.

In order to test the similarity of American consumption patterns to those in other countries, patterns in the United Kingdom and in the European Economic Community were compared with American data. Comparable figures of saturation for a number of products in the United States, the United Kingdom, and the Common Market show a striking similarity in ranking. The Coefficient of Concordance for the three countries is $+ .91$.

Another measure of the similarity is the degree of lead of the United States over lower-income countries. If the low-saturation products are the most highly elastic, as is observed from the American data, a high-income country such as the United States might be expected to be further in the lead in ownership of lower-saturation items. A comparison of the rankings of products by saturation in the United States with the ranking by the ratio of Common Market saturation to United States saturation shows a Spearman's Coefficient of $+ .71$. A comparison of the rankings of products by saturation in the United States with the ranking by the ratio of Common Market saturation to United States saturation also yields a coefficient of $+ .71$. The American data do seem to give a fair reflection of ownership patterns, at least in Western Europe.

In addition, there is a little evidence that the American data are not bad reflections of ownership patterns in some other parts of the world. Paroush's calculations of the order of acquisition of consumer durables in Israel demonstrate a pattern similar to that in the United States and Western Europe. Paroush ranks the order of acquisition of durables in Israel as radio, gas cooker, refrigerator, washing machine, electric mixer, and vacuum cleaner.[10] The saturation figures for the United States show only a reversal of the last two items. Paroush's figures are for "order of acquisition" and not for saturation, but there does appear to be a similarity in his results for Israel and those of this study for the United States.

Of course, there are other problems with the two measures. Elasticities change over time, falling after the new product stage —elasticities were calculated at a point in the middle of the period which was being studied in order to minimize the effect of changing elasticities. There are other problems, but none of them seems to provide support for an argument that measures would be systematically distorted in a way that would support the hypotheses. The risk seemed to be that of finding no correlation due to scatter in the data.

The results of correlation tests seemed to confirm the hypotheses. The correlation of the income nature of the product and American export performance was strong. Equations of the following forms were fitted to the data:

1. $R = a + b \log S_{no}$
2. $R = a + b \log S_{no} + c \cdot e$
3. $R = a + b \log S + c \cdot e$
4. $R = a + b \cdot e$
5. $R = a + b \cdot e + c \cdot S$

Where R = ratio of 1962–63 average exports by value to 1952–53 average exports,

S_{no} = ratio of the number of items owned to the number of households reporting,

S = fraction of households owning at least one of the item,

and e = income elasticity of ownership.

Equation 4 gave the best results for a single independent variable. (See Table 1.) With the income elasticity of ownership as the predictor of export performance, 80 per cent of the variance in the data is explained. The regression coefficient was a positive 3.17. Adding saturation as a predictor gave no significant increase in the explained variance, due to the colinearity of saturation and elasticity. There does appear to be a strong correlation between

Table 1. Characteristics of Regression Equations

	(1)	*(2)*	*(3)*	*(4)*	*(5)*
a	10.745	5.380	4.829	.784	1.399
b	−2.404	−.908	−.696	3.171	2.786
c		2.512	2.656		−.717
F	21.32	37.13	40.63	74.46	36.33
For each coefficient, standard error	.521	.456	.482	.367	.668
		.512	.504		1.034
For each variable, correlation coefficient squared	.530	.530	.524	.803	.803
		.766	.803		.601
Multiple correlation coefficient	.728	.895	.903	.896	.893

American export performance and the income nature of the product.

Of course, it could be argued that this correlation is not due to a comparative advantage of the United States in high-income products but rather that the United States is simply sharing in an overall growth in world trade in these items. To test whether this might be the case, the performance of American exports of these products was compared with the world growth in exports for products which were included in Maizels' study.[11] A positive association would indicate that the United States may simply be sharing in world growth. A negative Spearman's Coefficient indicated that some sort of actual comparative advantage in these products exists for the United States.

Product Variations

The trade cycle model would predict that the United States would perform better as an exporter of a more sophisticated version of a product compared with a less sophisticated version, if sophistication can be assumed to make a product more attractive to high-income consumers. One would expect early foreign manufacture to be of a simpler, low-income version while American products are becoming more sophisticated, in cases where such modifications are possible. The United States would have comparatively lower costs due to savings from the economies of scale resulting from production of luxury versions for a larger home market.

A comparison of American and foreign prices for various models of some of the products in the study supports this proposition. Figure I shows American, German, and in some cases Japanese prices for various models of home freezers. The reader will note that the American price line has the smallest slope, the German the next, and the Japanese the steepest, demonstrating comparatively cheaper prices in the United States for the more sophisticated versions. Unfortunately, the number of products in the sample which could be classified reasonably unambiguously by sophistication was small. However, the contention that the United States has a comparative advantage in the luxury versions seems to be borne out by the four products for which the hypothesis could be tested.

The patterns for the other two variables are not quite clear, but there is evidence of the existence of the predicted influences.

Economies of Scale

The predictions about the export performance for products with different "income appeals" were based on the assumption of increasing returns-to-scale. Foreign production was assumed to begin only when the market in the country was large enough to support production at a level such that costs were below United States marginal cost plus transportation and duties. One would expect products which have, in some sense, different returns-to-scale to have different export patterns.

As a crude measure of economies of scale related to market size the number of plants manufacturing the product in the United States was taken. An index of dispersion was calculated for each

Figure I. Freezers: Price vs. Capacity

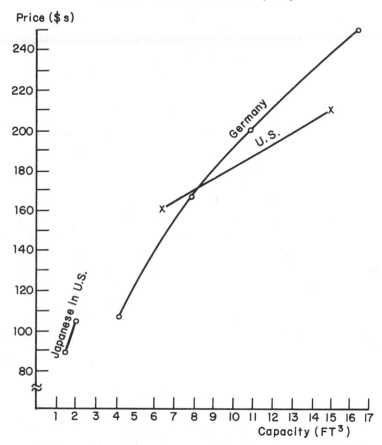

Prices for U.S. freezers are from the *Sears Roebuck Catalog,* Fall and Winter, 1965. All prices are for the lowest priced model of the size given.

Prices for German freezers are from the *Neckermann Katalog,* No. 169, Sept. 1, 1965–Mar. 1, 1966. Prices are converted at DM 4 = $1, and capacity at 1 cu. ft. = 28.3 ltrs.

Prices for Japanese freezers are from *Sears Roebuck Catalog,* Spring and Summer, 1966, for Japanese imports.

product by assuming that each plant in the four-digit SIC industry containing the product was the same size as the average plant in the group.[12]

The index of dispersion was plotted against the ratio of 1962–63 average exports to 1952–53 average exports for each of the products and against 1962–63 average exports as a percentage of 1963 factory shipments. The resulting scatter diagrams do indicate that there is probably a relationship between scale and export performance as predicted. It appears that exports have performed better for products where the index of dispersion is low. There is also some evidence that a certain degree of concentration is necessary before exports amount to a large percentage of production. This is not simply an oligopoly effect. Apparently, in cases where the number of companies is small but the number of plants is large, exports are small as a percentage of output.

Unfortunately, the number of products for which the index of dispersion could be calculated was not large enough to allow for a multiple correlation test with the index of dispersion and income elasticity as independent variables and United States export performance as the dependent variable. From the limited sample, though, it appears that the data are in agreement with the hypotheses about the relationship of changes in exports and the percentage of output exported to economies of scale.

Transportation and Tariffs

In order to test the effect of transportation and tariffs on the United States export patterns, a value per unit weight index was calculated and the tariffs for the United Kingdom, the European Economic Community, and Canada were collected. No common pattern was found for the three areas for the tariffs on an individual product.

It was assumed that shipping costs per unit value would be an inverse function of value per unit of weight. The model would predict that, given a sufficient degree of concentration such that exports are possible, those products which have lower transportation costs, i.e., higher value per unit weight, would perform better as exports. The coefficient of rank correlation was calculated for exports as a percentage of shipments and the value per unit weight for items which had an index of dispersion less than 25. The percentage of exports to shipments is positively correlated with the value per unit weight (Spearman's Coefficient of + .71). In order to test for cross correlation with the other variables, Spearman's Coefficients were calculated for rankings of value per unit weight and income elasticity of ownership and for rankings of value per unit weight and saturation. No significant correlation was found. The transportation costs do appear to be significant in determining the volume of exports.

Conclusions

American export performance of consumer durables for the period 1952–63 does seem to be consistent with the predictions of the cycle model. Income elasticities of products, economies of scale, and transportation costs appear to be significant determinates of American exports of consumer durables.

Most of the cycle models combine both demand and supply elements to yield a theory of international trade. The problem remains of reconciling these theories with the factor-cost models. There is no inconsistency between the findings of Leontief and the cycle model. It may be, and is in fact very likely, that new high-income products are more labor-intensive than the same products later in the product life cycle when production processes have become standardized.[13] Hence, it is not surprising to find that American exports are more labor-intensive than the domestic industries which imports are replacing. Keesing's study[14] demonstrated that the United States exports products embodying a large amount of technical skill. His results are also perfectly consistent with the cycle model. No doubt, new products in general do require more technically skilled labor. However, it seems unlikely that the supply-oriented models can adequately explain the behavior of American exports of consumer durables. It is difficult to explain the very different behavior of exports of room air conditioners, electric dishwashers, and slide projectors from those of ranges, refrigerators, and irons simply on the basis of factor inputs. It is unlikely that the difference in requirements of skilled labor inputs in these two groups of products is sufficient to give the United States a cost advantage great enough to explain the different export behavior. However, if demand characteristics are introduced, a plausible explanation is forthcoming.

FOOTNOTES

1 Gary C. Hufbauer, *Synthetic Materials and the Theory of International Trade* (London: Gerald Duckworth and Co., 1965).

2 Gordon K. Douglass, "Product Variation and International Trade in Motion Pictures," unpublished doctoral dissertation, Massachusetts Institute of Technology, 1963.

3 Seev Hirsch, *Location of Industry and International Competitiveness* (Oxford: The Clarendon Press, 1967).

4 Raymond Vernon, "International Investment and International Trade in the Product Cycle," *Quarterly Journal of Economics*, Vol. LXXX (May 1966), pp. 190–207.

5 *Ibid.*

6 Compare with the concept of "representative demand" in Staffan Burenstam Linder, *An Essay on Trade and Transformation* (Stockholm: Almqvist & Wiksell, 1961), p. 87.

7 Vernon, *op. cit.*

8 *1961 Starch Consumer Survey*, Daniel Starch and Company.

9 The sample included all products which were included in the Starch data and which had a separate classification in the U.S. export statistics, as reported by the U.S. Department of Commerce in *United States Exports of Domestic and Foreign Merchandise Commodity, by Country of Destination*, FT 410, 1952–1963 (Washington: Government Printing Office).

10 Jacob Paroush, "The Order of Acquisition of Durable Goods," in Bank of Israel *Bulletin*, No. 20, Jerusalem, December 1963, pp. 56–73.

11 A. Maizels, A. R. Thomas, and L. Boross, "Trends in World Trade in Durable Consumer Goods," *National Institute Economic Review*, No. 6, November 1959, p. 16.

12 Adjustments were made to the classification of room air conditioners.

13 See Hirsch, *op. cit.*, and Vernon, *op. cit.*

14 Donald Keesing, "Labor Skills and Comparative Advantage," *American Economic Review*, Vol. LVI (May 1966), pp. 249–258.

Appendix

Table A-1. Income-Elasticity and Saturation Levels for
20 Consumer Durables, 1961

Product	Income-elasticity of ownership (e)	Saturation (S) Number of households owning one of item divided by number of households reporting	Saturation (S_{no}) Total number owned divided by number of households reporting[a]
Outboard Motors	0.886	.084	
Movie Cameras	1.482	.132	
Still Cameras	0.558	.656	
Slide Projectors	1.526	.096	
Automobiles	0.457	.756	.940
Mixers	0.382	.670	
Irons	0.042	.968	
Refrigerators	0.032	.984	
Ranges	0.020	.988	
Freezers	0.463	.194	
Dishwashers	2.112	.051	
Washers	0.157	.748	
Dryers	1.248	.191	
Radios	0.091	.986	1.678
Televisions	0.147	.902	1.405
Record Players	0.642	.501	.578
Air Conditioners	0.808	.105	
Vacuum Cleaners	0.342	.735	
Electric Clocks	0.214	.747	
Recreational Boats	0.823	.006	

[a] Where multiple ownership was reported.

Table A-2. Percentage of Households Owning Certain Consumer Durables
in the United States, the United Kingdom, and the
European Economic Community

Product	U.S. % of House-holds Owning	Rank	U.K. % of House-holds Owning	Rank	E.E.C. % of House-holds Owning	Rank
Irons	97	11	91	11	81	11
Refrigerators	96	10	30	5	40	8
Radios	91	9	76	9	79	10
Televisions	90	8	82	10	34	7
Automobiles	77	7	32	6	28	5.5
Vacuum Cleaners	73	6	72	8	42	9
Mixers	69	5	5	4	21	4
Record Players	50	4	39	7	28	5.5
Two or More Automobiles	18	3	3	3	1	2
Movie Cameras	13	2	2	2	2	3
Dishwashers	6	1	0	1	0	1

Coefficient of Concordance = 0.905

SOURCE: Calculated from data in *The European Common Market and Britain*, Basic Report, Reader's Digest Association, Inc., 1963.

Louis T. Wells, Jr.

Table A-3. Relative Lead of the United States in High Saturation
and Low Saturation Products

Product	Rank by Ratio of E.E.C. Saturation to U.S. Saturation (1)	Rank by Saturation in U.S. (2)	Rank by U.S. Income-Elasticity of Ownership (3)
Irons	2	1	2
Refrigerators	5	2	1
Radios	1	3	3
Televisions	6	4	4
Automobiles	7	5	7
Vacuum Cleaners	3	6	5
Mixers	8	7	6
Record Players	4	8	8
Movie Cameras	9	9	9
Dishwashers	10	10	10

Spearman's Coefficient for (1) and (2) = .71
Spearman's Coefficient for (1) and (3) = .71

Table A-4. Ratio of 1962-1963 Average Exports to 1952-1953 Average Exports

Product	Ratio (units)	Ratio (value)
Outboard Motors	2.88	4.18
Movie Cameras	5.17	4.14
Still Cameras[a]	3.65	4.66
Slide Projectors	1.57	4.66
Automobiles	0.95	0.99
Mixers	1.29	1.25
Irons	1.71	1.56
Refrigerators	0.46	0.47
Ranges	0.79	0.87
Freezers[b]	3.41	2.65
Dishwashers	10.58	8.50
Washers	1.20	1.35
Dryers	n.a.	n.a.
Radios	1.30	1.42
Televisions	1.29	1.04
Record Players	1.12	1.81
Air Conditioners	4.60	3.59
Vacuum Cleaners	2.07	1.78
Electric Clocks	1.01	1.04
Recreational Boats	2.17	4.40

[a] Ratio 1962 exports to average 1952–1953 exports.

[b] Exports to Canada not included.

SOURCE: Calculated from U.S. Department of Commerce, Bureau of the Census, *United States Exports of Domestic and Foreign Merchandise, Commodity by Country of Destination*, FT 410, Washington, 1952, 1953, 1962, 1963.

Table A-5. United States' Share in Growth of World Exports

Product	Rank by Growth in World Trade 1950–1958[a]	Rank by Growth in U.S. Exports, 1952–53 to 1962–63
Radios and Televisions	1	5
Record Players	2	2
Refrigerators	3	7
Ranges[b]	4	6
Vacuum Cleaners[b]	5	3
Washers	6	4
Still Cameras	7	1

Spearman's Coefficient $= -.63$

[a] A. Maizels, A. R. Thomas and L. Boross, "Trends in World Trade in Durable Consumer Goods," *National Institute Economic Review*, No. 6, November 1959, p. 16.

[b] Although the categories for these products in Maizels' study were not identical to ours, they were considered to be close enough for comparison.

Table A-6. Index of Dispersion (1963) and Value per Unit Weight

Product	Index of Dispersion	Value/Weight ($/lb)
Outboard Motors	8.7	3.9
Movie Cameras	2.2	16.7
Still Cameras	5.7[a]	5.0
Slide Projectors	2.3	3.2
Automobiles	54.0	0.6
Mixers	—	2.0
Irons	—	2.4
Refrigerators	—	0.7
Ranges	52.0	0.8
Freezers	2.7	1.4
Dishwashers	—	1.1
Washers	2.1	0.7
Dryers	6.1	0.5
Televisions	138.0	3.1
Radios	41.7	4–10[b]
Record Players	14.0	1.6
Air Conditioners	5.0[c]	1.0
Vacuum Cleaners	13.0	2.0
Electric Clocks	—	4.7
Recreational Boats	180.0[d]	1.2

[a] 1958 data.
[b] The range of models was too wide to arrive at a meaningful number.
[c] Unadjusted calculation yielded 56.
[d] Probably overstated.

SOURCE: Index of dispersion calculated from *Industry Reports*, Department of Commerce 1963 Census of Manufactures. Value/weight calculated from price and shipping weights for cheapest model in *Sears Roebuck Catalog*, Fall and Winter 1965. Where export data were available by type, a weighted average was calculated.

Table A-7. Value per Unit Weight and Exports

Product	Rank by Value per Unit Weight (1)	Rank by Percentage of Shipments Exported (2)	Rank by Income Elasticity (3)	Rank by Saturation (4)
Slide Projectors	4	1	1	9
Movie Cameras	1	2	2	8
Outboard Motors	3	3	4	10
Refrigerators	6	4	10	1
Still Cameras	2	5	6	4
Freezers	8	6	7	6
Washers	7	7	9	2
Vacuum Cleaners	5	8	8	3
Dryers	10	9.5	3	7
Record Players	6	9.5	5	5

Spearman's Coefficient (1) and (2): .706
Spearman's Coefficient (1) and (3): .353
Spearman's Coefficient (1) and (4): −.180

NOTES TO FIGURE A-1:

Prices for U.S. refrigerators are from the *Sears Roebuck Catalog*, Fall and Winter, 1965, except for the 6.2 cu. ft. model, which is a locally quoted discount price for a G.E. model. The next larger G.E. model is also lower in price, comparable to the Sears model used.

Prices for German refrigerators are from the *Neckermann Katalog*, No. 169, September 1, 1965, March 1, 1966. Prices are converted at DM4 = $1 and capacities at 1 cu. ft. = 28.3 ltrs.

Prices for the 1.5 cu. ft. and 2 cu. ft. Japanese freezers are from the *Sears Roebuck Catalog*, Spring and Summer, 1966. Prices for the larger Japanese refrigerators are from "Tokai Electric Company," case written by Mr. Shoto Fujieda of the Keio Business School, ICH 8M31, 1962 data. Prices are converted at Yen 362 = $1.

Figure A-1. Refrigerators: Price vs. Capacity

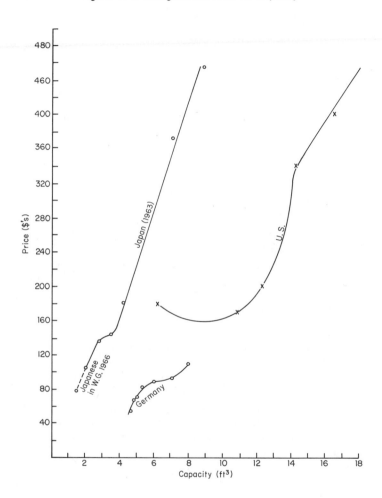

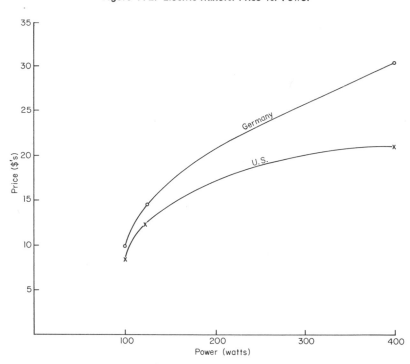

Figure A-2. Electric Mixers: Price vs. Power

Prices for U.S. mixers are from the *Sears Roebuck Catalog*, Fall and Winter, 1965.

Prices for the German mixers are from the *Neckermann Katalog*, No. 169, September 1, 1965, March 1, 1966. Prices are converted at DM4 = $1.

Prices were taken for mixers having comparable features for a given motor output.

Figure A-3. Transistor Radios: Price vs. Number of Transistors

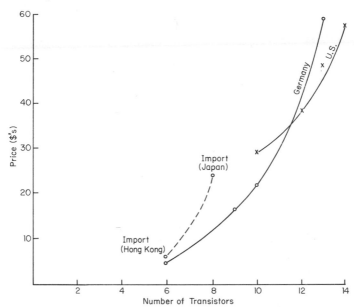

Prices for U.S. transistor radios are from *Sears Roebuck Catalog,* Fall and Winter, 1965.

Prices for the German transistor radios are from the *Neckermann Katalog,* No. 169, September 1, 1965, March 1, 1966. Prices are converted at DM4 = $1.

Prices for Japanese and Hong Kong transistor radios are from the *Sears Roebuck Catalog,* Fall and Winter, 1965.

Radios were chosen which had similar characteristics for a given number of transistors (e.g., number of bands received, number of diodes).

Figure A-4. Index of Dispersion vs. Export Performance

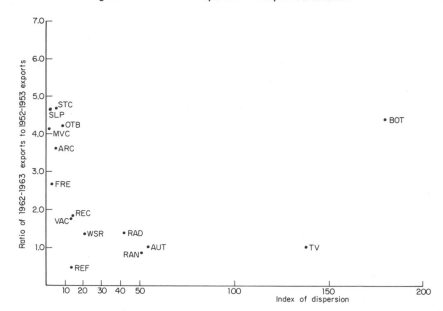

NOTE: For an explanation of the observation for recreational boats, see Louis T. Wells, Jr., "Product Innovation and Directions of International Trade," unpublished doctoral dissertation, Harvard Business School, 1966.

Figure A-5. Index of Dispersion vs. Percentage of Total Shipments Exported

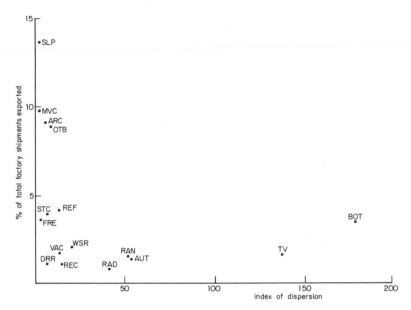

NOTE: For an explanation of the observation for recreational boats, see Louis T. Wells, Jr., "Product Innovation and Directions of International Trade," unpublished doctoral dissertation, Harvard Business School, 1966.

The Neotechnology Account of International Trade: The Case of Petrochemicals

ROBERT B. STOBAUGH

(Reprinted by permission of *Journal of International Business Studies*, Fall 1971)

Robert B. Stobaugh

Robert Stobaugh is Associate Professor at the Harvard University Graduate School of Business Administration. He has an S.B. degree in Chemical Engineering from Louisiana State University and holds the D.B.A. degree from Harvard University.

He has held positions in several multinational companies in the United States, Europe, the Middle East, and South America. He served as Alternate Member of President Johnson's Public Advisory Committee on Trade Policy (1968), and as an expert witness before the Congressional Joint Economic Subcommittee on Foreign Economic Policy (1970), before the U.S. Tariff Commission on international trade policy for high-technology products (1970), and in the Federal Court on transfer pricing within multinational enterprises (1969).

He authored the monograph, Effects of "Geneva Supplementary Agreement" on United States Exports and Imports, *which was prepared as testimony before the Committee of Ways and Means, U.S. House of Representatives (1968 and 1970); a petrochemical report for the Cabinet Task Force on Oil Import Control (1970); articles on international trade and investment in the* Harvard Business Review *and* The Review of Economics and Statistics; *and two books on manufacturing policy in the petrochemical industry. Currently he is completing books on international trade and investment and on the financial management of multinational enterprises.*

The Neotechnology Account of International Trade: The Case of Petrochemicals

Since the publication of the Leontief paradox in 1953, there has been a proliferation of theories and studies intended to provide a better explanation of observed trade patterns than does the traditional factor proportions theory.[1]

Authors of the newer theories have relaxed some of the restrictive simplifications of the traditional factor proportions theory, as defined in the Heckscher-Ohlin-Samuelson model, such as two homogeneous factors of production (capital and labor), constant returns-to-scale of production functions, international identity of production functions and factors, international similarity of preferences, and perfect competition.

Two of the newer theories have emphasized the dynamic aspects of international trade, one focusing on the production factors—the technological gap theory of Posner and Hufbauer[2]—and the other focusing on marketing factors—the product life cycle theory of Vernon.[3] These two theories have so many elements in common that any exact distinction between them is arbitrary.[4] Johnson combined them with a scale-economy theory into one "neotechnology" account of international trade, which he then includes as part of a modified factor proportions theory.[5]

The research described in this paper concerns world trade in petrochemicals and springs from Vernon's product life cycle theory;

AUTHOR'S NOTE: I benefited from discussions with Professors Edith Penrose, Raymond Vernon, and Louis T. Wells, Jr. The research was partially financed by the Ford Foundation and the Harvard Business School as part of a broader study of "The Multinational Enterprise and the Nation State," coordinated by Professor Raymond Vernon.

therefore it also is part of Johnson's neotechnology account of international trade. In fact, after the early stage in the life of a petrochemical, product quality becomes standardized; then technological changes become a major determinant of economic behavior. Hence, the observed changes in economic behavior in the petrochemical industry could be referred to as a "technological life cycle" rather than a "product life cycle," but the latter term is used in this paper for consistency with other studies.

According to Vernon's exposition, the life cycle of products that save labor or appeal to high incomes can be divided into three parts, with certain specified international trade patterns.[6] Initially, in order to minimize communication costs during the time when a product is nonstandardized, a manufacturer makes the product in a high-income, large-market country—typically the United States. This original producing country becomes an exporter to other consuming countries. Second, production begins in other major industrial nations, which begin exporting to the United States and third-country markets. Finally, during the third stage, when competition becomes keen, the product very standardized, and the technology standardized so that relatively unskilled labor can be used in the production process, the less developed countries because of their low labor costs become exporters of the product; the United States becomes a net importer of the old product and shifts its resources into the manufacture of newer products.

The empirical studies to date have provided evidence consistent with this general line of reasoning: U.S. exports shift to newer products[7] and U.S. exports of high-income products hold up better than low-income products;[8] the exports of manufactured goods from Greece, Japan, and Central America tend to be standardized products originally developed elsewhere;[9] and in general the exports of manufactured goods from less developed countries tend to be from relatively mature industries although not necessarily labor-intensive ones.[10]

This paper shows the usefulness of the product life cycle model in explaining world trade in petrochemicals and presents refinements that are suggested by trade in petrochemicals. Some important economic characteristics affecting trade in petrochemicals and bringing out the necessity of adding some refinements to the product life cycle theory are: Labor costs are relatively small compared with raw material costs, product quality is standardized at an early time in the product's life, the production process has substantial economies of scale and requires a "lumpy" investment in which capacity can be added only in large steps.

Most studies of the product life cycle have focused on *categories* of products; thus, there is the problem of a change in "mix" of products over time. The study presented here differs in that it examines world trade and investment for nine *individual* petrochemicals (in SITC 512). World production of these nine petrochemicals exceeds $4 billion and the value of U.S. exports exceeds $100 million; these petrochemicals are used in the manufacture of a variety of polymers and other organic chemicals which, in turn, are used primarily in the manufacture of synthetic materials— plastics, fibers, and rubbers. These petrochemicals are believed to be representative of petrochemical products, which account for about $20 billion of U.S. sales and $80 billion of world sales.*

The Birth of a Petrochemical

Market size is the major factor in determining the initial country of production of petrochemicals and the materials made from them. The United States and Germany, the countries that have the largest domestic markets (omitting the USSR), have accounted for most introductions of such products. All nine petrochemicals in this study initially were introduced commercially in the United States or Germany;[11] furthermore, 46 of the 53 most important plastics, man-made fibers, and rubbers were introduced commercially in either the United States or Germany, with the United Kingdom and Italy accounting for the remainder.[12]

The marketing opportunities are more likely to be recognized in a country with a large market than in one with a small market. There are several reasons why the producer prefers to build his first commercial plant in a country with a large market.

---

* Appendix A contains information on the selection of petrochemicals for this study and on their relation to the remainder of the chemical industry.

First, there is a need for a considerable amount of communication between the customers and the personnel in the pilot plant producing samples for the customers. For chemical products there is usually a long and complex development process during which trial quantities of the product are made for the customers.[13] The pilot plant is located in a large-market country in order to minimize communication difficulties; there is an advantage in locating the initial commercial plant near the pilot plant so that the pilot plant operating personnel are available to form the nucleus of the commercial plant's work force, and so that the research and development personnel are available for consultation. Furthermore, although chemical products reach "standardized" quality more rapidly in their product life cycles than items such as radios, there is still much negotiation between the manufacturer and the customer over product quality for some time after the initial commercial plant has been built.[14] As a result, marketing costs for new chemical products are high compared with what they are when the product is mature, declining from about 23% of sales price to 2% of sales price as a product goes from introduction to maturity (Exhibit 1). Locating the initial commercial plant in a country with a large market minimizes these marketing costs.

Exhibit 1. Selling Expenses for Chemical Products

	Estimated Cost as % of Sales	
Item	*New Product*	*Old Product*
Customer technical service	8.0%	0.5%
Selling expense	15.0	1.5
Total	23.0%	2.0%

SOURCE: Roger Williams, Jr., "Why Cost Estimates Go Astray," *Chemical Engineering Progress*, LX (April 1964), p. 18.

A second reason for the producer's preferring a country with a large market results from the large economies of scale inherent in the production of chemicals. The producer wants to build a large plant and at the same time wants to avoid the risk of depending on the export market for a large percentage of the plant output. This risk results from the specialized nature of most plants producing chemicals in large volumes—the plants could not be converted easily to the production of other chemicals if changes in trade barriers closed an export market.

Furthermore, the producer probably perceives that factor costs abroad are not radically different from those in his home country. And the producer is unlikely to make a major search for the location with the lowest factor costs because as a monopolist or near monopolist he faces a low price elasticity of demand.

Certain external economies are critical in the development of new chemical products; for example, scientists and engineers are needed[15] and are likely to be available in a country with a large market for chemicals. However, even though a supply of technical manpower is a necessary condition for the introduction of new chemicals, it is not a sufficient condition for the introduction of petrochemicals, which typically have large economies of scale in the production process. Countries such as Switzerland, with a supply of technical manpower but a relatively small market, have not been the kind of market in which new petrochemicals have been introduced.

To summarize, there are a number of relationships making it desirable to locate the first commercial plant in a large-market country: Close communication between the plant and customers is needed. Also, the producer does not want to depend on the export market for too large a share of plant output. Furthermore, because of a relatively low price elasticity of demand for the product, the producer has little incentive to search for a location with lower costs, especially as he probably expects them not to be radically different from those in his home country.

The Start of Exports

In those cases in which production begins initially in the United States, a market develops abroad some time later and exports begin. Consumption increases in the United States and in the foreign markets as a result of three factors: increases in market saturation due to the diffusion of knowledge about the product, increases in consumer income, and decreases in product price.[16] The American producer prefers expanding his U.S. plant in order to serve these markets abroad.[17] There is a relatively low incremental manufacturing cost of production from the existing plant; furthermore, the rapid growth of the U.S. market during the early stages of the product life cycle means that the producer, in addition to providing capacity for the home market, also can provide with a minimum of risk the capacity necessary to serve the foreign markets. If the foreign markets eventually are lost, the producer knows that soon his expanded home market will be able to consume all the output of his plant.

In those cases in which production begins initially outside the United States, the large American market induces an early production date in the United States; furthermore, the large market enables the American producer to expand rapidly and to lower his costs because of large economies of scale. However, as will be shown later, a relatively weaker export performance on the part of U.S. producers results because of competition in the world markets from the initial producing country; and, of course, the initial producing country has one important advantage: the longer experience of its manufacturers helps them to reduce production costs because of the "learning curve" effect of cumulative production experience.[18]

Regardless of whether production initially is started abroad or in the United States, there is a lag of several years and often as long as 20 years between the time commercial production begins in the United States and the time U.S. exports begin.[19] This lag results because the individual foreign markets are served very early by exports of end products—plastics, rubbers, and fibers, for example—rather than petrochemical intermediates such as styrene monomer. Eventually the individual foreign markets become large enough to justify construction of a plant to manufacture the end products. But since economies of scale relative to market size usually are larger for petrochemicals than for end products,[20] the erection of a plant to produce the end product in a given country typically precedes the erection of a petrochemical plant. During this lag in a given country between the time the plant to produce the end product goes onstream and the time the petrochemical plant goes onstream, American exports provide the petrochemicals used as raw materials for these foreign plants making the end product.

Although the export performance of the United States is weaker when production initially commences abroad rather than in the United States, the time lag between commencement of U.S. production and commencement of U.S. exports seems to be the same regardless of whether the product is produced initially abroad or in the United States. For the products in this study, the lag for both classes averaged about 14 years.[21] Two countervailing forces apparently cancel one another. On the one hand, the development of markets abroad begins with the commencement of production in the initial producing country rather than with production in the United States. Therefore, by the time production commences in the United States, foreign markets already are available, thus encouraging U.S. exports soon after U.S. production has commenced. On the other hand, the U.S. plant initially has less experience than the initial producer abroad.

These exports to nonproducing countries often are referred to as "technological gap" exports; in fact, as consumption in individual foreign nations approaches a sufficient size to support an economic-sized plant, plants begin to be constructed in these countries. As the size of the market is the most important determinant of when production is begun in a country,[22] such gaps might better be referred to as a "market size gap" rather than a "technological gap."

As more manufacturers in more countries begin production, the U.S. share of the total foreign market begins to decline. At the same time, U.S. exports begin to grow at a slower rate than American consumption, so U.S. exports *as a percentage of U.S. production* begin to decline. This decline has occurred for most products in this study (Exhibit 2). Under this model, once production starts abroad it typically experiences a greater percentage growth than in the United States; and, once exports start from abroad, these foreign exports experience a greater percentage of growth than

American exports. This is illustrated in Exhibit 3 for low-density polyethylene, which is used in this illustration because data on world trade for the nine petrochemicals in this study were not available to the author. However, the trade patterns shown in Exhibit 3 are believed to apply to petrochemicals in general because low-density polyethylene normally is classified as a petrochemical and has many of the economic characteristics of the nine

Exhibit 2. Decline in U.S. Exports as a Percentage of U.S. Production, Seven Petrochemicals, 1914 to 1969

Products First Produced in United States	*Year of Export Peak*	*U.S. Exports as % of U.S. Production, Average for Products in Sample*	
		In Peak Year	*In 1969*
CH[a]	1967	47%	35%
OX	1960	87	70
PX	1965	25	22
Average		53%	42%
Products First Produced Abroad			
AN	1963	27%	24%
MN	1964	14	2
PN	1943	16	1
SM	1969[b]	18	18[b]
Average		19%	11%

[a] For descriptions of the individual products, see the Appendix.

[b] U.S. exports of SM had not yet reached a peak—exports during 1969 were an all-time high.

SOURCES: Production data from U.S. Tariff Commission, *Synthetic Organic Chemicals—U.S. Production and Sales.* Export data from Bureau of the Census, *U.S. Exports of Domestic and Foreign Merchandise, FT–410.* These sources were supplemented by data from files of a consulting firm and from chemical industry trade journals.

NOTE: Export data for the other two products in the study—IP and VC —are not available.

petrochemicals in this study. Labor costs are relatively small compared with raw material costs, and the production process has substantial economies of scale and requires a "lumpy" investment. The quality of low-density polyethylene is changed more often than those of the petrochemicals in this study, but not to such an extent that a producer can gain a major competitive lead over other producers by continually changing the quality.

Before the decline in the relative importance of U.S. exports begins, an export peak higher than the chemical industry average of about 4% of U.S. production[23] is reached. These export peaks

Exhibit 3. Low-Density Polyethylene Production and Exports

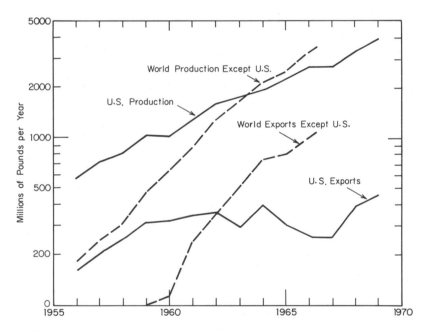

SOURCE: World-wide production and trade data are very difficult to obtain for individual products. These data came from United States Industries, Inc., and were reported in the Arthur D. Little, Inc., report in the Appendix of the Chemco Group's submittal to the Cabinet Task Force on Oil Import Control, 1969.

expressed as a percentage of production are substantial for those products first produced in the United States; for the products in this study, they averaged 53% compared with 19% for products first produced abroad (Exhibit 2). Further evidence of the effect of a production lead on exports is indicated by the significant negative correlation ($\bar{R}^2$ = .69) between the imitation lag of the United States and the peak that American exports reached as a percentage of American production (Exhibit 4).

U.S. Exports Later in the Product Life Cycle

Although U.S. exports decline in relative importance, their growth in absolute terms is a different story. The sizes of new plants continue to become larger, because consumption continues to grow and there are very large economies of scale in the production process; to illustrate, if two petrochemical plants were built at the same time using similar technology with one having a capacity of 2X and the other a capacity of 1X, then when both plants operated at maximum capacity, the one with an output of 2X would have operating costs per pound of product about 30% to 40% lower than the plant with an output of 1X.[24] As a result, even though a foreign nation's market might eventually be large enough to support a plant of an economic size, this day is postponed by the continuing increase in the economic sizes of new plants. Therefore, the volume of the export market grows in absolute terms; albeit, the United States begins to share with other producing nations these markets in countries without production.

U.S. exports continue because of a second phenomenon: U.S. manufacturers export to some foreign countries that have already begun production of the product. There are several reasons for U.S. exports to these producing countries: there may be only one source of supply in the foreign country but the local customers might desire several sources of supply, or a multinational enterprise might export to its subsidiary in the producing nation. Both are common situations in the chemical industry. Furthermore, new capacity in the chemical industry generally can be added only in fairly large lumps;[25] thus, as consumption rises steadily, periodic

Exhibit 4. Imitation Lag and U.S. Export Peak,
Seven Petrochemicals, 1914 to 1969

Products First Produced in United States	Imitation Lag of U.S., Average for Products in Sample	U.S. Export Peak as % of U.S. Production, Average for Products in Sample
OX	−15[a]	+87
CH	−7	+47
PX	−6	+25
Average	−9	+53
Products First Produced Abroad		
AN	+7	+27
PN	+7	+16
SM	+4	+18
MN	+3	+14
Average	+5	+19

[a] This negative imitation lag of 15 years means that the United States started production 15 years before any other country.

SOURCES: Production data from U.S. Tariff Commission, *Synthetic Organic Chemicals—U.S. Production and Sales.* Export data from Bureau of the Census, *U.S. Exports of Domestic and Foreign Merchandise, FT–410.* These sources were supplemented by data from files of a consulting firm and from chemical industry trade journals.

NOTES: (1) Export data for the other two products in this study—IP and VC—are not available.

(2) The coefficient of correlation, r, between "imitation lag" and "U.S. export peak as a percentage of U.S. production" for these seven products is -0.86 ($R^2 = .74$ and $\overline{R}^2 = .69$). This coefficient is significant at greater than 95% confidence level; if the observation for OX is omitted, the resulting coefficient would not be statistically significant.

shortages and surpluses exist in any given country. Because the producer in a foreign country does not want to depend on the export market for too large a share of the output of any plant, especially during the early and intermediate stages of the product life cycle before world trade has become large relative to the size

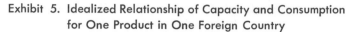

Exhibit 5. Idealized Relationship of Capacity and Consumption for One Product in One Foreign Country

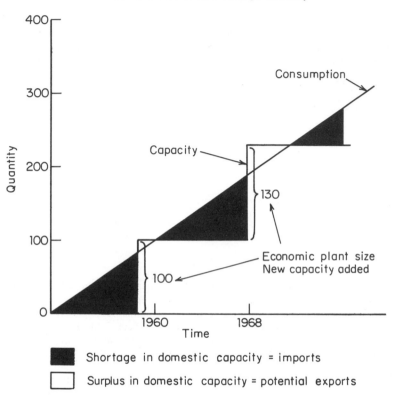

Shortage in domestic capacity = imports

Surplus in domestic capacity = potential exports

of a typical plant, he is likely to build a new plant only when the domestic market can consume most of the plant output. This pattern is depicted in Exhibit 5. The case of styrene monomer (SM) in Germany supplies a specific example of this phenomenon. U.S. exports of SM to Germany were negligible in the few years prior to 1964 and 1965; however, in 1964 and 1965 they approximated $10 million yearly. In 1966 they dropped off sharply as a new SM plant began production in Germany.[26] Other foreign markets replaced the German market so that total U.S. exports of SM were essentially the same in 1966 and in 1965.

These "balancing exports" become very important once many of the foreign countries with large markets commence production. In fact, after a petrochemical reaches a mature stage in its life cycle, these balancing exports exceed the so-called "technological gap" or "market size gap" exports (i.e., exports to nonproducing countries). For the products in this study, U.S. exports of individual products to countries producing the products at the time of the exports increased from 12% of total U.S. exports of the products during an early stage of the life cycle to 62% of total U.S. exports of the products during a mature stage of the life cycle.[27]

Primarily because of these balancing exports, the quantity of U.S. exports of individual petrochemicals typically does not decline to lower levels, at least in *absolute* terms. To be sure, in some years a shortage of the product in the United States results in a cutback in exports, since the U.S. producer typically gives priority to the domestic market. However, as soon as new plants are brought into production in the United States, exports resume in substantial quantities. For the products in this study, by 1969 only two had clearly passed their export peaks expressed in absolute terms. These two peaks had been reached in the early 1960s, after one product had been produced in the United States for 38 years and the other for 46 years;[28] and for one of these products (synthetic methanol), a new export peak was being predicted for the early 1970s because of a technological innovation's being adopted in the United States prior to adoption by other countries; and by mid-1971 it appeared that these predictions might be realized at an early date.[29] For the remaining seven products in this study, export peaks expressed in absolute terms had not yet been reached by the late 1960s even though these seven products had been produced in the United States for periods of 20 to 40 years.

The lack of recognition of the existence of balancing exports by managers of U.S. chemical companies has contributed to a belief that after reaching a peak, U.S. exports would experience a permanent decline, approach zero, and stay there. This belief has contributed to a shortage of chemical products in the United States and abroad—at times chemicals have been rationed by the U.S. producers in both the U.S. and the export markets.[30]

The general belief that the United States will lose most of its export market for an individual product is not restricted to the chemical industry; international executives in a variety of industries feel that "most markets will eventually be closed to exports [because of high tariffs or the erection of a competing plant]."[31]

The Future

The product life cycle model suggests that late in the life of the product, after product quality has been standardized and competition has become severe, less developed countries—with low production costs—would export to the advanced countries. In addition to standardized product quality and keen competition, another factor should encourage the development of export plants in less developed countries: technology for the production of mature products often is readily available for purchase.[32]

Under these conditions any country with lower production costs than other nations for the production of certain products should become a major exporter of such products. In electronics this has happened in mature products as nations such as Taiwan, with low labor costs, have become major exporters to developed nations. However, few such developments have taken place in the petrochemical industry. For example, only one of the 350 plants in the world that manufacture any one of the nine petrochemicals in this study was built in a less developed country without a large domestic market for the consumption of the product.[33] In this case the less developed country was one that had low raw material costs rather than low labor costs—the potential labor savings were not sufficiently large to offset the capital risk of building a plant solely for exports.

Looking to the future, however, there is evidence that the nations having low-cost raw materials because of large oil and gas supplies might become major exporters of mature petrochemicals. If this trend develops, two criteria will determine which products are produced initially for exports and in which nations they will be produced.

The first criterion is that products made from natural gas, such as ammonia and methanol, will be the first made in oil-producing nations for export, as natural gas is produced with crude oil and is flared in some oil-producing nations. Hence, the opportunity cost of this gas is zero (although at times some benefit can be obtained by reinjecting the gas into the ground). Still, the production of mature chemicals for exports will not be limited to those made from natural gas, because officials of oil-producing nations with nominal oil-producing costs and with 40 or so years of reserves will place a very low value on a barrel of oil used in petrochemical production.

A second criterion that affects the products for which export plants will be constructed is the ratio of world trade in that product to the output of one economic-sized plant: the higher this ratio the less risk the owner of one economic-sized plant takes in depending to a large extent on the export market for his sales. In other words, a large world trade in a product relative to the capacity of a given plant presents more opportunities for the output of this plant to be absorbed in the export market than if world trade were relatively small compared with the plant capacity. Thus, given two products made from natural gas, such as ammonia and methanol, export plants will be constructed first for ammonia, because world trade in relation to the capacity of one economic-sized plant to make ammonia is much larger than that in the case of methanol.

Sketchy evidence and speculation suggest that this pattern is evolving as several plants to manufacture ammonia primarily for the export market are either under construction or nearing completion in the oil-rich nations,[34] and it is clear that sales are being made on the basis of low price (India claims to have obtained the lowest priced ammonia in the world from Iran).[35]

Summary

The product life cycle theory, as part of a broader neotechnology account of world trade, provides an explanation for certain production and trade patterns observed for petrochemicals.

The plants to manufacture commercial quantities of petrochemicals initially are built in a country with a large domestic market, such as the United States or Germany.

Exhibit 6, based on the patterns described in this article, tells the story of U.S. exports. These exports begin some years after U.S. production and *as a percentage of U.S. production* reach a peak substantially higher than the average for the U.S. chemical industry. The decline from the peak begins as more nations commence the manufacture and export of petrochemicals. However, the time required for the U.S. export peak to be reached is relatively long—some 25 years after the commencement of U.S. production.

On the other hand, it is not clear that U.S. exports decline in terms of *absolute quantity*—only two of the nine products in this study have experienced a clear descent from a peak; these descents occurred in the early 1960s after some 30 to 40 years of U.S. production. And for one of these two products a new peak is being predicted in the early 1970s as new technology is being adopted now (1971) in the United States prior to being adopted abroad. This continual increase in the absolute level of U.S. exports for so many years is the result of sales to countries in which production of the product has already commenced. One factor encouraging these countries to import from time to time is the need to balance supply with consumption, since local supply can be added only in "lumps" while consumption proceeds smoothly. These shifts in trade depend not on shifts in factor costs but on lumpiness in the production process.

Late in the product life cycle the relative costs of the factors of production begin to exert a major influence on trade patterns as scale, lumpiness, uncertainty, and communications become less important. Evidence suggests that for petrochemicals low-cost raw materials rather than low-cost labor will be an important factor affecting trade, and that countries with low-cost raw materials will become exporters of petrochemicals to countries with high-cost raw materials, regardless of the sizes of the respective markets of the two countries.

Exhibit 6. Typical Pattern of U.S. Exports of Petrochemicals

Relative to U.S. Production

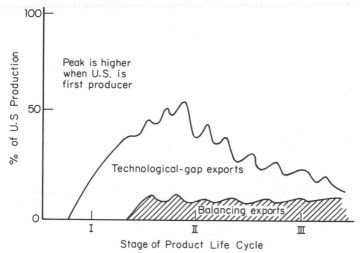

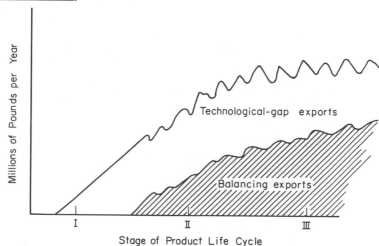

FOOTNOTES

1 These are summarized in G. C. Hufbauer, "The Impact of National Characteristics and Technology on the Commodity Composition of Trade in Manufactured Goods," in Raymond Vernon (ed.), *The Technology Factor in International Trade* (New York: National Bureau of Economic Research, 1970), pp. 145–232.

2 M. V. Posner, "International Trade and Technological Change," *Oxford Economic Papers*, XIII (October 1961), pp. 323–341; and G. C. Hufbauer, *Synthetic Materials and the Theory of International Trade* (Cambridge: Harvard University Press, 1966).

3 Raymond Vernon, "International Investment and International Trade in the Product Life Cycle," *Quarterly Journal of Economics*, LXXX (May 1966), pp. 190–207.

4 Hufbauer, "The Impact of National Characteristics and Technology on the Commodity Composition of Trade in Manufactured Goods," p. 149.

5 Harry G. Johnson, "The State of Theory in Relation to the Empirical Analysis," in Vernon, *The Technology Factor in International Trade*, pp. 9–21; and Harry G. Johnson, "Comparative Cost and Commercial Policy Theory for a Developing World Economy," Wicksell Lectures of 1968, mimeographed.

6 Vernon, "International Investment and International Trade in the Product Cycle," *loc. cit.*

7 Seev Hirsch, *Location of Industry and International Competitiveness* (Oxford: The Clarendon Press, 1967); and Robert B. Stobaugh, "Systematic Bias and the Terms of Trade," *The Review of Economics and Statistics*, XLIX (November 1967), pp. 617–619.

8 Louis T. Wells, Jr., "Test of a Product Life Cycle Model of International Trade," reprinted in this book.

9 Sotirios G. Mousouris, "Export Horizons of Greek Industries" (unpublished doctoral dissertation, Harvard Business School, 1967); Yoshihiro Tsurumi, "Technology Transfer and Foreign Trade: The Case of Japan, 1950–1966" (unpublished doctoral dissertation, Harvard Business School, 1968); and Jose R. de la Torre, "Exports of Manufactured Goods from Developing Countries; Marketing Factors and the Role of Foreign Enterprise" (unpublished doctoral dissertation, Harvard Business School, 1971).

10 Hal B. Lary, *Imports of Manufactures from Less Developed Countries* (New York: National Bureau of Economic Research, 1968), p. 97.

11 Chemical and trade journals and private correspondence with manufacturers; for data see Robert B. Stobaugh, "The Product Life Cycle, U.S.

Exports, and International Investment" (unpublished doctoral dissertation, Harvard Business School, 1968), p. 71.

12 Hufbauer, "Synthetic Materials and the Theory of International Trade," pp. 131–134.

13 A survey showed an *average* of six years and two months between the inception of the idea and the start of commercial production, with an average of 540 possibilities considered for every one commercialized. H. M. Corley (ed.), *Successful Commercial Chemical Development* (New York: John Wiley & Sons, Inc., 1954), p. 137.

14 Corley, *op. cit.*, pp. 142, 237.

15 Gruber, Mehta, and Vernon, "The R&D Factor in International Trade and International Investment of U.S. Industries," reprinted in this book; and Roger Williams, Jr., "Why Cost Estimates Go Astray," *Chemical Engineering Progress*, LX (April 1964), p. 18.

16 The steady increase in consumption and decline in price is shown in Robert B. Stobaugh, "Away from Market Concentration: The Case of Petrochemicals" (tentative title), *Working Paper* (Cambridge, Mass.: Marketing Science Institute, 1972).

17 For a typical expression of this preference, see statement by Lammot du Pont Copeland, President of du Pont, *The General Electric Forum*, April–June 1964, p. 16.

18 For the application of the learning curve to a process industry, see W. B. Hirschman, "Profit from the Learning Curve," *Harvard Business Review*, XLII (January–February 1964), pp. 125–139.

19 First production dates were obtained from chemical trade journals and private correspondence with chemical manufacturers, and first dates of U.S. exports were obtained from chemical trade journals and from private files of a consulting firm. Of the nine products in this study, extensive export data are available only for seven—a relatively few observations from which to draw statistical conclusions; however, for a statistical analysis of such small samples, see Robert B. Stobaugh, "The Product Life Cycle, U.S. Exports, and International Investment," p. 98.

20 As an illustration, there were 17 vinyl chloride monomer (intermediate product) plants compared with 29 polyvinyl chloride (end-product) plants) in the U.S. in 1965. Wickham Skinner and David C. D. Rogers, *Manufacturing Policy in the Plastics Industry* (Homewood, Illinois: Richard D. Irwin, Inc., 1970), p. 29.

21 Stobaugh, "The Product Life Cycle, U.S. Exports, and International Investment," Chapter III.

22 Robert B. Stobaugh, "Where in the World Should We Put That Plant?" *Harvard Business Review*, XLVII (January–February 1969), pp. 129–136.

23 The United States chemical industry exported $2.4 billion out of total sales of $36 billion in 1965, or 6.7%, according to *The Chemical In-*

dustry, Organization for Economic Cooperation and Development, Paris, 1967, pp. 16, 143. The ratio of United States chemical exports to total United States chemical industry sales for the years 1929, 1939, 1948, 1957, and 1961 varied from 4% to 6%. Jules Backman, *Foreign Competition in Chemicals and Allied Products* (Washington: Manufacturing Chemists' Association, 1965), p. 6. U.S. exports as a percentage of U.S. production would be less than these percentages because these are a percentage of industry sales, which are less than production because of captive uses by manufacturers.

24 Stobaugh, "Away from Market Concentration: The Case of Petrochemicals."

25 For discussions of "lumpy" production functions, see Jacob Viner, "Cost Curves and Supply Curves," *Zeitschrift für Nationalekonomie*, III (1931), pp. 23–46; reprinted with supplementary note in American Economic Association, *Readings in Price Theory* (Homewood, Illinois: Richard D. Irwin, Inc., 1952), pp. 198–233; George Stigler, "Production and Distribution in the Short Run," *Journal of Political Economy*, XLVII (June 1939), pp. 305–327; Alan S. Manne (ed.), *Investments for Capacity Expansion: Size, Location and Time Phasing* (London: George Allen & Unwin Ltd., 1967), pp. 44–45; and John Haldi and David Whitcomb, "Economies of Scale in Industrial Plants," *Journal of Political Economy*, LXXV (August 1967), pp. 373–385.

26 "A 440-million-pound/year styrene (SM) plant by Badische Anilin & Sodafabrik," *Oil, Paint and Drug Reporter*, April 18, 1966, p. 9.

27 A Gompertz-type curve, "smoothed by eye," was used to classify the products' growth into stages of a product life cycle. For further details, see Stobaugh, "The Product Life Cycle, U.S. Exports, and International Investment," Chapter II.

28 Synthetic phenol was first produced in the United States in 1913 and reached an export peak in absolute quantity in 1960, and synthetic methanol was first produced in the United States in 1926 and reached an export peak in absolute quantity in 1964. *Ibid.*, Chapter III.

29 Barry Hedley, Walter Powers, and Robert B. Stobaugh, "Methanol: How, Where, Who—Future," *Hydrocarbon Processing*, XLIX (July 1970), p. 135; and "How Will They Close the Gap?" *Chemical Week*, CVIII (May 19, 1971), p. 47.

30 Hufbauer, *Synthetic Materials and the Theory of International Trade*, pp. 101–102; and Robert B. Stobaugh, "Effects of Proposed 'ASP Package' on U.S. Chemical Exports and Imports," in *Foreign Trade and Tariff Proposals*, Hearings before the Committee on Ways and Means, House of Representatives, 90th Congress, July 1, 1968, p. 4686.

31 Yair Aharoni, *The Foreign Investment Decision Process* (Boston: Division of Research, Harvard University Graduate School of Business Administration, 1966), p. 183.

32 Robert B. Stobaugh, "Using Technical Know-How in a Foreign Investment and Licensing Program," *Proceedings* of the Chemical Marketing Research Association, Houston, February 1970.
33 This was a CH plant in Trinidad; see Stobaugh, "The Product Life Cycle, U.S. Exports, and International Investment," Chapter IV.
34 Earl V. Anderson, "Arabs and Their Oil," *Chemical and Engineering News*, XLVIII (November 16, 1970), pp. 58–72.
35 "Iran Gets NH_3 Order from India," *European Chemical News*, XVIII (February 27, 1970), p. 8.

APPENDIX

Information Concerning Products in This Study

Selection of Products for the Study

Five criteria were used in the selection of individual chemicals: (1) the author would be expected to be knowledgeable about the product because of past experience; (2) the manufacture of the product would not be tied to a national resource that could not be easily transported, i.e., the products would be "foot-loose" manufactured goods; (3) the product would have characteristics that enable it to be traded internationally; (4) there would be a sufficient number of producing facilities in the world to allow a test of the model; (5) adequate data would be available on the location and timing of world production facilities.

Some 12 "foot-loose" manufactured chemical products were chosen from a list appearing in a series of journal articles written by the author and from a booklet published by the author's former employer.[1] From this list of 12 products, two were deleted because freight costs for transport between continents were so high relative to value of product that international trade had been negligible, and one was deleted because adequate data could not be obtained on world production facilities.

---

[1] A series of 14 journal articles appeared in *Hydrocarbon Processing* between September 1965 and August 1967 as a Petrochemical Guide series. The booklet reference is Monsanto Company, *Facts about Monsanto and the Hydrocarbon Division*, not dated, but published about 1964.

The nine products studied are:

Abbreviation	Name	Principal Use
AN	Acrylonitrile	Fiber
CH	Cyclohexane	Fiber
IP	Isoprene	Rubber
MN	Synthetic methanol	Plastics
OX	Ortho-xylene	Plastics
PN	Synthetic phenol	Plastics
PX	Para-xylene	Fiber
SM	Styrene monomer	Plastics
VC	Vinyl chloride monomer	Plastics

The abbreviations are used in the text to refer to the individual products.

The nine products are organic chemicals produced in the United States in large volumes—greater than 100 million pounds per year. Each product is commonly referred to as a "petrochemical" because each can be manufactured by using petroleum as a basic raw material, although they can also be manufactured from other raw materials. While these products are used principally in the manufacture of plastics, synthetic rubbers, and synthetic fibers, as shown above, they also have a number of miscellaneous industrial uses.[2]

The number of years that had passed since their commercialization varied from 21 years for the "youngest" to 62 years for the "oldest," as of 1969.

Relationship of Products in This Study to Remainder of Chemical Industry

The products in this study were produced in about 100 plants in the United States in 1969. The total U.S. production of these products in 1969 was valued at $1 billion, or about 5% of the total petrochemical industry sales of more than $20 billion. This compares with total U.S. chemical industry sales of about $50 billion in 1969.

---

[2] More details concerning markets and manufacturing are presented for AN, CH, IP, OX, PN, PX, SM, and VC in my *Petrochemical Manufacturing and Marketing Guide*, Vols. I and II (Houston: Gulf Publishing Company, 1966 and 1968); and MN in *Hydrocarbon Processing* (June, July, August, September, 1970).

The total number of plants world-wide manufacturing these products totaled about 350 in 1966. This compares with a world total of some 1,100 petrochemical plants,[3] many of which manufacture other products in addition to those in this study. The total world production of these nine petrochemicals was valued at $4 billion, or about 5% of the total world sales of petrochemicals of about $80 billion.[4]

U.S. exports of these nine petrochemicals were about 5% of total U.S. exports of petrochemicals, or slightly over $100 million. World trade in these nine petrochemicals has not been estimated.

---

[3] "Focus on Naphtha," *Petroleum Press Service*, XXXIV (December 1967), p. 447.

[4] For industry estimates see the Arthur D. Little, Inc., and the Stanford Research Institute estimates in the submittals to the Cabinet Task Force on Oil Import Control, 1969.

PART II

COUNTRY STUDIES

The R&D Factor in International Trade and International Investment of United States Industries

WILLIAM H. GRUBER, DILEEP MEHTA, AND RAYMOND VERNON

(Reprinted by permission of the *Journal of Political Economy*, Vol. 75, No. 1, February 1967)

William H. Gruber

William Gruber is President of Research and Planning Institute, Inc., and Director of the Northeastern University Research Program on the Management of Science and Technology. He has had faculty and research relationships at the Sloan School of Management, Massachusetts Institute of Technology, and the Harvard University Graduate School of Business Administration. He is a graduate of the Wharton School, University of Pennsylvania, and has a Ph.D. in Economics from M.I.T.

His publications include Factors in the Transfer of Technology, *edited with Donald G. Marquis (Cambridge: The M.I.T. Press, 1969);* "Management of Large Firms at the Technological Frontier" *in* European Business, *1969; and* "The Technology Factor in a World Trade Matrix," *with Raymond Vernon, in Raymond Vernon, editor,* The Technology Factor in International Trade *(New York, National Bureau of Economic Research, Columbia University Press, 1970).*

Dileep Mehta

Dileep Mehta is Associate Professor of Business at the Columbia University Graduate School of Business. Previously he was a Visiting Professor at the Indian Institute of Management in Ahmedabad and an Assistant Professor of Management and Instructor at the Massachusetts Institute of Technology. He holds the B-Com. degree from the University of Bombay, India, the S.B. in Industrial Management from M.I.T., and the D.B.A. degree from Harvard University.

His publications include articles in Management Science *and* Journal of Financial and Quantitative Analysis. *He is currently working on an analytical study of the management of working capital.*

Raymond Vernon

Raymond Vernon is the Herbert F. Johnson Professor of International Business Management at the Harvard University Graduate School of Business Administration. At various times, he has served as the Director of the Overseas Development Advisory Service of the University, and as Acting Director of its Center for International Affairs. He holds the Ph.D. degree from Columbia University.

He is the author of The Dilemma of Mexico's Development *(Cambridge: Harvard University Press, 1963);* Manager in the International Economy *(Englewood Cliffs: Prentice-Hall, 1968); and* Sovereignty at Bay: The Multinational Spread of U.S. Enterprises *(New York: Basic Books, 1971). He is also the editor and a contributor to* The Technology Factor in International Trade.

The R&D Factor in International Trade and International Investment of United States Industries

In the last ten or fifteen years, the field of international trade theory has been in continuous ferment.[1] The received doctrine drawn from the mainstream of Smith-Ricardo-Mill-Marshall-Heckscher-Ohlin has been re-examined from many different angles. Sometimes, there have been strongly revisionist reactions, such as those encountered in the economic development area.[2] In other contexts, the emphasis has been mainly on the further testing and refinement of the doctrine of comparative advantage and the role of factor endowments.

Much of the discussion of U.S. trade performance in recent years has taken for granted the main premises of classical and neoclassical theory. A considerable part of the debate over the interpretation of the Leontief paradox and much of the discussion of the implications of other recent empirical work have concentrated on questions of national factor endowments, or the response of national production functions to different factor prices, or other issues readily compatible with the classical theoretical structure. Leontief, for instance, was inclined to "explain" his familiar paradox by asserting that skilled labor may be relatively cheap in the U.S. economy.

Nonetheless, one can also detect an echo of the discontent voiced

---

NOTE: Gruber's contribution to this work was financed by a grant from the M.I.T. Center for Space Research funded by NASA, while the work of Mehta and Vernon was financed by a grant from the Ford Foundation to the Harvard Business School for the study of multinational enterprise and nation states. Calculations were done at the M.I.T. Computation Center.

111

so effectively by Williams in 1929, a discontent based on the view that classical doctrine is not structured to deal efficiently with the trade implications of a number of forces that may be of major consequence in any descriptive and analytical work (see Hoffmeyer, 1958; MacDougall, 1957; Linder, 1961; Kindleberger, 1962). For the most part, the literature of dissent seems to have sprung out of efforts to explain the foreign trade patterns of the United States, especially the country's exports of manufactured goods. U.S. labor, it has been observed, is higher priced than labor abroad, to an extent which greatly exceeds any productivity differences (Kreinin, 1965). To be sure, U.S. capital is cheaper and less tightly rationed. But the effective interest rate for major industrial borrowers only differs by a few percentage points among the advanced countries. This difference hardly seems enough to explain the strength and persistence of U.S. exports in manufactured products.

From capital and labor cost considerations, therefore, attention has turned to questions of innovation, of scale, of leads and lags (Posner, 1961; Freeman, 1963, 1965; Hirsch, 1965; Hufbauer, 1965; Wells, 1966). Approaches of this sort have tended to stress the possibility that the United States may base its strength in the export of manufactured goods upon monopoly advantages, stemming in the first instance out of a strong propensity to develop new products or new cost-saving processes. This propensity has usually been credited either to the demand conditions that confront the American entrepreneur or to the scale and structure of enterprise in U.S. markets. In any case, the propensity has given American producers a temporary advantage which has been protected for a time either by patents or by secrecy. Eventually, the monopoly advantage has been eroded; but by that time, the U.S. producers have seized the advantage in other products.

Of late, the tendency has been to search for hypotheses which "explain" not only the apparent strength in U.S. exports of manufactured products but also the apparent propensity of U.S. producers of those very products to set up manufacturing facilities abroad (see, for example, Polk, Meister, and Veit, 1966; Vernon, 1966). This line of speculation takes off from the observation that entrepreneurs in the United States are surrounded by a structure of domestic demand for producer and consumer goods that is in some respects a forerunner of what will later be found in other countries. Labor is costly in relation to its productivity, while capital is comparatively plentiful, facts which influence the nature of the demand for producer goods. And per capita incomes are high by international standards, a fact which creates unique consumption patterns. This means that entrepreneurs in the United States are likely to be willing to gamble on the innovation of labor-saving and affluent-consumer products at an earlier point in time than their overseas competitors.

The hypotheses go on to project certain characteristic sequences in the foreign trade of products that have been innovated in the United States. According to the assumption, although the new products that satisfy high-income or labor-substituting wants may have their earliest and largest markets in the United States, some demand for them is generally assumed to exist elsewhere. And in the course of time, that demand will normally grow. For a time, then, the United States will have an oligopoly position in supplying foreign markets. And this oligopoly position will be strongest with respect to the products of those U.S. industries which have been making the largest research and development effort.

According to the hypotheses of this genre, overseas investment eventually comes into the picture partly because the large-scale marketing of technically sophisticated products demands the existence of local facilities and partly because the protection of the oligopoly position of the U.S. producer eventually requires such investment. The threat of competition in foreign markets may come from local sources or from other outside producers, as the original technology-based oligopoly position of the U.S. producer in any given product begins to be eroded. At this point, with profits on exports being threatened, the U.S. company may see a high prospective marginal yield in an investment in local facilities, provided such facilities will help to buttress its existing market position.

A chain of hypotheses as complex as these needs extensive testing before it can gain much in credibility. This brief paper is much less than an adequate test of the chain. But it does contribute modestly to the credibility of the chain for some industries. At the same time, however, the data suggest that simple univariate explanations of the complex causal chain may be dangerous; that while the relevant explanations may involve "research" or "technology" or similar factors in one form or another, the causal role played by such factors may well be rather different from one industry to another.

Research and Trade[3]

All roads lead to a link between export performance and R&D. Whether one accepts the cheap-skilled-labor hypothesis of Leontief or the oligopoly hypotheses in the tradition of Williams, one expects to see a link between exports and research effort. Table 1 provides a simple set of data typical of the evidence which relates research effort by U.S. industry to U.S. trade performance in 1962. The positive correlation between the "research effort" measures, R_1 and R_2, and the "export performance" measures, E_1 and E_2, is evident to the eye. The five industries with the greatest "research effort" are also the five industries with the most favorable trade position.[4] When the five industries with the highest research effort are separated off from the other fourteen industries, it begins to grow clear that the export strength of U.S. industries is centered in the group of five; in fact, the fourteen remaining industries exhibit a net import rather than a net export balance for the year 1962.

In speaking of "export strength," however, one has to exhibit a certain caution. The phrase may have many different meanings, and a word or two about the measures contained in Table 1 will be helpful to clarify some of the concepts involved.

Measure E_1, a ratio of exports to total sales in each industry, can hardly be thought of as a measure of U.S. comparative advantage for the industry. Such a measure, after all, is not only a function of the competitive position of U.S. industry; it also reflects, *inter alia*, the structure of demand overseas as compared with the United States, as well as the effects of transport and tariff frictions on international trade.

Measure E_2—namely, the excess of exports over imports taken as a percentage of sales—goes a little way in the direction of allowing for the effects of demand differences and trading frictions. We observed earlier that differences in demand, rather than in competitive position, might account for a low level of U.S. exports at an earlier stage in a product's development; but there is a respectable body of opinion for the view that in products for which U.S. demand differs considerably from demand in foreign markets, the risk of heavy imports from abroad is not very great.[5] Where demand differences were holding down exports, therefore, they might also be expected to hold down imports. The same is true of transport frictions; if these were responsible for a poor export showing, it would not be utterly unreasonable to suppose that the same forces might be discouraging imports.

It is slightly reassuring to observe, therefore, that both measures of export performance act in a remarkably parallel fashion, generally reflecting a strong export position for research-oriented industries and a weak export position for industries without large research inputs. To be sure, the parallelism cannot be said to prove too much; the so-called correction provided by the second measure need not wipe out all biases of the sort mentioned earlier, if they exist. But we propose to show, as the analysis progresses, that the simple ratio of exports to sales is not wholly misleading as a measure of international competitive strength.

There is still another kind of problem which data of the sort presented in Table 1 may well involve. Each unit of observation in Table 1 is an "industry," arbitrarily defined. Each such "industry" can be proliferated into two or more, by schism. Has the arbitrary grouping used in Table 1 provided an impression of the export importance of the research-oriented industries which distorts the absolute contribution of these industries to the U.S. economy? The data in Table 2 lay that fear to rest. The figures show that the five industries with the strongest research effort accounted for 72.0% of the nation's exports of manufactured goods, though they were responsible for only 39.1% of the nation's total sales of such goods. The same five industries were also responsible for 89.4% of the nation's total R&D expenditures and 74.6% of the company-financed R&D expenditures. The five industries concerned,

Table 1. Research Effort and World Trade Performance by United States Industries, 1962

Industry Name[a] and SIC Number	Research Effort		Export Performance	
	Total R&D Expenditures as % of Sales (R_1)	Scientists-Engineers in R&D as % of Total Employment (R_2)	Exports as % of Sales (E_1)	Excess of Exports over Imports, as % of Sales (E_2)
Transportation (37)	10.0	3.4	5.5	4.1
Aircraft (372)	27.2	6.9	8.4	7.6
Transportation (other than aircraft) (- - -)	2.8	1.0	4.2	2.6
Electrical machinery (36)	7.3	3.6	4.1	2.9
Instruments (38)	7.1	3.4	6.7	3.2
Chemicals (28)	3.9	4.1	6.2	4.5
Drugs (283)	4.4	6.6	6.0	4.8
Chemicals (other than drugs) (- - -)	3.8	3.7	6.2	4.4
Machines (non-electrical) (35)	3.2	1.4	13.3	11.4
Rubber and plastic (30)	1.4	0.5	2.0	1.3
Stone, clay, and glass (32)	1.1	[b]	1.9	−0.2
Petroleum and coal (29)	0.9	1.8	1.2	−0.8
Fabricated metal (34)	0.8	0.4	2.1	0.7
Primary metal (33)	0.6	0.5	3.1	−1.8
Nonferrous metal (333)	0.8	0.5	4.2	−4.7
Ferrous metal (- - -)	0.5	0.4	2.5	−0.2
Leather (31)	0.6	0.1	1.7	−3.4
Printing and publishing (27)	0.6	0.2	1.7	1.1
Tobacco (21)	0.3	0.2	2.2	2.1
Food (20)	0.2	0.3	0.9	−1.2
Textile (22)	0.2	0.3	3.4	−1.1
Furniture and fixtures (25)	0.1	0.2	0.7	[b]
Lumber and wood (24)	0.1	[b]	2.0	−6.2
Paper (26)	0.1	0.3	2.1	−3.5
Apparel (23)	0.1	[b]	0.7	−2.1
All 19 industries:	2.0	1.1	3.2	0.6
5 industries with highest research effort	6.3	3.2	7.2	5.2
14 other industries	0.5	0.4	1.8	−1.1

therefore, represent both the heart of U.S. export strength in manu-factured products and the heart of its industrial research effort.

In groping for some credible measure of comparative advantage, however, it is not necessary to stop with the measures presented in Tables 1 and 2. Still another set of measures can be devised which relates U.S. industry export performance to the export per-formance of the same industry localized in prospective competitor countries. In this case, the "normalizing" variable becomes the total industry exports of all the countries concerned, rather than the total shipments of U.S. industry. Neither normalizer is wholly with-out latent error as a measure of comparative advantage. But the use of another approach offers an opportunity to expose any lurk-ing anomalies and to generate more information about the under-lying forces.

The results of the new approach are presented in Table 3. In general, the figures in the table tend to add a little more credence to the view that the export performance measures used in earlier tables are a function of the international competitive strength of the U.S. industries they represent.

The extreme left-hand column of Spearman coefficients in Table 3 presents measures of correlation between (1) the indi-cated measures of each U.S. industry's research effort and (2) U.S. exports in each industry taken as a percentage of the exports of the OECD countries in the industry.[6] The resulting relationships are practically indistinguishable from the rank correlations between R&D and export performance calculated from the data in Table 1.

In the next two columns of Table 3, however, almost all these relationships fall apart. In these columns, U.S. exports to the world are "normalized" by calculating them respectively as a ratio to (1) United Kingdom world exports and (2) German world exports. The result is that, suddenly, almost all the statistically significant

---

NOTES TO TABLE 1:

(a) Industries arranged in descending order of research effort, defined by R&D expenditures as a percentage of sales.

(b) Less than 0.05%.

SOURCE: See Statistical Appendix.

Table 2. Distribution of Research Effort, Sales, and Exports Among United States Industries, 1962

Industry Name[a] and SIC Number	Percentage Distribution				
	Total R&D Expenditures	Company Financed R&D Expenditures	Scientists and Engineers in R&D	Sales	Exports
Transportation (37)	45.6	24.1	25.3	13.5	19.7
Aircraft (372)	36.7	9.3	21.1	3.7	8.9
Transportation (other than aircraft (- - -)	9.0	14.7	4.2	9.5	10.8
Electrical machinery (36)	21.1	17.7	27.1	8.5	9.4
Instruments (38)	4.0	4.9	5.9	1.6	3.0
Chemicals (28)	10.5	18.6	16.7	7.9	13.0
Drugs (283)	1.8	3.9	3.5	1.2	1.9
Chemicals (other than drugs) (- - -)	8.7	14.7	13.2	6.7	11.1
Machines (non-electrical) (35)	8.2	12.9	10.3	7.6	26.9
Rubber and plastic (30)	1.2	2.1	1.0	2.5	1.4
Stone, clay, and glass (32)	1.0	2.0	1.1	2.7	1.4
Petroleum and coal (29)	2.7	5.7	1.7	8.9	2.8
Fabricated metal (34)	1.3	2.4	2.2	5.1	2.9
Primary metal (33)	1.5	3.3	2.5	7.4	6.1
Nonferrous metal (333)	0.6	1.4	1.0	2.5	2.8
Ferrous metal (- - -)	0.9	1.9	1.6	4.8	3.3
Leather (31)	0.2	0.4	0.2	1.2	0.5
Printing and publishing (27)	0.5	0.9	0.3	2.5	1.1
Tobacco (21)	0.1	0.2	0.1	1.4	0.8
Food (20)	1.1	2.4	2.7	15.5	3.9
Textile (22)	0.2	0.5	1.4	3.8	3.5
Furniture and fixtures (25)	[b]	0.1	0.3	0.3	0.2
Lumber and wood (24)	[b]	0.1	[b]	1.7	0.9
Paper (26)	0.6	1.3	1.0	3.6	2.0
Apparel (23)	[b]	0.1	0.2	3.4	0.6
All 19 industries:	100.0	100.0	100.0	100.0	100.0
5 industries with highest research effort	89.4	78.2	85.3	39.1	72.0
14 other industries	10.6	21.8	14.7	60.9	28.0

[a] Industries arranged in descending order of research effort, defined by R&D expenditures as a percentage of sales. [b] Less than 0.05%.

SOURCE: See Statistical Appendix.

Table 3. World Exports of U.S. Industries Related to
World Exports of OECD Countries, 1962
(Spearman Coefficient of Rank Correlation for Indicated Cell)

Industry Characteristics	*U.S. World Exports in 1962 as % of World Exports of*			
	OECD Countries[a] *(1)*	*United Kingdom (2)*	*West Germany (3)*	*France (4)*
Total R&D expenditures as % of sales	+0.68	+0.28[b]	+0.08[b]	+0.60
Scientists and engineers in R&D as % of total employment	+0.64	+0.37	+0.24[b]	+0.59

[a] Although Japan did not join the OECD until after 1962, Japan is included in the data.

[b] These coefficients are not significant at the 5% probability level. All other coefficients in the table are significant at that level or at a lower probability level.

SOURCE: See Statistical Appendix.

relationships disappear. What this means, of course, is that the United Kingdom and the German export profiles must be very much like that of the United States. Wherever the United States has a large volume of exports, the United Kingdom and Germany also have a large volume of exports.

Does this mean that all our prior indications of the causes of U.S. export strength were misleading? Not at all. It means rather that the United Kingdom and Germany, also being at the top of the advanced country list with relatively high incomes and a relatively heavy stress on industrial innovation and product development, derive their export strength from roughly the same characteristics as those that govern U.S. export performance. Their export performance differs from that of the other OECD countries in the same general way that U.S. export performance differs from that of the OECD countries.

Table 4. Characteristics of R&D Activity in United States,
United Kingdom, West Germany, and France, 1962

	United States	*United Kingdom*	*West Germany*	*France*
Number of scientists and engineers in R&D ('000's full-time equivalents)	435.6	50.7	40.1	28.0
R&D personnel as % of working population	1.0	0.6	0.4	0.4
R&D expenditure (billions of U.S. dollars) [a]	17.5	1.8	1.1	1.1
R&D as % of GNP[a]	3.1	2.2	1.3	1.5
R&D expenditures performed in the business sector as % of total national R&D expenditures	71.0	63.0	61.0	48.0

[a] No adjustment was made for differences in relative factor prices.

SOURCE: Freeman and Young (1965, pp. 71–72).

The extreme right-hand column of Table 3 offers some parallel data for U.S. exports in relation to those of France. These data are more tantalizing than they are revealing. When French exports to the world are used as the normalizer, as the table shows, the significant correlations return; French exports evidently have a profile much more nearly corresponding to the less developed of the OECD countries than to those of the United Kingdom and Germany.

The common view of French industry does paint a picture of an institution that is different in structure, in outlook, and in innovational habits from the industry of the United States, the United Kingdom, and Germany. Table 4 indicates that French industrial research is not on a smaller scale, relatively speaking, than that of Germany. The research tends to be controlled, however, to a greater degree by government institutions which are said to have less concern with industrial applications. Furthermore, French industry's ingenuity, as illustrated by the automobile producers, is said to be devoted to satisfying highly differentiated, highly individual tastes. Up to a point, such innovation might have the same export possibilities as the differentiated products of the United States, the United Kingdom, and Germany. Pushed very far, however, stress on this kind of output has the effect of encouraging an industrial structure which is not highly concentrated, hence a structure which reflects few scale economies in either production or (more importantly, in this context) in research, servicing, or sales. The sale of products for the overseas markets, especially products that have high technical inputs, cannot easily be achieved by an industry of small firms whose innovational stress borders on artistry. The U.S. model of the highly concentrated mass innovator seems more closely to approximate the effective pattern for the successful exporter.

We now come to another group of measures, slightly different in approach, which appear to offer some added evidence of the sources of U.S. export strength. In Tables 1, 2, and 3, it should be remembered, we were concerned with analyzing and comparing the world exports of each U.S. industry, expressing those exports by various relative measures. Table 5 disaggregates the data into U.S. trade with Europe and U.S. trade with non-Europe. It will be observed that in every case there is a better relationship between research intensity and trade with non-Europe than there is in trade with Europe. In fact, as far as trade with Europe is concerned, there is no significant relationship between (1) R&D as a percentage of sales and (2) trade advantage as measured by the excess of exports over imports as a percentage of sales.

The U.S. margin of competitive strength in the research-intensive industries is challenged by Europe, therefore, more effectively than by other countries. This is almost self-evident and has already been suggested by the data on the United Kingdom and German trade patterns. We propose shortly to show that part of the result was due, beyond much doubt, to the patterns of U.S. industry's investments in overseas productive facilities. But before we turn to that phase of the analysis, it will be useful to pin down more firmly what is meant by the research-intensive industries.

Table 5: Research Effort and Trade Performance with Europe and
Non-Europe by United States Industries, 1962
(Spearman Coefficient of Rank Correlation for Indicated Cell)

Industry Characteristics	Trade of U.S. Industries with Europe		Trade of U.S. Industries with Non-Europe	
	Exports as % of Sales	*Excess of Exports over Imports as % of Sales*	*Exports as % of Sales*	*Excess of Exports over Imports as % of Sales*
Total R&D expenditures as % of sales	+0.63	+0.35 [a]	+0.73	+0.78
Scientists and engineers in R&D as % of total industry employment	+0.65	+0.48	+0.74	+0.67

[a] Not statistically significant at the .05 level. All other coefficients are significant at that level or lower.

Characteristics of Research-Intensive Industries

So far the presentation has referred to research-intensive and research-oriented industries, as if a research orientation were synonymous with new-product orientation, and as if new-product orientation were the most likely characteristic of those industries to be linked with their export strength. However, a number of different industry characteristics are related to research effort, and some of these characteristics may provide equally plausible explanations of export performance. This proves to be an especially important point because of the message projected by the data in Table 6.

That table begins by reassuring us in one respect. It indicates that the industries with the strongest research effort are also those with the strongest new-product orientation. But the table goes on to demonstrate that a high research and development effort in an industry is closely correlated with various other characteristics. The table demonstrates that industries with a heavy complement of scientists and engineers in research and development also have a heavy complement of scientists and engineers in production, as well as in sales. To a considerable extent, therefore, high technical effort at any stage of the design-production-marketing process is associated with high technical effort at all the other stages.

The measures in Table 6 tell us more, however. They indicate that the intensity of the research and development effort is greatest in industries in which the degree of employment concentration is high, and in industries in which large firms are particularly dominant.

So far, the statistical picture is familiar enough.[7] Where the statistics begin to break some new ground is in their indication that the large-scale high-concentration pattern is not associated with high capital intensity. To be sure, high indirect labor costs *are* positively correlated with high research effort; and high indirect labor costs could well be consistent with high capital intensity. But the picture of high capital intensity is virtually dispelled by the two final measures in Table 6. Here, two fairly sensitive measures of capital intensity fail to display any systematic relation with high research effort.[8]

These findings, when drawn together, paint a fairly consistent picture. They suggest the existence of national markets in which economies of large scale and barriers to entry stem from the requirements of successful product innovation and successful marketing, rather than from capital intensity.[9] The forces that determine the propensity to gamble on product innovation are no doubt extraordinarily complex and lend themselves only grudgingly to easy generalization. A firm that can spread its research risks over a large number of efforts will have a more predictable payout in any finite period than one which does not have the resources for a large number of tries, especially if the anticipated yield on any single effort is not systematically different for large firms than for small.

William H. Gruber, Dileep Mehta, Raymond Vernon

Table 6. Relationship Between Measures of Intensity of Research Effort and Other Characteristics in United States Industries[a]

Industry Characteristics	Spearman Coefficient of Rank Correlation for Indicated Cell			Average of Industry Characteristics	
	Total R&D Expenditures in Industry Sales, 1962	Company Financed R&D Expenditures as % of Industry Sales, 1962	Scientists and Engineers in R&D as % of Total Industry Employment, 1962	5 Most Research-Intensive Industries	14 Other Industries
Research and technology:					
% of companies indicating majority of R&D efforts for new products, 1958	+0.63	+0.64	+0.51	(b)	(b)
Scientists and engineers in R&D as % of total industry employment, 1962	+0.81	+0.82	+1.00	3.2%	0.4%
Scientists and engineers in production as % of total industry employment, 1962	+0.76	+0.79	+0.92	2.1	0.8
Scientists and engineers in sales as % of total industry employment, 1962	+0.84	+0.87	+0.86	0.9	0.1

Scale and concentration:					
Index of employment concentration, 1958[c]	+0.66	+0.66	+0.59	47.0	21.1
Index of asset scale, 1961[d]	+0.48	+0.47	+0.60	67.1	46.1
Index of sales scale, 1961[e]	+0.58	+0.57	+0.70	35.0	21.1
Cost characteristics:					
Indirect labor costs as % of value added, 1957	+0.64	+0.63	+0.68	24.7	17.2
Depreciation expenses as % of value added, 1957	−0.11[f]	−0.08[f]	+0.03[f]	4.3	5.3
Net fixed assets as % of value added, 1957	−0.09[f]	−0.03[f]	+0.09[f]	31.0	41.0

[a] The number of industries for which relationships in the table could be calculated was not the same throughout. In some cases data were not available for some industries.

[b] Not available.

[c] The index, calculated for each SIC 2-digit industry, consists of a ratio whose numerator is employment in constituent SIC 4-digit industries in which the largest 8 firms accounted for 60% or more of 2-digit total employment, and whose denominator was total employment in the 2-digit industry.

[d] The index, calculated for each SIC 2-digit industry, consists of a ratio whose numerator is the assets of firms with $50 million or more in assets, and whose denominator is total assets in the industry.

[e] The index, calculated for each SIC 2-digit industry, consists of a ratio whose numerator is sales in firms with one-half billion or more in assets, and whose denominator is total assets in the industry.

[f] These coefficients are not significant at the 5% probability level. All other coefficients in the table are significant at that level or at a lower probability level.

Source: See Statistical Appendix.

Once the new product has been invented, scale continues to play a part in success. The sale of technically complex producer goods, for instance, requires a detailed understanding of the needs of customers, a continuing sales service, readily accessible spare parts, and a high level of research activity to keep the product competitive. The act of exporting to foreign markets, therefore, represents a marketing investment which one would expect to be associated with significant scale economies.

In sum, one derives a picture of high research effort being correlated with industries that experience substantial trade surpluses. These research-intensive industries, although large and concentrated, are not systematically capital intensive. It is in these industries that the U.S. trade advantage lies.

Trade and Investment in Foreign Manufacturing Subsidiaries

Neither the theory of international trade nor the theory of international capital movements has much to offer in explanation of managerial decisions to invest in production facilities abroad. International trade is explained largely in comparative advantage and factor endowment terms; long-term capital movements are seen largely as a reflection of the process of equating the marginal efficiency of capital in different countries. Yet, intuitively, one is aware that the prospective foreign investor, debating whether to invest in a production facility in a foreign market, is engaged in an evaluation process which juggles a number of additional major variables.

One way of looking at the overseas direct investments of U.S. producers of manufactures is that they are the final step in a process which begins with the involvement of such producers in export trade. The export trade of the United States, according to the data presented, is heavily weighted with products that demand large scientific and technical inputs in the selling process. Products of this sort, as we noted earlier, ordinarily demand an apparatus for learning customer needs and for subsequent technical servicing and consulting. Once such an organization has been established for sales purposes, the marginal costs of setting up a facility for production may be sharply reduced; for "marginal cost" in this context should be read not solely as a direct money expenditure but also as a measure of the pain of acquiring information regarding a country, negotiating for entry in a foreign economy, altering the company's organization to accommodate the new element, and tolerating the high subjective risks involved in a novel venture. Once the marginal costs are reduced in this sense, the probability that the venture may appear economical is, of course, enhanced. Whence it follows that industries with comparatively high export sales of products involving scientific and technical aspects in their sales and servicing, *ceteris paribus*, will have a high propensity to invest in manufacturing subsidiaries in the markets they serve.

This hypothesis appears particularly plausible if additional factors are considered. The research-intensive industries tend to be highly concentrated and suggest the existence of strong oligopoly forces. It is in such industries that rule-of-thumb measures of success, such as "maintaining our share of world markets," can be expected to enter most strongly into the investment decisions. In industries with lower concentration characteristics, the individual firm presumably finds share stability a less reliable gauge of its long-run survival or profit-maximizing prospects than in industries in which the principal rivals are few in number. In the oligopoly industries, therefore, individual firms are likely to consider foreign investments as important forestalling tactics to cut off market preemption by others. And they are likely to feel obliged to counter an investment by others with an investment of their own.

The available figures on foreign direct investment by U.S. enterprise do nothing to undermine the credibility of these hypotheses. The figures in Table 7 indicate in various ways that the propensity for U.S. industry to build facilities or otherwise to invest abroad, when "normalized" by the U.S. investment level, is higher in the research-oriented industries than in other industries. The figures on sales by U.S. subsidiaries abroad exhibit the same general characteristics as those for investment; when "normalized" by sales in the United States, sales of U.S. subsidiaries abroad are weighted heavily in favor of the research-oriented groups. The figures in the table have to be interpreted with a certain caution since invest-

Table 7. Plant and Equipment Expenditures, Investment Expenditures,
and Sales in the United States and Foreign Countries
by United States Industries[a][b]

	4 Research-Intensive Industries (Billions of Dollars)	*14 Other Industries (Billions of Dollars)*	*Ratio of 4 Research-Intensive Industries to 14 Other Industries*
Plant and equipment expenditures, 1958–64:			
In U.S.	$ 32.7	$ 50.8	64.4%
In Europe, by U.S.-owned subsidiaries	4.3	1.6	266.3
In non-Europe, by U.S.-owned subsidiaries	3.9	3.0	133.4
Direct investment, 1964:[c]			
In U.S.	71.7	94.9	75.6
In U.S.-owned subsidiaries in Europe	4.5	2.0	227.5
In U.S.-owned subsidiaries in non-Europe	5.2	4.9	106.0
Sales, 1962:			
In U.S.	143.4	205.7	69.7
By U.S.-owned subsidiaries in Europe	8.4	3.7	227.0
By U.S.-owned subsidiaries in non-Europe	8.7	7.3	119.3

[a] Data on the petroleum industry, SIC 29, are not included because not available for all parts of the table.

[b] Some of the data on the scientific instruments industry, SIC 38, are not available separately and have to be included in the "14 other industries" totals. This tends to blur slightly the otherwise sharp differences between the research-intensive industries and the other industries.

[c] For United States, the figures presented represent total equity interest; for the non-U.S. data, the figures are equity and debt in foreign subsidiaries owned by U.S. parents.

SOURCE: See Statistical Appendix.

ments in the non-Europe areas are heavily weighted with resource-oriented activities, such as paper and food processing. But the very limited conclusion suggested above obviously holds.

The figures in Table 8 permit slightly deeper probing of the investment patterns of U.S. industries in foreign countries. In this table, the focus is on the relationship between U.S. exports and the sales of U.S. subsidiaries located abroad. For this purpose, the sales of U.S. subsidiaries have been adjusted to exclude sales to the United States by U.S. subsidiaries abroad. The figures in the table, therefore, begin to approach a comparison between U.S. exports and foreign sales which could conceivably (but need not necessarily) be export substituting from the U.S. viewpoint.

Once again, some familiar patterns emerge. In the European area, the sales of U.S. subsidiaries are more important in relation to U.S. exports than in the non-European areas; if subsidiary sales are a substitute for U.S. exports, then the process would seem to have gone further in Europe than elsewhere. The tendency for Europe to have a higher ratio of subsidiary sales to exports than non-Europe is true both for the research-intensive and the other industries, but the research-intensive industries exhibit the tendency to a somewhat more marked degree. All this is consistent with expectations. Where scale factors are important, large markets are more likely to stimulate the ultimate commitment of a production facility than small markets.

The one new morsel of information which the table affords is an indication of the extent to which the "other" industries of the United States have moved their overseas operations from the sphere of exports to that of sales through overseas subsidiaries. In these industries, as we have repeatedly observed, neither exports nor overseas investment have much prominence, at least when "normalized" by the level of activities of those industries in the United States. However, of the two externally directed activities, exports and foreign subsidiary sales, the export position appears even less prominent than the subsidiary sales position. In terms of Table 8, the ratio of subsidiary sales to exports is fairly high.

There are at least two observations worth making concerning

Table 8. U.S. Exports and Foreign Subsidiary Sales to Elsewhere than U.S. by U.S. Manufacturing Industries in 1962 [a]

Industry Name [b] and SIC Number	U.S. Exports (Millions of Dollars)			Sales by Foreign Subsidiaries [c] (Millions of Dollars)			Foreign Subsidiary Sales Related to Exports (Per Cent)		
	Total	Europe	Non-Europe	Total	Europe	Non-Europe	Total	Europe	Non-Europe
Transportation (37)	$ 2,819	$ 315	$ 2,504	$ 6,590	$ 3,235	$ 3,355	233.8	1027.0	134.0
Electrical machinery (36)	1,344	273	1,071	2,553	1,210	1,343	190.0	443.2	125.4
Chemicals (28)	1,866	627	1,239	4,280	1,745	2,535	229.4	278.3	204.6
Machinery (non-electrical) (35)	3,846	1,070	2,776	3,263	2,045	1,218	84.8	191.1	43.9
Rubber and plastic (30)	193	43	150	1,322	455	867	685.0	1058.1	578.0
Primary and fabricated metal (33, 34)	1,286	367	919	1,946	710	1,236	151.3	193.5	134.5
Food (20)	553	187	366	3,287	1,180	2,107	594.4	631.0	575.7
Paper (26)	289	88	201	755	80	675	261.2	90.9	335.8
Other [d]	1,721	408	1,313	2,777	1,225	1,552	161.4	300.1	118.2
All 18 industries:	13,917	3,378	10,539	26,773	11,885	14,888	192.4	351.8	141.3
4 most research intensive	9,875	2,285	7,590	16,686	8,235	8,451	169.0	395.0	111.3
14 other industries	4,042	1,093	2,949	10,087	3,650	6,437	249.6	333.9	218.3

[a] Data on the petroleum industry, SIC 29, are excluded because figures for foreign direct investment and foreign subsidiary sales are not available.

[b] Industries arranged in descending order of research effort.

[c] Sales to the United States have been deleted from the total sales of foreign subsidiaries leaving only sales to local markets and to other countries by such subsidiaries.

[d] Data on the scientific instruments industry, SIC 38, are not available separately and have to be included with the "14 other industries." This tends to blur slightly the otherwise sharp differences between the research-intensive industries and the other industries.

Source: See Statistical Appendix.

the high ratios of subsidiary sales to exports in these "other industries." One fits well enough into the theme of this article; the other opens wholly new avenues of inquiry.

The observation that fits fairly well has to do with the present export position of these "other" industries. Time was, some decades ago, when the United States was a heavy exporter of most of the materials included in "other industries"—paper, food, rubber and metal products, in particular. In the course of time, the initial trade advantage of U.S. industries in these products was eroded. In partial response, these industries set up overseas subsidiaries to service their erstwhile export markets. The subsidiaries did not always do precisely what their parents had done by way of exports; while the subsidiaries of the rubber companies may have taken over the tire markets once serviced by their parents' exports, the subsidiaries of the food companies no doubt engaged in many new activities which could not have been supported by way of exports. In any event, in the end, subsidiary sales were a means by which contact with foreign markets was maintained.

But there is obviously another phenomenon involved. U.S. firms, such as those in food distribution and food processing, are commonly found investing in foreign markets for reasons which have little to do with salvaging an export position. Some of these firms, in effect, are seeking to sell a technique of production, finance, marketing, or general organization; this is certainly the interpretation to be placed on most of the investments of the U.S. food-processing and food-distributing industry in Europe. It is not sufficient, therefore, to explain U.S. overseas investment with a simple set of hypotheses based on the protection of markets previously acquired.

As a more complete explanation is developed of the forces behind U.S. overseas investment, the issue of market defense and market protection will no doubt play a part. But the strengths that derive from research and from the capacity to organize and maintain large complex organizations will surely figure in some independent sense as well.

Further research on the functioning of research and development in the creation of new products, new processes, and new systems, and on the forces that lead to industrial concentration and large-scale operations will be particularly fruitful in shedding more light on the problems that have been only partially answered in this paper.

Major Limitations of the Data

The following weaknesses of the data should be considered when the findings presented in the paper are evaluated: (1) the conversion of activity from SITC to SIC is only approximate in some cases; (2) the definition of R&D as used by companies in National Science Foundation reports differs between firms and industries; (3) the SIC two-digit level aggregates dissimilar industries; (4) research and development data is gathered at the company level, and this distorts the inputs by industry for diversified firms; (5) there is often not a complete matching of industry classification for various measures of activity (for example, scale data are by company while employment data are by establishment); (6) some goods should not be expected to move in international activity (for example, newspapers), and this lowers the ratio of trade performance to sales; (7) trade with Canada may not be a result of the forces under examination, but may result from the partial integration of the two economies; (8) activities related to natural resources have, in general, not been eliminated; (9) other forces, such as the differential impact of the "Buy American" provision of U.S. foreign aid have not been considered; (10) indirect exports have not been evaluated (for example, shipments of instrumentation from SIC 36 that enter into airplanes that are exported by SIC 37).

Fortunately, none of these limitations would affect the ordinal division of manufacturing activity into the five most research-intensive industries and the fourteen less research-intensive industries. There still would be a substantial gap between the fifth and sixth industries in order of research intensity.

These weaknesses, together with the arbitrary definition of the industries and the differences in the size of industries, have led us to use the methodology of dividing manufacturing activity into five research-intensive and fourteen less research-intensive industries. The summation of manufacturing activity into two classes of activity helps to make manifest the differences that exist between the research-intensive and the less research-intensive industries. This measure is less subject to the enumerated statistical weaknesses and is in harmony with the measures of Spearman rank correlation that were given. But it does not permit a disregard for the very substantial limitations that are inherent in the data.

FOOTNOTES

1 For authoritative summaries, see J. Bhagwati (1964) and J. Chipman (1965a, 1965b).

2 This school is epitomized by the writings of Economic Commission for Latin America (see Baer, 1962).

3 Attempts to quantify the relationship between research and trade have begun to appear in the literature. The French have coined the term "technological balance of payments," and some quantitative measures of this concept are presented in Freeman and Young (1965, pp. 51–55, 74). The relationship between the employment of scientists and engineers and trade position has been tested by Keesing (1966). Keesing's findings in that paper and in some unpublished work parallel and agree with some of the findings in the first section of this paper.

4 The Spearman rank coefficient for the association between R_1 and E_1, as those terms are defined in Table 1, is $+0.69$; between R_1 and E_2, is $+0.79$; between R_2 and E_1, $+0.74$; and between R_2 and E_2, $+0.69$. All coefficients are significant at the 1 per cent level. Pearson least-squares coefficients give similar results. In these correlation measures and in others presented hereafter, twenty-two sets of paired observations, rather than nineteen, are used, since each of the three-digit industries shown in Tables 1 and 2 provides the basis for a separate observation.

5 Characteristic of this view is the case made in Linder (1961).

6 The ratio of U.S. exports to the sum of the exports of a group of nations has been called "trade competitive power" by Donald Keesing. He found that there was a rank correlation of $+0.60$ between (1) "trade competitive power" and (2) scientists and engineers as a percentage of total employment for a sample of thirty-five non-natural-resource processing industries (Keesing, 1966, p. 256).

7 Compare, for instance, the findings in Worley (1962).

8 This result is consistent with analyses done by George E. Delehanty, in which he finds that the ratio of non-production employment to production employment in U.S. industries is more closely correlated with the degree to which scientists and engineers are in the work force of the industry than with the capital:labor ratio of the industry (see Delehanty, 1962).

9 This, of course, is hardly a new thought. See Bain (1956). See also C. Freeman's observations about the "reasons for the United States lead" in electronics (Freeman, 1965, p. 51).

REFERENCES

Baer, Werner. "The Economics of Prebisch and ECLA," Part 1, *Econ. Development and Cultural Change*, X, No. 2, Part I (January, 1962), 169–82.

Bain, Joe S. *Barriers to New Competition*. Cambridge, Mass.: Harvard Univ. Press, 1956.

Bhagwati, J. "The Pure Theory of International Trade: A Survey," *Econ. J.*, LXXIV, No. 293 (March, 1964), 1–84.

Chipman, John. "A Survey of the Theory of International Trade," Part 1, *Econometrica*, XXXIII, No. 3 (July, 1965), 477–519. (*a*)

————. "A Survey of the Theory of International Trade," Part 2, *ibid.*, No. 4 (October, 1965), pp. 685–760. (*b*)

Delehanty, George E. "An Analysis of the Changing Proportion of Non-Production Workers in U.S. Manufacturing Industries," unpublished doctoral thesis, M.I.T., 1962.

FTC-SEC. *Quarterly Financial Reports*, 1st Quarter, 1965. Washington: Government Printing Office, 1965.

Freeman, C. "The Plastics Industry: A Comparative Study of Research and Innovation," *Nat. Inst. Econ. Rev.*, No. 26 (November, 1963), pp. 22–62.

————. "Research and Development in Electronic Capital Goods," *ibid.*, No. 34 (November, 1965), pp. 40–91.

Freeman, C., and Young, A. *The Research and Development Effort in Western Europe, North America and the Soviet Union*. Paris: OECD, 1965.

Hirsch, S. *Location of Industry and International Competitveness*, Oxford: The Clarendon Press, 1967.

Hoffmeyer, Erik. *Dollar-Shortage*. Amsterdam: North-Holland Publishing, 1958.

Hufbauer, G. C. *Synthetic Materials and the Theory of International Trade*. London: Duckworth, 1965.

Keesing, Donald B. "Labor Skills and Comparative Advantage," *A.E.R. Proc.*, Vol. LVI, No. 2 (May, 1966).

Kindleberger, C. P. *Foreign Trade and the National Economy*. New Haven, Conn.: Yale Univ. Press, 1962.

Kreinin, Mordechai. "The Leontief Scarce-Factor Paradox," *A.E.R.*, LV, No. 1 (March, 1965), 131–40.

Linder, S. B. *An Essay in Trade and Transformation*. Stockholm: Almqvist & Wiksell, 1961.

136   *William H. Gruber, Dileep Mehta, Raymond Vernon*

MacDougall, Sir Donald. *The World Dollar Problem*. London: Macmillan, 1957.

National Industrial Conference Board. *The Conference Board Record*, April, 1964.

National Science Foundation. *Basic Research, Applied Research, and Development in Industry, 1962*, NSF 65–18. Washington: Government Printing Office, 1965.

———. *Basic Research, Applied Research, and Development in Industry, 1963*, NSF 66–15. Washington: Government Printing Office, 1966.

OECD. *OECD Statistical Bulletins. Foreign Trade Series B, Analytical Abstracts Jan.–Dec. 1962*. Paris: OECD, 1963.

Polk, Judd, Meister, I. W., and Veit, L. A. *U.S. Production Abroad and the Balance of Payments*. New York: National Industrial Conference Board, 1966.

Posner, M. V. "International Trade and Technical Change," *Oxford Econ. Papers*, XIII, No. 3 (October, 1961), 323–41.

United Nations Department of Economic and Social Affairs. *Trade Statistics, according to SITC*, Series D, Vol. XII, Nos. 1–20. New York: United Nations, January–December, 1962.

U.S. Bureau of the Census. *Census of Manufactures, 1958*, Vol. I, *Summary Statistics*. Washington: Government Printing Office, 1961.

———. *U.S. Census of Population: 1960 Subject Reports Occupation by Industry*, Final Report PC (2)–7C. Washington: Government Printing Office, 1962.

U.S. Bureau of Labor Statistics. *Employment of Scientific and Technical Personnel in Industry, 1962*, Bull. No. 1418. Washington: Government Printing Office, 1964.

———. *Employment and Earnings Statistics for the United States, 1909–64*. Washington: Government Printing Office, 1965.

U.S. Department of Commerce. *Survey of Current Business*. Washington: Government Printing Office, various dates.

U.S. Treasury Department, Internal Revenue Service. *Statistics of Income 1961–62. Corporation Income Tax Returns*. Washington: Government Printing Office, 1964.

Vernon, Raymond. "International Investment and International Trade in the Product Cycle," *Q.J.E.*, May, 1966.

Wells, L. T., Jr. "Product Innovation and Directions of International Trade," unpublished doctoral dissertation, Harvard Bus. School, 1966.

Williams, J. H. "The Theory of International Trade Reconsidered," *Econ. J.*, XXXIX (June, 1929), 195–209.

Worley, J. S. "The Changing Direction of Research and Development Employment among Firms," in Universities–National Bureau Committee for Economic Research, *The Rate and Direction of Inventive Activity*. Princeton, N.J.: Princeton Univ. Press, 1962.

STATISTICAL APPENDIX

Tables 1 and 2*

1. Research and development: Industry research and development expenditures in 1962 from NSF 66-15, page 83 for total research and development, and NSF 65-18, page 105 for company-financed research and development. The National Science Foundation divides these figures by the sales of the responding firms that do research and development in order to get a ratio of research and development expenditures as a percentage of sales. This seemed to be inadequate for our purpose of developing an index of research intensity for an industry as it omitted the sales of the firms that do not do research and development. We divided by total industrial sales as measured by the *FTC-SEC Quarterly Financial Reports*. NSF lumped some industries together [22 + 23; 24 + 25; 21, 27 + 31]. We estimated industry inputs by disaggregating the NSF data by the ratios of scientists and engineers in these industries as reported in U.S. Bureau of the Census (1962, Table 2). It is unlikely that errors resulting from this method of estimation would affect the findings because of the very small amounts of research and development to be allocated in these seven industries. In this case, a little bit more or less of a very small amount will cause insignificant errors.

2. Scientists and engineers in research and development in 1962 from B.L.S. Bulletin No. 1418 (1964, p. 35). Employment by industry taken from B.L.S. (1965).

3. Exports and imports from OECD (1963, nos. 1, 5).

Tables 3 and 5

1. World exports of U.S. and all OECD countries (OECD, 1963, nos. 1–6). Japan was not included in the OECD until after 1962, and her world exports taken from the U.N. Department of Economic and

---

* Where data are used again in subsequent tables, they are not referenced. For example, scientists and engineers as a percentage of total employment is a variable used in Tables 3 and 5 as well as in Tables 1 and 2.

Social Affairs (1962). In order to be able to perform parametric tests, a range of values from 0.2 to 5.0 was set. For example, a positive value divided by zero would give a measure of absolute advantage equal to 5.0. Similarly, a zero divided by a positive number would be given a value of absolute disadvantage of 0.2. The conversion from SITC to SIC was done according to the accompanying tabulation.

Table 6

1. The percentage of companies indicating majority of research and development efforts for new products from the 1958 McGraw-Hill Survey of Capital Spending.

2. Scientists and engineers in production and in sales as a percentage of total industry employment in 1962 from B.L.S. Bulletin No. 1418 (1964, p. 35).

3. Index of employment concentration: *The Conference Board Record* (1964, p. 52).

4. Index of asset scale, 1961, and index of sales scale, 1961: U.S. Treasury Department Internal Revenue Service (1964, Table 2).

5. Cost characteristics: U.S. Bureau of the Census (1961, Table 3).

Table 7

1. Plant and equipment expenditures from 1958 to 1964 in the United States: U.S. Department of Commerce (July, 1961, p. 29; and September 1965, p. 6). Plant and equipment expenditures of U.S. corporations in Europe and non-Europe: U.S. Department of Commerce (October, 1960, p. 20; September, 1961, p. 21; and September, 1965, p. 29).

2. Direct investment in the United States in 1964: FTC-SEC (1965). For U.S.-owned subsidiaries in Europe and non-Europe: U.S. Department of Commerce (September, 1965, Table 5, p. 27).

3. For sales in the United States in 1964: FTC-SEC (1965). For sales of U.S.-owned subsidiaries in Europe and non-Europe: U.S. Department of Commerce (November, 1965, p. 19).

Table 8

See sources for Table 7.

	SIC	*SITC*
Food and kindred products	20	013, 023, 024, 032, 046, 047, 048, 053, 055, 061, 062, 091, 099, 111, 112
Tobacco products	21	122
Textile mill products	22	65
Apparel and related products	23	84
Lumber and wood products	24	63, 243
Furniture and fixtures	25	82
Paper and allied products	26	64
Printing and publishing	27	892
Chemicals and allied products	28	5
Drugs	283	541
Chemicals (other than drugs)	. . .	5 minus 541
Petroleum and coal products	29	332
Rubber and plastic products, n.e.c.	30	62, 893
Leather and leather products	31	611, 612, 613, 83, 85
Stone, clay, and glass products	32	661, 662, 663, 664, 665, 666
Primary metal	33	67, 68
Nonferrous metal	333	68
Ferrous metal	. . .	67
Fabricated metal products	34	69
Machinery except electrical	35	71
Electrical machinery	36	72
Transportation equipment	37	73
Aircraft and parts	372	734
Transport (other than aircraft)	. . .	73 minus 734
Instruments and related products	38	86

The Relationship Between the Income and Price Elasticities of Demand for United States Exports

(Reprinted by permission of *The Review of Economics and Statistics*, Vol. LII, No. 3, August 1970)

F. Michael Adler

Michael Adler is Associate Professor of Finance and International Business at the Columbia University Graduate School of Business. He was previously Assistant Professor at Columbia and at the Wharton School, University of Pennsylvania, and Research Assistant at the Harvard University Graduate School of Business Administration. He is an Associate Editor of The Journal of Finance *and has served as consultant to the U.S. Departments of Treasury and State on matters pertaining to direct investment overseas. He holds B.S. and M.S. degrees from Carnegie-Mellon University and the D.B.A. degree from Harvard University.*

He co-authored Overseas Manufacturing Investment and the Balance of Payments *(Washington: Government Printing Office, 1968), and has published articles on foreign investment in* The Columbia Journal of World Business, Law and Contemporary Problems, *and* The Bankers Magazine.

The Relationship Between the Income and Price Elasticities of Demand for United States Exports

Recent empirical studies in international trade, by Junz and Rhomberg [10], Krenin [14] and in a major contribution, by Houthakker and Magee [6], have stressed the importance of different price and income elasticities of demand for exports and imports among countries as determinants of trade patterns. However, questions as to why such differences in elasticities arise remain open. An important component of the problem is whether the price and income elasticities of demand for individual exporters' products vary systematically across customer markets. This paper attempts partially to address the latter issue by examining the elasticities of United States exports of manufactured goods. The major finding is that a relationship exists between the competitiveness of United States manufactured goods exports in various foreign countries and the nature of the customer market. The result has implications, outlined below, for projections of future United States trade balances.

* AUTHOR'S NOTE: The author has benefited from critical comments on earlier drafts made by Professors H. G. Grubel, G. C. Hufbauer, P. B. Kenen, N. Leff and R. Vernon. None shares any responsibility for errors. Thanks are extended to R. R. Rhomberg who supplied the price data used. Research support was provided in part by the Graduate School of Business, Columbia University.

143

Hypotheses

In any foreign country United States manufactured goods vie for market share with products from the set of all other competing suppliers. If the American goods differ materially from others' exports, they will face different price and income elasticities of demand. This section develops two hypotheses based on a synthesis of recent additions to the theory of the consumer and to the analysis of sources of United States comparative advantage. The first is that the difference between the income elasticities of United States and competitors' goods in each foreign market should be related to the difference between the respective price elasticities. The second is that the market appeal of the kinds of manufactures exported by the United States should be stronger in the advanced than in the less developed countries. These hypotheses can conveniently be discussed using the notation of a model which relates changes in United States market shares in individual foreign markets to the relevant elasticities.

For each country i, two import demand equations are specified:

$$Q_{1it} = Q_{1it}(y_{it}, p_{1t}, p_{2t}) \tag{1}$$
$$Q_{2it} = Q_{2it}(y_{it}, p_{1t}, p_{2t}) \tag{2}$$

where Q_{1it} is the ith country's imports of manufactured goods from the United States during year t in 1958 dollars; Q_{2it} is country i's manufactures imports from the set of all other exporters, excluding the United States; y_{it} represents the ith country's national income in 1958 dollars; p_{1t} is the United States export unit value index; and p_{2t} is a weighted average of the export unit value indices of the major competing suppliers as described in [10].[1] The model incorporates assumptions made elsewhere. Domestic production and price variables, which empirically added little in previous work [6, p. 112], are omitted.[2] Similarly, to avoid specification error, the price elasticities of export supply in the United States and elsewhere are implicitly assumed to be infinite.[3] Finally, the price and income variables are assumed to be mutually independent.[4] For simplicity, the i and t subscripts can temporarily be dropped.

By differentiation of the ratio of (1) over (2),

$$\frac{d(Q_1/Q_2)}{Q_1/Q_2} = \left[\frac{\partial Q_1/Q_1}{\partial y/y} - \frac{\partial Q_2/Q_2}{\partial y/y}\right] \frac{dy}{y}$$

$$+ \left[\frac{\partial Q_1/Q_1}{\partial p_1/p_1} - \frac{\partial Q_2/Q_2}{\partial p_1/p_1}\right] \frac{dp_1}{p_1}$$

$$+ \left[\frac{\partial Q_1/Q_1}{\partial p_2/p_2} - \frac{\partial Q_2/Q_2}{\partial p_2/p_2}\right] \frac{dp_2}{p_2}.$$

$$(3)$$

Rewriting (3), proportional changes in the United States market share in each customer market can be expressed by:

$$\frac{d(Q_1/Q_2)}{Q_1/Q_2} = (E_1 - E_2)\frac{dy}{y} + (e_{11} - e_{21})\frac{dp_1}{p_1}$$

$$+ (e_{12} - e_{22})\left(\frac{dp_2}{p_2}\right); \qquad (4)$$

where e_{jk} is the partial elasticity of Q_j with respect to p_k, and E_j is the partial elasticity of Q_j with respect to y. On the plausible assumption that the price cross elasticities are equal, (4) becomes

$$\frac{d(Q_1/Q_2)}{Q_1/Q_2} = (E_1 - E_2)\frac{dy}{y} + (e_{11} - e_{22})\frac{dp_2}{p_2}$$

$$+ (e_{11} - e_{12})\left(\frac{dp_1}{p_1} - \frac{dp_2}{p_2}\right). \qquad (5)$$

Equation (5) reflects explicitly the effects on United States export market shares of competition between the United States and competitive suppliers in individual third-country export markets. Under usual conditions, the income elasticities and price cross elasticities will be positive, while e_{11} and e_{22} will be negative. Consequently only $(e_{11} - e_{12})$, the "elasticity of substitution" in Junz and Rhomberg [10], can unambiguously be identified as negative. *Ceteris paribus*, United States export market shares abroad will be depressed (raised) when United States export prices rise (fall) faster than other exporters'. However, if both foreign incomes and other suppliers' prices are rising (falling) the adverse impact of inflation in the United States will be offset (aggravated) to the extent that $E_1 > E_2$ and $|e_{22}| > |e_{11}|$. Over the 1953–1963 period of the study, United States export prices and customer country incomes rose while competitors' export prices tended to decline.

A growing body of literature suggests that $(E_1 - E_2)$ and $(e_{11} - e_{22})$ should be related in United States export markets and that jointly, the magnitudes of both differences should vary with the level of development of the importing country. Let us see how these hypotheses arise.

Kravis, later supported by Lary, recognized that the composition of United States manufactured goods exports tends continually to shift towards new products [13, 16]. Such products have been defined by Vernon and Keesing, independently, as technologically advanced, human-capital and research and development intensive [4, 11, 12]. On the supply side, Vernon has argued that externalities, such as government R&D support and the existence of jobbing firms, render the United States the most likely place for the initial production of new goods [21]. More probably, the United States, the world's highest income market, is where frequently they will first be demanded. The new products, which may include producer goods designed to increase efficiency by capital-labor substitution, are more commonly identified as differentiated consumer goods, including durables, developed specifically in response to the increasingly sophisticated tastes of high income consumers [cf. 21]. According to Becker [1], such individuals have the highest opportunity costs of time and therefore stand to gain most from the time-savings available from buying branded goods and time and labor saving devices. Sales of new products in the United States tend to follow a "life cycle" which depends upon how long they retain their superiority as replacements for competing goods and techniques [21].

Foreign demand for, and therefore exports of, each new, high-technology good tend to appear shortly after its introduction in the United States. According to Posner and Hufbauer, there follows a period of "technological gap" exports which depend for their existence on the monopolistic determinants (e.g., patent protection, scale economies) and the duration of the "imitation lag" [7, 19]. Once foreign markets expand sufficiently and the technology is transferred, foreign production of each good will begin and the erstwhile United States exports will cease to grow and may decline. To say that high-technology products feature prominently in the United States export mix is, consequently, to hypothesize that the composition of United States manufactures exports is continually shifting towards goods in the early stages of their product life cycles. As exports of one good taper and fall off, other products must take its place.

Marketing studies in the United States and the United Kingdom reveal that the price elasticity of demand for successful new products in their early stages is relatively low essentially because substitutes for such products are imperfect [2, 20].[5] Such reasoning gives rise to part of the present hypothesis. The more perfect the substitutability between United States goods and others in a foreign market, the more the price elasticities will tend to be equal. Imperfect substitutability implies unequal elasticities. When $|e_{11}| > |e_{22}|$ there are better substitutes for United States goods than for others'. Equivalently, the more United States manufactures are differentiated from, are considered superior replacements for, and are in an earlier product stage than competitors' products, the smaller $|e_{11}|$ will be relative to $|e_{22}|$.

Similar considerations determine the difference, $(E_1 - E_2)$, between a country's income elasticities of demand for United States goods as opposed to competitors' manufactures. Three of the requisite links in the chain of propositions were forged by Wells [22]. In the United States, successful, new high-technology products tended to exhibit high income elasticities of demand in the early stages of their product lives. These income elasticities declined as the products aged and competitive substitutes were introduced. Independently, a close correspondence existed in a sample of twenty consumer durables between income elasticities and other measures of consumer preferences such as saturation. Finally, his evidence indicated that consumption patterns in America and other developed countries were similar. Wells' results suggest the following interpretation of the difference, $(E_1 - E_2)$, in the present study. Equal income elasticities will be taken to indicate that the customer market requires little product differentiation, at least by country of origin or age of product, among the manufactures in its import mix. When $(E_1 - E_2) < 0$, United States manufactures may be less adapted to local tastes than competitors' goods. Conversely, we may posit that the more positive the difference between E_1 and E_2, the more likely it is that the goods desired from the United States fill better a unique set of consumer requirements and are in an earlier cycle stage than the products imported from other manufacturers.

The first of our two hypotheses follows as an important implication of considerations which Johnson has identified as part of the theory of monopolistic competition in international trade [9]. If product cycle effects exert an operative influence on United States manufactures exports, then the larger E_1 is relative to E_2, the smaller $|e_{11}|$ should be compared to $|e_{22}|$, and vice versa.

Finally, following Linder's thesis that trade grows mainly among equally developed countries, each of which exports products for which a representative home demand exists [17], Vernon has suggested that United States exports of high-technology, human-capital-intensive products initially go to those foreign markets the nature of whose consumer demand is most similar to the United States [21]. The similarity should be least pronounced in the less-developed markets which by and large will require less product differentiation because high-income consumption constitutes only a small fraction of total demand. For the majority of the relatively standardized manufactures entering the import mixes of such countries, the technology will be widespread among the advanced nations, a number of which can therefore provide alternative, substitute sources of supply [5]. In contrast, the similiarity to the United States should be greatest among the advanced countries which should therefore comprise the markets in which the United States is likely to enjoy its strongest position either as temporary monopolist of specialties unavailable elsewhere or as the main alternative source for residual imports of technology-intensive goods which are produced locally. Our second hypothesis then follows.

The more developed the export market, the better should be the market share competitiveness of United States manufactures, and the higher E_1 and $|e_{22}|$ should be relative to E_2 and $|e_{11}|$ respectively.

Empirical Results

The empirical analysis consists of first estimating the differences $(E_1 - E_2)$ and $(e_{11} - e_{22})$ for thirteen countries, using eleven annual observations apiece, and then using the resulting elasticities as data to test the hypotheses. The following logarithmic model provides directly estimates of the parameters of equation (5):

$$\log (Q_1/Q_2)_{it} = a_{0i} + a_{1i} \log y_{it} + a_{2i} \log p_{2it} + a_{3i} \log (p_1/p_2)_{it}. \tag{6}$$

In (6), a_{1i} estimates $(E_1 - E_2)$; a_{2i} estimates the difference in the price elasticities, $(e_{11} - e_{22})$, and will be positive when $|e_{11}| > |e_{22}|$ since dp_2/p_2 was negative for the period as a whole in each of the customer markets; a_{3i} represents the (negative) elasticity of substitution and the variables themselves are defined as before. It should be noted that equation (6) differs substantially from the models of demand for United States exports estimated by Houthakker and Magee in [6] and by Junz and Rhomberg in [10]. The Houthakker-Magee model was applied to the present data to check their quality. The results, which can be obtained directly from the author, were in good agreement with theirs. No separate comparison with the Junz and Rhomberg findings was performed since their estimated elasticities of substitution are biased.[6]

Turning now to table 1, the fit as measured by R^2 is not uniformly good. Many of the coefficients seem relatively inaccurate, judging from the t values, and four sign reversals occur in the a_3 column.[7] However, the values and signs of the a_1 and a_2 coefficients seem, for reasons to be detailed, generally to accord with prior expectations. Since the data and the cardinal magnitudes of the computed elasticities quite evidently will not support elaborate procedures, the hypotheses of section I will be tested nonparametrically.

Table 1. United States Exports of Manufactured Goods by Destination

$$\log(Q_1/Q_2) = a_0 + a_1 \log y + a_2 \log p_2 + a_3 \log(p_1/p_2)$$

	a_0	a_1	a_2	a_3	R^2/D.W.
Mexico	−10.06	−1.41	11.08	7.82	0.78
	(−0.77)	(−2.15)	(2.08)	(1.08)	2.42
Venezuela	4.78	−0.70	3.72	−0.45	0.89
	1.06	(−1.98)	(2.99)	(−0.46)	2.39
Japan	8.66	−0.56	−0.36	−2.50	0.69
	(0.94)	(−2.05)	(−0.59)	(−0.50)	2.03
France	3.96	−0.48	2.54	−1.02	0.90
	(1.06)	(−2.43)	(2.14)	(−0.43)	2.78
Italy	0.78	−1.04	7.16	4.37	0.91
	(0.24)	(−6.29)	(5.06)	(3.74)	3.03
Canada	−4.18	0.10	3.94	−0.96	0.66
	(−0.13)	(1.51)	(0.71)	(−1.05)	2.20
Bel-Lux	4.11	−0.07	−0.42	−2.49	0.85
	(2.66)	(−1.85)	(−3.7)	(−2.17)	2.43
Sweden	−7.84	−0.66	1.04	3.66	0.51
	(−1.74)	(−2.28)	(2.26)	(1.29)	2.50
Netherlands	2.08	0.39	−2.76	−2.71	0.47
	(0.36)	(2.58)	(−0.84)	(−0.75)	1.89
U.K.	−2.25	0.42	−0.68	−1.04	0.71
	(−0.50)	(2.32)	(−1.16)	(−1.22)	2.95
W. Germany	0.21	1.39	0.90	−4.61	0.79
	(0.03)	(2.89)	(0.85)	(−1.09)	1.46
Australia	−10.22	0.62	−6.41	2.08	0.85
	(−2.63)	(2.44)	(−2.64)	(0.76)	1.86
India	5.63	3.65	−2.09	−11.83	0.55
	(0.95)	(3.82)	(−0.37)	(−2.79)	1.92

NOTES: Numbers in parentheses are t-ratios. $Q_2 = Q_T - Q_1$, where $Q_T =$ each country's total imports of ITC groups 5, 6, 7 and 8, adjusted as in [8, pp. 36–37], and deflated by its import unit value index; $Q_1 =$ reported United States exports of manufactured goods to each country deflated by the United States export unit value index. For y, United Nations national income estimates were converted to constant 1958 dollars, using unpublished United Nations purchasing power parity exchange rates [see 18]. The price data, supplied by R. R. Rhomberg, are described in [10, p. 261].

SOURCES: [8], [10], [23], [24], [25], [26].

Four rankings are presented in table 2. Column 1 ranks the thirteen countries in the sample according to the magnitude of the change in the United States share of each country's imports of manufactured goods over the entire 1953–1963 period. As a matter of interest, Q_1/Q_2 declined in the first eight countries, remained unchanged in the Netherlands and rose only in the bottom group of four. If market share changes can be taken as indicating the competiveness of United States manufactures abroad, column 1 ranks United States customer markets from where the United States was least to where it was most competitive.

Column 2 ranks the countries according to the difference between E_1 and E_2. The order is from the most negative to the most positive of the a_1 coefficients reported in table 1, with no adjustments. Column 3 provides a ranking according to the difference between

Table 2. Country Rankings

Change in U.S. Market Share[a] $\Delta(Q_1/Q_2)$	Difference Between Income Elasticities[b] $a_1 = E_1 - E_2$	Difference Between Price Elasticities[b] $a_2 = e_{11} - e_{22}$	Average 1953–1963 Net Income/Capital[c] NI
Mexico	Mexico	Mexico	Mexico
Venezuela	Italy	Italy	Japan
Japan	Venezuela	Canada	Italy
France	Sweden	Venezuela	Venezuela
Italy	Japan	France	Netherlands
Canada	France	Sweden	France
Bel-Lux	Bel-Lux	Germany	Germany
Sweden	Canada	Japan	Bel-Lux
Netherlands	Netherlands	Bel-Lux	Australia
U.K.	U.K.	U.K.	Canada
Germany	Australia	India	U.K.
Australia	Germany	Netherlands	Sweden
India	India	Australia	

SOURCES: [a] Underlying data: see notes to table 1.
[b] Table 1.
[c] Average National Income/Average Population [23].

the price elasticities, from the most positive to the most negative of the unadjusted a_2 values in table 1. The ranking indicates that the demand for United States products was relatively most price-elastic in Mexico and relatively least in Australia. Column 4, which excludes India for reasons discussed below, is self-explanatory.

Spearman rank correlation coefficients between pairs of table 2 columns are listed in table 3. Most are significant at the one per cent level. The results confirm the first hypothesis of section I. Market conditions abroad are such that, the larger and more positive $(E_1 - E_2)$ the more likely it is that the price elasticity of foreign demand will be lower for United States goods than for other suppliers'. In addition, the characteristics of consumer demand in foreign markets are detectably related to United States market share performance. Theory predicts tautologically that if foreign demand is more income and less price elastic for American goods than for others, the competitiveness of United States goods will be enhanced. The data indicate that these effects were sufficient for United States goods to maintain or improve their market position in the bottom five of the thirteen countries in column 1 of table 2 despite adverse trends in United States export prices.[8] Less optimistically, the differences in elasticities were not large enough to preserve United States market shares in such traditional or growing trading areas as Canada, some European nations, Latin America and Japan.

The test of the Linder-Vernon hypothesis that United States competitiveness should be greater in the advanced than in the less-developed countries is more oblique. India's position in the rankings is anomalous. The unexpected strength of her apparent preference for United States manufactures over others' may be due to the distorting impact of tied United States aid and import controls. Excluding India, the market share ranking of the remaining twelve countries in column 1 of table 2 was correlated with their order according to average, 1953–1963 net income per capita in column 4. The Spearman coefficient, reported in table 3, is $r = 0.69$ with $t = 3.07$. Partial confirmation for the second hypothesis is therefore available if per-capita incomes can be accepted as an index of development. United States competitive-

Table 3. Spearman Rank Correlations: Coefficients and *t* Values

	$E_1 - E_2$	$e_{11} - e_{22}$	*NI*
$E_1 - E_2$	—	0.762 (3.92)	—
$\Delta(Q_1/Q_2)$	0.89 (6.35)	0.764 (3.96)	0.69 (3.07)

$t_{a=0.01} = 3.11$
SOURCE: Table 2.

ness in foreign markets is directly correlated with higher incomes. That, in addition, incomes, $(E_1 - E_2)$, $(e_{11} - e_{22})$ and market share changes tend systematically to vary together is evidenced by the coefficient of concordance among all four columns of table 2, each excluding India: $W = 0.75$, with Snedecor's $F = 9.0$, which is significant at the one-percentage level. However, the relationship between income and the parameters of consumer demand functions bears further study. While the positions of Mexico, Venezuela and Japan in column 1 seem plausible, intuitively it is not obvious why the United Kingdom, Germany and Australia should appear so much more receptive to United States goods than, say, Canada.

Conclusions

The results reported above support quite startlingly the hypothesis that product-cycle factors affect United States export performance. By substituting direct estimates of the parameters of foreign import demand functions, they improve upon previous work which found that United States income demand elasticities, taken as indicators of income elasticities and market receptivity abroad, performed well as predictors of United States success in exporting [22]. Further work might test the data underlying [6] specifically for the presence of product cycle effects. For example, Houthakker and Magee found that United States manufactures exports are considerably less price elastic than United States imports of manufactured goods. This result would follow if United States imports were in a later cycle stage than United States exports. In contrast, United States exports were not more income elastic than United States imports. The reversal bears closer examination. One suspects, however, that major progress awaits data improvements and, in particular, price series disaggregated by country and industry.

The omens for the future of the United States trade balance in manufactures are not auspicious. The present results reinforce the likelihood, established in [6] of further deterioration in erstwhile United States surpluses. Favorable United States trade balances with other advanced countries may depend to a large degree on America's ability to maintain a technological lead, reflected in a high rate of development and introduction of new products. Any present technological gap may, however, be ephemeral. Recent upsurges in direct investment abroad have probably accelerated transfers of knowhow, especially in Europe [8]. In any case, the bulk of United States manufactures exports go to countries, other than Australia, India, the United Kingdom and Germany, where income and price elasticities of demand for American and competitors' goods tend to be similar. It might be argued that as per-capita incomes rise abroad, an increasing number of countries will pass the threshold and become customers for high-technology goods. By that time, however, the United States can expect to face stiffer competition from other developed countries. Few factors, if any, will serve to offset the adverse market-share impact of continuing relative increases in United States export prices. If, in addition, others' demand for United States exports is less income elastic than United States demand for imports—as Houthakker and Magee have shown, anti-inflationary trade deficits must be expected to materialize. In the future the United States may increasingly have to look to its capital, rather than its current, account to finance expenditures abroad.

FOOTNOTES

1 Data definitions and sources are discussed further in the footnotes to Table 1.

2 No domestic price data were available. Earlier versions of this paper reported attempts to incorporate a local production variable both in a one-equation model and in the reduced form of a two-equation model. However, in both cases, collinearity between local production and income was very high, reducing to unacceptable levels the accuracy of estimated elasticities.

3 The assumption seems reasonable. The quantities required by any single importer will not generally be so large as to exert pressure on capacity constraints in exporting areas. Equally the possibility that importers act as monopsonists can be ruled out.

4 Changes in United States and others' export prices are assumed to leave unchanged home market price levels, the difference between the quantities produced and demanded locally, and foreign incomes. All export prices are measured by indices of F.O.B. export unit values rather than by indices of each supplier's delivered prices in each market. Differences or changes over time in transportation costs and tariffs among pairs of exporters and importers are ignored, or held constant. Efforts to distinguish statistically between pre- and post-EEC periods, using the methodology in [3], failed. Therefore, intra-period curve shifts are assumed to be absent.

5 Indeed, imperfect substitutability is the goal for products introduced as superior replacements for older goods and is enhanced by product differentiation. Less persuasively, marketeers argue that the price elasticity will be low because the new goods are supposedly bought for non-price reasons by rich consumers who are largely insensitive to prices. But then, the income elasticities of the new goods should also be low, contradicting the life cycle hypothesis. The argument is a little different if the new product is a producer good, which performs old functions more cheaply. Industrial buyers will pay a higher price for superior equipment based on the savings to be realized by replacing older machines.

6 The model in [10] corresponds to the specification $\log (Q_1/Q_2)_t = c_0 + c_{1t}$ $\log (p_1/p_2)_t + c_{2t}t$: c_{1t} can provide an unbiased estimate of the elasticity of substitution, defined as $[\partial(Q_1/Q_2)/(Q_1/Q_2)]/[\partial(p_1/p_2)/(p_1/p_2)]$, only if p_2 is assumed or constrained to be constant. If p_2 varies, as was historically the case, $\text{plim } c_{1t} = a_{3t} + a_{2t} (r/1 - r)$, where a_{3t} and a_{2t} are defined in equation (6) and r is the expected value of the (negative) correlation coefficient between $\log p_2$ and $\log p_1$.

7 Comparably, Junz and Rhomberg obtained positive elasticities of substitution for Japan, Sweden and all industrial countries combined [10, p. 240]. Houthakker and Magee obtained positive elasticities of United States exports with respect to relative prices in the cases of Mexico and Sweden [6, p. 117] whereas, using a similar model, the present data produced positive elasticities for Sweden and Australia. Dynamic effects may account for some of the unacceptable positive coefficients in each of the studies [cf. 6, appendix B]. Of the eight countries where autocorrelation seems to be present, seven have Durbin-Watson ratios which exceed 2. Only Germany's falls substantially below 2. The prevalent serial correlation is negative indicating an upward bias in the standard errors of the coefficients. However, attempts to eliminate or to explain the serial correlation all failed. The quality of the fit was reduced in regressions which adjusted for serial correlation using the Cochrane-Orcutt iterative technique but which used up an additional degree of freedom. Plots of the residuals suggested that the first three observations might have produced the negative serial correlation in several of the cases where Q_1/Q_2 declined. But tests of subperiods (see footnote 4) were inconclusive and regressions omitting the first three data points, leaving four degrees of freedom, were less accurate than those presented. The omission of (unavailable) domestic prices was immediately suspect. However, if the errors in the log-log model are not truly multiplicative, the effect will be the same as if there were a missing variable. The importance of dynamic factors remains an open question.

8 A similar conclusion is available from the cross-country regression: $\Delta(Q_1/Q_2)_i = b_0 + b_1 a_{1i} + b_2 a_{2i}$, where a_{1i} and a_{2i} are the values from table 1. The rank correlation procedure was chosen for the reasons given in the text, and also because the rank listings provide clearly visible patterns. The coefficient of concordance among the first three columns of table 2 $= W = 0.87$, with Snedecor's $F = 13.4$ which is significant at the one percentage level.

REFERENCES

[1] Becker, G. S., "A Theory of the Allocation of Time," *The Economic Journal*, LXXV (Sept. 1965).

[2] Buzzell, R., T. Levitt, and R. Frank, *Marketing: An Introductory Analysis* (New York: McGraw-Hill, 1964), 243–244.

[3] Chow, G. C. "Tests of Equality between Subsets of Coefficients in Two Linear Regressions," *Econometrica*, 28 (July, 1960).

[4] Gruber, W., D. Mehta, and R. Vernon, "The R&D Factor in International Trade and International Investment," reprinted in this book.

[5] Hirsch, S., *Location of Industry and International Competitiveness* (Oxford: The Clarendon Press, 1967).

[6] Houthakker, H. S., and S. P. Magee, "Income and Price Elasticities in World Trade," *The Review of Economics and Statistics*, LI (May, 1969).

[7] Hufbauer, G. C., *Synthetic Materials and the Theory of International Trade* (Cambridge: Harvard University Press, 1966).

[8] Hufbauer, G. C., and F. M. Adler, *Overseas Manufacturing Investment and the Balance of Payments*, U.S. Treasury Tax Policy Research Study No. 1. (Washington, D.C.: U.S. Government Printing Office, 1968).

[9] Johnson, H. G., "International Trade Theory and Monopolistic Competition Theory," chapt. 9 in [15].

[10] Junz, H., and R. R. Rhomberg. "Price and Export Performance of Industrial Countries, 1953–1963," *I.M.F. Staff Papers*, July, 1965.

[11] Keesing, D. B., "Labor Skills and Comparative Advantage," *American Economic Review*, LVI (May, 1960).

[12] Keesing, D. B., "The Impact of Research and Development on U.S. Trade," *The Journal of Political Economy*, 75 (Feb., 1967).

[13] Kravis, I., "Availability and Other Influences on the Commodity Composition of Trade," *The Journal of Political Economy*, LXIV (Apr., 1956).

[14] Kreinin, M., "Price Elasticities in International Trade," *The Review of Economics and Statistics*, XLIX (Nov., 1967).

[15] Kuenne, R. E., (ed). *Monopolistic Competition Theory: Studies in Impact* (New York: John Wiley and Sons, Inc., 1967).

[16] Lary, H. B., *Problems of the United States as World Trader and Banker* (Princeton: National Bureau of Economic Research, Princeton University Press, 1963), pp. 30–32, 52.

[17] Linder, S. B., *An Essay on Trade and Transformation* (Stockholm: Almqvist & Wiksell, 1961).

[18] Maizels, A., *Industrial Growth and World Trade* (Cambridge: Cambridge University Press, 1963).

[19] Posner, M. V., "International Trade and Technical Change," *Oxford Economic Papers*, 13 (Oct., 1961).

[20] Salter, W. E. G., *Productivity and Technical Change* (Cambridge: Cambridge University Press, 1960) p. 133.

[21] Vernon, R. "International Investment and International Trade in the Product Cycle," *The Quarterly Journal of Economics*, LXXX (May, 1966).

[22] Wells, L. T., Jr., "Test of a Product Cycle Model of International Trade: U.S. Exports of Consumer Durables," reprinted in this book.

DATA SOURCES

[23] International Monetary Fund, *International Financial Statistics*, various issues.

[24] United Nations, *Commodity Trade Statistics*, 1953–1964.

[25] United Nations, *Statistical Yearbook*, 1965.

[26] United Nations, Statistical Office, unpublished data.

R&D Factors and Exports of Manufactured Goods of Japan

YOSHIHIRO TSURUMI

Yoshihiro Tsurumi

Yoshihiro Tsurumi is Associate Professor at the School of Business, Queen's University, Kingston, Ontario (on leave). He currently holds an appointment as a Visiting Associate Professor at the Harvard University Graduate School of Business Administration and is engaged in research of Japanese-based multinational enterprises. Formerly he taught at Keio University, Tokyo, where he received the B.A. and M.A. degrees in Economics. He also holds the M.B.A. and D.B.A. degrees from Harvard University. He has served as a consultant to the governments of Japan, Canada, and the United States in the area of international trade, investment, and labor.

His publications include "Myths that Mislead U.S. Business Managers in Japan," Harvard Business Review, *July-August 1971; "Economic Costs of Foreign Direct Investments in Canada: Computer Simulations,"* The Proceedings *of the 1971 Meeting of the Association of Canadian Schools of Business; and with Dr. H. Tsurumi, Queen's Economic Department, "Oligopolistic Model of a Japanese Pharmaceutical Company," presented at the Second World Congress of the Econometric Society, Cambridge, England, to be published in* Readings in Managerial Economics *(Englewood Cliffs: Prentice-Hall, forthcoming).*

R&D Factors and Exports of Manufactured Goods of Japan

Of late, the expressions "technology gap" and "product life cycle" have been added to the vocabulary of international trade.[1] While these two phrases emphasize different effects of a nation's level of technology in shaping international trade, both are based on the assumption that, at a given time, some technology is not universally shared by all trading nations. However, technology— a body of manufacturing and administrative knowledge and skill that enables industrialists to produce specific products or to render services—is transferrable from one country to another. With the aid of such transfer agents as technicians, blueprints, publications, and sample products, industrialists and government planners in the lagging countries make conscious efforts to absorb foreign techniques and to modify and adapt them to the specific market and industrial conditions of their country. And eventually, they even come to possess such a high level of scientific and technological knowledge that they begin to produce technological innovations themselves. When this happens, the nation that used to import foreign technology joins the other industrialized nations in exporting technology, and often capital, to other nations.

Japan is frequently cited as the example of a nation which has during the last one hundred years grown industrially through her concerted efforts to absorb and adapt Western technologies.[2] The rapid industrial growth of Japan during the post-World War II period has motivated a number of research efforts to illuminate the effects of technological progress upon her industrial growth. One

161

calculation claims that over 60% of Japan's economic growth during the years 1950–1960 was due to technological progress.[3]

During Japan's rapid growth, her export trade shifted radically both in composition and in destination. Japan's trade with the industrialized nations grew faster than her trade with the underdeveloped world. By 1964 Japanese exports going to more advanced countries reached 50% of her total exports; and this percentage is still increasing. At the same time, Japan's share in the world trade of manufactures is increasing. In 1960 Japan held approximately 7% of total world trade of manufactures. By 1964 she held over 10% of total world trade of manufactures.

When Tatemoto and Ichimura encountered a Japanese version of the Leontief Paradox in the 1950s, they speculated that the phenomenon was due to Japan's unique economic and geographical position, which makes Japan a "capital abundant" nation relative to her Asian neighbors and other developing nations and a "labor abundant" country relative to the industrialized nations of the Western Hemisphere.[4] At that time, as Tatemoto and Ichimura noted, approximately three-quarters of Japan's exports were being shipped to the underdeveloped nations. The remaining sections of this paper will examine the dual nature of Japanese exports—those to less developed countries and those to more developed countries —and whether the Tatemoto-Ichimura hypothesis provides an adequate explanation of recent Japanese trade patterns.

The Tools of Analysis

Three indices, the Relative Share Index (R.S.I.), the Relative Share Index of Trade with Asian Nations (R.S.I.A.), and Japan's Dependence on Asia (J.D.O.A.), were devised to represent the export profiles of Japanese manufactures. Manufactured product groups were selected from SITC 3-digit product groups and, in some cases, from 4-digit product groups which appeared in the *Commodity Trade Statistics* of the United Nations.[5] The three indices were computed as follows:

The Relative Share
Index (R.S.I.) of Product $=$
Group i of Country j

$$\dfrac{X_{ji}}{\displaystyle\sum_{k=1}^{13} X_{ki}} \cdot \dfrac{\displaystyle\sum_{i=1}^{n} X_{ji}}{\displaystyle\sum_{i=1}^{n} \sum_{k=1}^{13} X_{ki}}$$

Where,

X_{ji}: export of product i from country j to the world
X_{ki}: export of product i from country k to the world
n : the number of SITC (Standard International Trade
Classification) product groups selected

In order to compute the Relative Share Index of country j the
total world export market of manufactures is defined as the sum
of the manufactures exported from 13 industrialized nation: The
United States, United Kingdom, Italy, Japan, West Germany,
Netherlands, France, Belgium-Luxembourg, Sweden, Norway, Austria, Denmark, and Canada. Today, the manufactured exports of
these 13 nations make up over 95% of total world exports of
manufactures.

The Relative Share
Index of Trade with
Asian Nations (R.S.I.A.) $= \dfrac{X_{jai}}{X_{ji}}$
of Product Group i of Japan

$$\dfrac{\displaystyle\sum_{i=1}^{69} X_{jai}}{\displaystyle\sum_{i=1}^{69} X_{ji}}$$

Japan's Dependence on
Asia (J.D.O.A.) of $= \dfrac{X_{jai}}{X_{ji}}$
Product Group i

Where,

X_{jai}: export of product i from Japan to Asia
X_{ji} : export of product i from Japan to the world

The Relative Share Index reflects the competitive strength that
each of Japan's product groups commands in the world market
relative to the competitive strength of Japan's total exports of

164   *Yoshihiro Tsurumi*

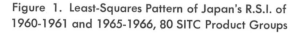

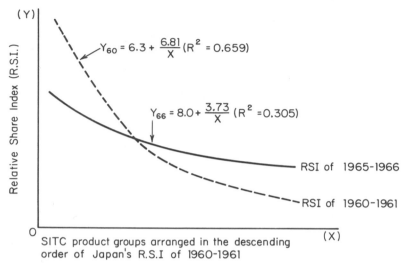

Figure 1. Least-Squares Pattern of Japan's R.S.I. of
1960-1961 and 1965-1966, 80 SITC Product Groups

$Y_{60} = 6.3 + \dfrac{6.81}{X}$ ($R^2 = 0.659$)

$Y_{66} = 8.0 + \dfrac{3.73}{X}$ ($R^2 = 0.305$)

RSI of 1965-1966

RSI of 1960-1961

SITC product groups arranged in the descending
order of Japan's R.S.I of 1960-1961

manufactured goods in world markets. And the direction of change
of the Relative Share Index for any product group indicates the
direction of change in Japan's export strength for the product
group.

Figure 1 depicts the level of the Japanese Relative Share Index
for the year 1965–1966 and that of the year 1960–1961. Both
of these can be described as having a hyperbolic shape. On the
abscissa of Figure 1, the 80 SITC product groups have been
arranged in descending order of Japan's Relative Share Index for
the year 1960–1961. The 1965–1966 array is determined by the
sequence established on the basis of the 1960–1961 data, so that
every SITC group is plotted for both years on a common vertical
line at the same distance to the right of the abscissa.

The 1965–1966 line retains its hyperbolic shape. But the high
end of the 1965–1966 R.S.I. data is lower and the low end is
higher than the 1960–1961 figures. This seems to indicate that
those SITC product groups of Japan which commanded a relatively strong position in the world export market were losing their

strength, while those Japanese SITC product groups which commanded a relatively weak position in the world export market had gained.

The Market Duality of the Exports of Japanese Manufactures

In 1965 Japan's trade with neighboring Asian nations accounted for over 65% of Japan's trade with the developing nations as a whole. For each SITC product group, Japan's profile of Asian trade is indicated either by the Relative Share Index of Trade with Asian Nations (R.S.I.A.) or by Japan's Dependence on Asia (J.D.O.A.). The index, R.S.I.A., shows each product group's relative dependence on Asia as a deviation from a norm. The index, J.D.O.A., describes each product group's absolute dependence on Asia. The two indices indicate the extent to which each of Japan's product groups relies on Asian market areas.

If the export profile of Japanese manufactures in the Asian market approximates the total picture of the Japanese export profile in the world in general for all the SITC product groups, the index values, R.S.I.A., of all the products involved will be close to unity. And the index values, J.D.O.A., will not show much variation from one SITC product to another. The findings are, however, quite different.

As shown in Figure 2, there appears to be a market duality in the exports of Japanese manufactures. The United Nations commodity trade statistics enable the calculation of 69 paired observations of R.S.I. and R.S.I.A. indices for Japan for the year 1965–1966. Of the 69 paired observations of R.S.I. and R.S.I.A., 53 pairs (77% of total observations) fell into the category in which an R.S.I. of over 1.00 was matched with an R.S.I.A. of less than 1.00, and vice versa. This means that the stronger the world position of a SITC product group in the Japanese export mix, the less it was dependent on Asian neighbors for export markets, and vice versa. Of the remaining 16 pairs of R.S.I. and R.S.I.A., 10 pairs fell into the category in which both R.S.I. and R.S.I.A. were smaller than 1.00. But 9 pairs out of these 10 showed R.S.I.A. values

Figure 2. Scatter Diagram of R.S.I. and R.S.I.A. of Japanese
Manufactured Goods, 1965-1966, 69 SITC Product Groups

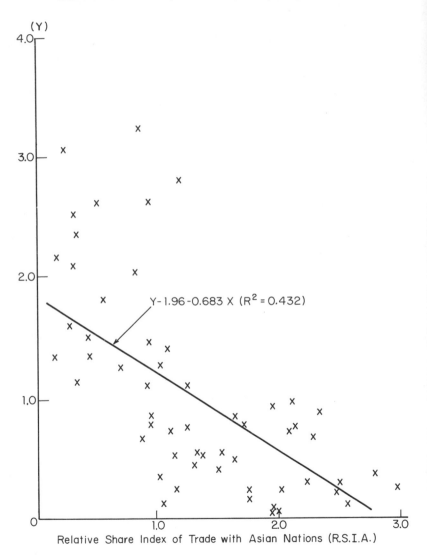

Relative Share Index of Trade with Asian Nations (R.S.I.A.)

which were materially greater than R.S.I. values, indicating that manufactures, the relative competitive position of which was still weak in the world export market, were relatively more dependent on Asian neighbors for their export market. Altogether, 62 paired observations out of 69 (90% of total observations) supported the contention that Japan relies heavily on her Asian neighbors for her exports of those manufactures in which she commands relatively weak competitive positions in the world export market at large and especially in the markets of industrialized nations.

Japan's Export Profiles and Capital Intensity Indicators of Manufacturing Industries

Japan does seem to have two distinct types of exports. But the Tatemoto-Ichimura hypothesis would indicate that capital intensity indicators would bear a positive relationship with the R.S.I.A. index and with the J.D.O.A. index of Japan. This does seem to be the case when capital intensity is measured by the Japanese data for the ratio of depreciation expenses to value added by manufactures and for the amount of net fixed assets per person employed. However, when the capital intensity of the industry is measured by the ratio of capital in use to total output, the prediction of the Tatemoto-Ichimura hypothesis is not supported. Table 1 summarizes the correlation tests: although none of the results is statistically significant at the 5% probability level, the correlation coefficients indicating the relationship between the two indicators of Asian export market profiles and two indicators of capital intensity have positive signs and are statistically significant at the 20% probability level. This may well lead one to speculate that if a more appropriate indicator of capital intensity of products, not the industry, were used, the relationship between Asian market profiles of Japanese manufactures in 1965–1966 and the capital intensive nature of the products may prove to be positive and significant. At any rate, the Tatemoto-Ichimura hypothesis cannot be clearly rejected with these tests.

Table 1. Relationship between Indicators of the Capital Intensity of
Japanese Manufacturing Industries and the Asian Export Market Profile of Japan, 1964

Asian Export Market Profile of Japan	*Simple Logarithmic Correlation for Indicated Cells*		
	Ratio of Capital in Use to Output	*Ratio of Depreciation Expenses to Value Added*	*Net Fixed Assets per Person Employed*
Relative Share Index of Trade with Asian Nations (R.S.I.A.), 1965–1966	−0.040[a]	+0.400[b]	+0.460[b]
Japan's Dependence on Asia (J.D.O.A.) of 1965–1966	−0.150[a]	+0.390[b]	+0.420[b]

[a] These coefficients are not statistically significant at the 5% probability level but significant at the 20% probability level.

[b] These coefficients are not statistically significant at the the 5% probability level.

SOURCE: *Kigyo Keiei no Bunseki* (Analysis of Corporate Management), Mitsubishi Economic Research Institute, Tokyo, November, 1965. *The U.N. Commodity Trade Statistics*, Statistical Paper Series D, the United Nations, New York, 1965 and 1966.

To be sure, of all the Japanese exports of manufactures of a given year, those products which are going to Asian markets appear to be more capital intensive than those products going to the rest of the world. All in all, however, the relationship between the capital intensity indicators and either R.S.I.A. or J.D.O.A. of Japan is very weak. The capital intensity of the manufacturing industries involved appears to be a poor explanatory variable of the export profiles of Japan.

Table 2 confirms these misgivings concerning the capital intensity of manufacturing industries as an explanatory variable of the export profiles of the Japanese manufacturing industries. None of the correlation tests demonstrates a significant relationship between Japan's export profile for a given year and the capital intensity indicators of the manufacturing industries involved.

What are, then, other characteristics of the exported manufactures of Japan? When arranged in the descending order of the Relative Share Index of Japanese manufactures (see Statistical Appendix), there is toward the end of the list a concentration of products of heavy and chemical industries such as iron and steel products, chemical synthetics, electronic and electrical equipment, rubber products, metal products, chemicals, plastics, nonferrous products, motor vehicles, metal-working machinery, precision machinery, drugs, and transport machinery such as aircraft. While the position of manufactures in this list cannot be explained by their capital intensity, the R&D efforts of these manufacturing industries appear to vary significantly from one product group to another. As was shown in Figure 2, the manufactures, the Relative Share Index of which is relatively small, are more dependent on Asian markets. Thus, the export market duality of the Japanese manufactures may well be explained by the material difference in R&D efforts from one manufacturing industry to another. High R&D-content products are being exported first to the developing nations, notably Asian nations, and then to the industrialized nations in the West as the Japanese manufacturing industries improve their technological competence.

Table 2. Relationship between Indicators of the Capital Intensity of Japanese Manufacturing Industries and the Export Profile and the Direction and the Magnitude of Change in the Export Profile of Japanese Manufacturing Industries, 1964

Export Profile Characteristics of Japan	Simple Logarithmic Correlation for Indicated Cells		
	Ratio of Depreciation Expenses to Value Added	Net Fixed Assets per Person Employed	Ratio of Capital in Use to Output
Relative Share Index (R.S.I.) of Japanese manufacturing industries 1965–1966	−0.240[a]	−0.270[a]	−0.100[a]
Change ratio of 1965–1966 R.S.I. to 1960–1961 R.S.I. of Japanese manufacturing industries	−0.230[a]	−0.120[a]	−0.107[a]

[a] These coefficients are not statistically significant at the 5% probability level.

SOURCE: *Kigyo Keiei no Bunseki* (Analysis of Corporate Management), Mitsubishi Economic Research Institute, Tokyo, November, 1965. *The U.N. Commodity Trade Statistics*, Statistical Paper Series D, the United Nations, New York, 1960, 1961, 1965, and 1966.

R&D Effort and Export Profiles

The direction of the change in Japan's export patterns seems more closely related to the R&D efforts of the Japanese manufacturing industries than to any other single factor we have been able to isolate. The R&D effort of Japanese manufacturing industries was measured by the following four indicators: (1) annual R&D expenditure, by industry, (2) cumulative R&D expenditure for a number of years, by industry, (3) the ratio of annual R&D expenditure to total annual sales, by industry, and (4) R&D personnel per 1,000 employees, by industry.

The relationship between R&D and Japanese export patterns is supported by the significant correlations between the change in the export profiles of Japanese manufacturing industries from 1960–1961 to 1965–1966 and the indicators of the R&D efforts of the Japanese manufacturing industries. The results of this statistical test are summarized in Table 3. All the results indicate that the relationship between the direction of change in the export profile of Japan (change ratio) and the R&D efforts of Japanese manufacturing industries are positive and statistically significant. These results support the contention that the technological effort of manufacturing industries of Japan (a follower nation, vis-à-vis, say, the United States) materially improved the competitive strength of her manufactures in the world market.

Japan's overall export profile as represented by the Relative Share Index of 1965–1966 is at best weakly related to R&D performances of the Japanese manufacturing industries. What hypothesis can we, then, submit to explain Japan's export profile for a given year? One plausible hypothesis is that the current level of R&D efforts of Japanese industries does not necessarily indicate the level of Japan's attained technological competence relative to the levels of technological competence of other leading industrialized nations. A case in point is the textile industry of Japan. Although the R&D efforts of this industry are rather small compared with those of other industries of Japan, the technological competence of this industry is probably as high as that of the textile industries of other industrialized nations. The same thing may

Table 3. Relationship Between Indicators of Cumulative Technological Experience of Japanese Manufacturing Industries and Export Profiles and the Direction and the Magnitude of Change in these Profiles of Japanese Manufacturing Industries, 1956-1964

Export Profile Characteristics	Simple Logarithmic Correlation for Indicated Cells				Spearman's Coefficients of Rank Correlation for Indicated Cells			
	R&D Expenditure 1964	R&D Expenditure 1956–1964	R&D Sales Ratio 1964	R&D Personnel per 1,000 Employees 1963	R&D Expenditure 1964	R&D Expenditure 1959–1964	R&D Sales Ratio 1964	R&D Personnel per 1,000 Employees 1963
Relative Share Index of Japanese industries 1965–1966	+0.115[a]	+0.208[a]	+0.250[a]	+0.215[a]	+0.150[a]	+0.270[a]	+0.320[b]	+0.280[a] +0.280[a]

Change ratio of 1965–1966 R.S.I. to 1960–1961 R.S.I. of Japanese industries								
+0.560[c]	+0.550[c]	+0.620[c]	+0.570[c]	+0.750[c]	+0.723[c]	+0.820[c]	+0.760[c]	+0.760[c]

[a] These coefficients are not significant at the 5% probability level.
[b] This coefficient is significant at the 20% probability level.
[c] These coefficients are significant at the 5% probability level.

SOURCE: *The U.N. Commodity Trade Statistics*, 1960, 1961, 1965 and 1966, *Kagaku Gijutsu Hakusho* (White Paper on Science and Technologies), The Agency of Science and Technology, Japan, August 1964, and *Gijutsu Koryutono Kansuru Chosa* (Study of Technological Activities), the Ministry of International Trade and Industry, Japan, March 1966.

be said of the shipbuilding industry of Japan. On the other hand, the electronics industry of Japan appears still to be behind those of other industrialized nations, notably that of the United States, although it is now investing much effort in its R&D activities.

It is often claimed that the postwar industrial growth of Japan owes much to the successful transfer of foreign technologies through licensing agreements to Japan. International licensing agreements can be effective vehicles of technological transfer. One study shows that Japanese manufacturing industries have been investing in their own R&D activities related to the foreign technologies that they import from licensors.[6] To be sure, the extent of such R&D work which the licensees perform depends upon the licensee's capability of absorbing the licensed technology, on the one hand, and upon any necessary reconditioning of the licensed technology to fit the nature of Japanese market demand, on the other.

In 1961 over one-fourth of R&D expenditures were devoted to absorptive activities which were designed to learn and absorb foreign technologies.[7] Assuming that by 1961 the Japanese manufacturing corporations had already accumulated a substantial amount of scientific and technological experience, the presence of a sizable degree of absorptive R&D activities as late as 1961 suggests that technology transfer through licensing agreements requires far more than the mere international movement of transfer agents like patent information, design, blueprints, prototype products, and persons knowing manufacturing technology. The rest of the R&D expenditures were devoted to renovative and innovative work designed to create new products or make material improvements over the technology learned from foreign sources.

If technology transfer via international licensing agreements influences the export profile of Japan, it does so through the improved supply capabilities of the Japanese manufacturing industries, not only in the sense that the industries can supply the old products at a reduced price but also in the sense that the industries can supply products of improved quality and even totally new products. The technological competence of the manufacturing industries for a given year, then, is indicated by their ability to absorb new foreign technologies as well as their ability to create improved production methods and products themselves.

In order to measure the attained level of technological competence of Japanese manufacturing industries relative to other leading industrialized nations as of 1966, both the nature and the frequency of the substantial improvements which the Japanese licensees made on licensed technologies during 1950–1964 were surveyed. The results of the survey are summarized in the Statistical Appendix. Such improvements were classified into six categories according to the nature of the improvements: namely, (1) distinctly new products and new production processes are created and industrially utilized on the basis of licensed technology; (2) patentable and totally new products are created and utilized on the basis of licensed technology; (3) the licensee achieved better results than the initial specifications of the licensed technology; (4) where technically too weak to command international competitiveness before, exportable products and processes are developed on the basis of licensed technology; (5) no distinct improvements are made over and above the initial specifications of the licensed technology; and (6) no specific information was available. Each category was computed as a percentage of total licensed technologies sampled by industry. The sample size, 1,132, amounted to 40% of all licensing agreements concluded during 1950–1964. And the combination of categories (1) and (2) was redefined as the Rate of Distinctive Renovations. The greater the Rate of Distinctive Renovations, the higher is the attained level of technological competence of the industry relative to the counterpart of other leading industrialized nations which are the licensors to Japan.

Certainly, there was no *a priori* guarantee that the licensees all used the same definition of "a distinctly new product" and "a distinctly new process." However, categories (2) and (4) were specific enough to warrant the assumption that responses from the licensees were trustworthy. And these two categories are independently verifiable. The author's random check of the responses confirmed this result. Category (1) represented a higher level of achievements than did category (3), indicating that the respondents of the questionnaire had reasonably differentiated between category (1) and (3). There is hope that any window dressing was slipped into category (3) rather than into category (1), because the achievements of category (1) must also be so apparent to the third party as to discourage blatant misrepresentations.

Table 4 summarizes both Spearman's coefficient of rank correlation and a coefficient of simple logarithmic correlation between the level of the export profile of Japan and the technological competence of the Japanese manufacturing industries. The fact that both coefficients were statistically significant at the 5% probability level enables one to infer that the export profile of a nation like Japan (a follower nation) is determined, among other things, by the technological competence of the nation which creates new products and new production processes.

Table 4. Relationship between the Export Profiles of Japan and the Technological Competence of the Japanese Manufacturing Industries, 1965-1966

Export Profile of Japanese Manufacturing Industries, 1965–1966	Rate of Distinctive Renovations, 1966 Spearman's coefficient of rank correlation for indicated cells	Rate of Distinctive Renovations, 1966 Simple logarithmic correlation for indicated cells
The Relative Share Index of the Japanese Manufacturing Industries, 1965–1966	+0.550[a]	+0.502[a]

[a] These coefficients are statistically significant at the 5% probability level.

To be sure, other economic factors in Japan, such as the size of the potential market, precipitated the process of dynamic economies of scale in the manufacturing sectors and thus enabled the postwar growth of the productive capability of Japan. In addition, a growing domestic market that has been protected from direct foreign competition either through importation of foreign goods or through direct foreign investment in Japan may have allowed the Japanese industrialists to concentrate on improving their manufacturing capabilities. Without direct foreign competition the competition and rivalry among Japanese industrialists are severe enough to pressure Japanese corporations into building up their technological capability. It has been observed that such competition among the Japanese companies enables speedy spread of new technology among the competitors.[8] And their increased productive capability in turn pressured them into seeking markets for their products abroad.

In Conclusion

The export market duality of Japanese manufactures still exists today. The manufactures which have not yet attained a strong competitive position in the world export market are demonstrating their exportability to Asia. The underlying forces which make Japanese manufactures competitive in Asian markets may be the combination of Japan's geographical proximity to Asia and the relative similarities of Japan's social and economic situations to Asia as opposed to, say, the United States to Asia. Additionally, the Asian markets which Japan has cultivated particularly through the shipments of industrial goods on the reparation agreements after the Second World War may have developed a certain degree of dependence on Japan.

This paper showed that high R&D content products of heavy and chemical industries of Japan were more dependent than other industries on Asian markets; their competitive positions in the world market at large were still weak. The manufactures which were dependent on Asia in a given year were typically concentrated on the tail end of the descending order of the Relative Share Index which measured the position of Japan in the world market.

Furthermore, the changing direction of Japan's export profile was related to the R&D effort of Japanese manufacturing indus-tries. And the export profile of Japan for a given year was posi-tively related to the technological competence of the Japanese industries relative to their counterparts in other industrialized nations. At the earlier stage of development, Japanese manufac-tures of high R&D-content industries are exported, sometimes exclusively, to the Asian nations. And only at the later stage of maturity are Japanese manufactures exported to the industrialized nations, as they gain worldwide competitive strength. There exists today a strong indication that R&D-intensive companies of Japan are consciously taking advantage of the duality of the Japanese export markets.[9] Often Asian markets serve as the testing ground for Japanese manufactures in the world market.

Japanese manufacturing industries have vigorously purchased technology, mainly from the United States, during the last decade. And the R&D efforts of Japanese manufacturing industries have been based largely on such acquired foreign technologies. Products and technologies which originated in the developed countries and were purchased by Japan are at some point in the future embodied in Japan's exports. Both absorptive and innovative R&D efforts of Japanese manufacturing industries first help Japan try out her new R&D-intensive products in Asia and later help Japan make inroads into the markets of the developed nations.

FOOTNOTES

1 See, for example: G. C. Hufbauer, *Synthetic Materials and the Theory of International Trade*, Harvard University Press, 1966; and R. Vernon, "International Investment and International Trade in the Product Cycle," *Quarterly Journal of Economics*, Vol. LXXX (May 1966), pp. 190–207.

2 B. K. Marshall, *Capitalism and Nationalism in Prewar Japan*, Stanford University Press, 1967: T. C. Smith, *Political Change and Industrial Development: Government Enterprise, 1868–1880*, Stanford University Press, 1955; Y. Tsurumi, Chapter II of "Technology Transfer and Foreign Trade: The Case of Japan, 1950–1966," unpublished doctoral dissertation, Harvard Business School, 1968.

3 *White Paper on the Economic Situation, 1961*, Economic Planning Agency, Tokyo, 1962.

4 M. Tatemoto and S. Ichimura, "Factor Proportions and Foreign Trade: The Case of Japan," *Review of Economics and Statistics*, Vol. XLI, No. 4 (November 1959), pp. 442–446.

5 *The Commodity Trade Statistics*, Statistical Paper Series D, United Nations, New York, 1960, 1961, 1965 and 1966.

6 Y. Tsurumi, *op. cit.*, pp. 224–231.

7 Y. Tsurumi, *ibid.*, Chapter IV.

8 Y. Tsurumi, *ibid.*, Chapter V.

9 This view is based on the interviews the author conducted among the top executives of the R&D intensive firms of Japan during the summer of 1969. These interviews were a part of an effort to illuminate the export strategy of R&D intensive firms in Japan.

STATISTICAL APPENDIX

1. SITC product classifications had to be reconciled with available industry classifications in order to complete empirical tests of the hypotheses. I used industry statistics which were based on *Sangyo Chu Bunrui* [the Intermediary Industry Classification] of the Japan Bureau of Statistics of Ministry of International Trade and Industry. The reconciliation of SITC statistics with Intermediary Industry Classification (IIC) statistics may complicate already arbitrary definitions of industry. Furthermore, the industry statistics, which are based on the records of reporting firms, may distort the industry statistics when the reporting firms' lines of products encompass more than one industry. However, there was no reason to believe that the IIC of Japan was any less or more arbitrary than the Standard Industrial Classification (SIC) of the United States. The following is the conversion table of SITC product groups into appropriate industry groups:

IIC Industry Groups	SITC Product Groups Assumed to Correspond
1. Cotton yarn, rayon textiles	651.3, 651.4, 651.7, 652, 653, 655
2. Woolen textiles	651.2
3. Synthetic fibers	266, 651.6
4. Apparel	654, 656, 657, 841
5. Pulp and allied products	641, 642
6. Plastics	581
7. Inorganic chemicals	561, 571
8. Organic chemicals	512, 551
9. Paint, indigo, pigments	513.5, 531, 533, 553, 554
10. Drugs	541
11. Other industrial chemicals	599
12. Petroleum products	332
13. Rubber products	631, 629.1
14. Leather products	611, 612
15. Stone, clay, and glass products	664, 665, 666
16. Iron and steel products	671, 673, 674, 675, 676, 678
17. Nonferrous metal products	682.2, 683.2, 684.2, 685.2, 686.2, 698, 812
18. Fabricated metals	691, 692, 693, 694, 695, 696, 697, 698, 812
19. Metal-working machinery	715
20. Other machinery	711, 712.5, 717.1, 718, 719
21. Electrical equipment	722.1, 725
22. Electronics, telecommunication equipment	714, 724, 861, 891
23. Motor vehicles	732
24. Ships	735
25. Rolling stock	731
26. Other transport machinery	733, 734
27. Precision machinery	862
28. Others	613, 821, 831, 842, 851, 897

2. The sensitivity of the testing methods to the ways the SITC statistics were reconciled with the IIC statistics was not ignored. Various sensitivity tests showed that the statistical correlation tests used in the text were not affected by either conversion of SITC groupings into IIC groupings or condensation of the original 28 IIC groupings into 27 groupings simply by eliminating those product groups classified as "other."

3. R&D efforts of an industry culminate in (1) the creation of new products, (2) the improvement of existing products, and (3) the improvement of production methods. These results are then incorporated in actual manufacturing activities, mainly through the industry's capital investment decisions. Therefore, a time lag exists before R&D efforts actually affect the market of manufactured goods. This time lag is determined by both the time required for R&D efforts and the time required for the capital investment to become effective in the actual production processes. This time lag, which I call the development lead time, is defined as follows:

Development lead time
of a manufactured product   =   (1) R&D time spent on the
in Japan   product
                                     +   (2) Production lead time
                                              required to produce the
                                              first marketable product
                                              for the Japanese market

The Ministry of International Trade and Industry of Japan received in mid-1963 answers to a questionnaire which had been sent out earlier to 1,920 Japanese manufacturing corporations which had a paid-in capital of 50 million yen or more as of the end of March 1962. Altogether, 1,039 corporations returned the questionnaire (the rate of return was 53.7%). This questionnaire solicited information concerning the development lead time of the "new products" and the "new production processes" which the corporation had successfully developed and utilized commercially from the end of the war up to the time of returning the answers. In total, 2,310 products and processes were reported with their estimated development lead times. The industry averages of the development lead time differed from 0.5 years for petroleum and coal products to 2.94 years for mining. The weighted average of development lead times for Japanese manufacturing as a whole was 2.35 years. Thus, it seems reasonable to assume that the R&D efforts of Japanese manufacturing industries were being incorporated into actual production activities with a two-year to three-year time lag. Consequently, as an independent variable to test the hypotheses in the text, the R&D data of Japanese manufacturing industries from 1959 to 1964 were used.

4. The R&D expenditures of the Japanese manufacturing industries is as follows:

Industry	R&D expenditures, 1964 (millions of yen)	R&D expenditures, 1959–64 (millions of yen)	R&D as % of sales, 1964
Textiles	5,061	26,484	0.53%
Pulp and allied products	2,191	9,824	0.40
Chemicals including drugs	21,143	104,906	2.00
Petroleum products	2,702	11,905	0.30
Plastics and synthetics	19,570	85,214	3.00
Rubber products	2,380	12,704	0.90
Stone, clay, and glass products	986	12,054	0.80
Iron and steel products	12,453	58,042	1.00
Nonferrous metals	4,262	21,209	0.81
Fabricated metal products	1,263	6,558	0.60
Construction and general machinery	14,430	59,723	1.20
Electrical equipment and machinery	10,520	49,030	1.80
Electronics, telecommunication equipment	32,242	155,873	3.20
Motor vehicles	13,975	59,131	1.30
Ship and boats	3,602	18,719	1.00
Other transport	2,519	8,623	0.52
Precision and optical instruments	2,734	13,476	0.95

SOURCE: *Kagaku Gijutsu Hakusho* [White Paper on Science and Technologies], the Agency of Science and Technology, Japan, August 1964, and *Gijutsu Koryutoni Kansuru Chosa* [Study of Technological Activities], The Ministry of International Trade and Industry, Japan, March 1966.

5. The number of R&D personnel per 1,000 employees by industry is as follows:

Industry	R&D personnel per 1,000 employees, 1963
Textile and apparel	20.07
Pulp and allied products	29.78
Chemicals	70.99
Petroleum products	29.83
Rubber products	34.09
Stone, clay, and glass products	29.37
Iron and steel products	26.54
Nonferrous metal products	36.81
Fabricated metal products	33.61
Machinery	37.69
Electrical and electronics machinery	55.23
Transport machinery	34.45

SOURCE: *Gitjutsu Doko Chosa Hokokusho* [Report on Current State of Technologies], Bureau of Technologies, Ministry of International Trade and Industry, Japan, May 1963.

6. The data on which Figure 1 was drawn are presented below in the descending order of Japan's R.S.I. of 1965–66 for each SITC product group.

SITC	R.S.I.		SITC	R.S.I.	
Descending order of Japan's R.S.I., 1965–66	*1960–61*	*1965–66*	*Descending order of Japan's R.S.I., 1965–66*	*1960–61*	*1965–66*
735	2.85	4.15	684.2	0.45	0.75
666	5.07	3.72	722.1	0.55	0.75
652	4.60	3.20	733	1.07	0.75
724	2.38	2.62	692	0.85	0.72
653	3.41	2.60	695	0.88	0.70
674	1.50	2.50	812	0.90	0.65
694	1.08	2.50	682.2	0.50	0.63
891	0.90	2.35	665	0.88	0.58
696	0.98	2.18	621	0.65	0.57
831	2.35	2.10	642	0.74	0.57
678	1.06	2.04	686.2	0.04	0.55
513.5	0.57	2.00	725	0.08	0.53
266	0.92	1.75	732	0.11	0.53
676	1.50	1.67	664	0.56	0.52
656	2.56	1.61	715	0.16	0.50
651.7	1.30	1.60	685.2	0.40	0.46
841	2.72	1.60	821	0.38	0.45
861	1.69	1.50	897	1.84	0.45
651.4	1.81	1.48	719	0.36	0.42
693	0.98	1.47	687.2	0.20	0.41
651.2	0.76	1.42	671	0.36	0.39
629.1	1.10	1.40	553	0.25	0.37
651.6	1.20	1.40	711	0.29	0.30
612	0.65	1.35	531	0.35	0.29
851	2.89	1.34	862	0.18	0.28
654	2.25	1.28	541	0.37	0.27
673	1.02	1.27	641	0.37	0.27

(continued on p. 186)

SITC	R.S.I.		SITC	R.S.I.	
Descending order of Japan's R.S.I., *1965–66*	*1960–61*	*1965–66*	*Descending order of Japan's R.S.I.,* *1965–66*	*1960–61*	*1965–66*
657	1.77	1.20	714	0.20	0.27
651.3	4.70	1.20	718	0.25	0.27
697	0.95	1.16	533	0.25	0.26
655	2.15	1.10	554	0.25	0.26
691	1.90	0.93	599	0.10	0.24
731	1.37	0.92	842	0.21	0.21
571	0.51	0.88	712.5	0.01	0.20
561	1.28	0.88	611	0.05	0.13
717.1	1.05	0.88	332	0.13	0.11
698	0.98	0.80	551	0.09	0.10
512	0.40	0.78	683.2	0.03	0.09
581	0.55	0.78	734	0.03	0.06
675	0.88	0.78	613	0.04	0.04

SOURCE: *Commodity Trade Statistics*, Statistical Paper Series D, the United Nations, New York, 1960, 1961, 1965, and 1966.

7. The conversion of SITC product group's Relative Share Index and change ratio into the Relative Share Index and change ratio of a corresponding industry was completed by computing the weighted average of both the Relative Share Index and the change ratio of SITC product grouped by industry. The weight was each product's share in the industry's total export value of the year 1965–66. The same procedure was followed when the R.S.I.A. and the J.D.O.A. of SITC product groups were converted into the same indices of the corresponding industry.

8. The indices, R.S.I.A., and J.D.O.A., indicating the extent to which specific manufacture groups of Japan depends on the Asian market for export are reproduced below:

SITC	R.S.I.A. 1965–66	J.D.O.A. 1965–66	SITC	R.S.I.A. 1965–66	J.D.O.A. 1965–66
266	1.27	0.385	683.2	2.00	0.610
332	2.60	0.790	684.2	2.19	0.665
512	1.23	0.374	691	2.14	0.655
531	2.53	0.770	692	2.16	0.650
533	2.47	0.750	693	0.91	0.275
541	1.78	0.540	694	0.34	0.102
551	1.97	0.600	695	0.81	0.245
553	2.80	0.850	696	0.19	0.057
554	3.04	0.925	697	0.33	0.100
561	3.00	0.915	698	0.97	0.295
571	1.68	0.400	711	2.28	0.690
581	1.68	0.514	712	1.05	0.212
599	2.02	0.615	714	0.35	0.106
611	0.82	0.249	715	1.61	0.490
612	0.46	0.139	717.1	2.38	0.725
629	1.10	0.356	718	1.50	0.346
641	2.50	0.755	719	1.50	0.458
642	1.54	0.465	722	0.53	0.670
651.2	1.56	0.472	724	0.53	0.162
652	0.86	0.262	725	1.36	0.415
653	0.96	0.290	731	1.97	0.600
654	0.76	0.230	732	1.17	0.355
655	1.28	0.386	734	1.93	0.590
656	0.48	0.146	733	1.12	0.342
657	0.07	0.021	735	3.14	0.950
664	0.85	0.320	812	0.88	0.268
665	0.80	0.243	821	0.68	0.206
666	0.31	0.095	831	0.31	0.095
671	1.00	0.304	841	0.30	0.090
673	1.04	0.314	851	0.14	0.044
674	1.25	0.380	861	0.41	0.123
675	1.68	0.510	862	1.75	0.534
678	0.85	0.258	891	0.36	0.110
682.2	2.30	0.700	897	0.24	0.071

SOURCE: *Commodity Trade Statistics*, the United Nations, Statistical Paper Series D, New York, 1965, and 1966.

9. The six categories of improvements made on licensed technology are shown as a percentage of total licensed technologies sampled.

Industry [a]	New products & processes (1)	Patentable table & new products (2)	Better than specifications (3)	Exportable products, processes (4)	No improvements made (5)	No information available (6)
Textiles (52)	5.5%	—	5.5%	—	75.0%	14.0%
Pulp and allied products (10)	10.0	30.0%	20.0	—	30.0	10.0
Synthetics (25)	24.0	28.0	28.0	8.0%	4.0	8.0
Chemicals (196)	17.4	13.3	28.0	3.8	35.4	2.1
Pigment, paint and oil (15)	46.5	—	20.0	13.3	13.3	7.5
Drugs (31)	3.2	6.2	9.7	9.7	71.2	—
Petroleum products (58)	—	1.7	8.6	—	84.0	5.7
Rubber products (29)	27.6	10.3	20.6	—	13.9	27.6
Stone, clay products (18)	5.5	27.8	38.9	5.5	22.3	—
Iron and steel products (59)	17.0	25.4	17.0	8.4	25.4	6.2
Nonferrous metals (62)	14.5	9.7	19.3	4.8	50.0	1.7
Fabricated metal products (26)	23.0	11.5	11.5	—	54.0	—
Machinery (239)	17.2	16.8	22.6	2.1	38.2	2.1
Electrical equipment (46)	21.7	8.7	37.0	4.3	28.3	—

Electronics, telecommunication equipment (173)	31.7	27.8	13.9	7.0	18.0	1.6
Motor vehicles (32)	18.7	15.6	21.9	12.5	28.1	3.2
Ships (3)	33.3	33.3	33.4	—	—	—
Other transport machine (49)	22.4	4.1	10.2	—	61.0	2.3
Precision instruments (9)	11.1	11.1	22.2	—	55.6	—
All industries (1,132)	19.0%	15.0%	19.6%	3.6%	38.8%	4.0%

(a) The figures in parentheses are the number of sampled license agreements.

SOURCE: With the use of _Gijutsukoryu ni Kansuru Chosa_ [Study of Technological Activities], Ministry of International Trade and Industry, Tokyo, March 1996, and _Registry of Licensing Agreements and Foreign Capital,_ Economic Research Institute, Tokyo, May 1967, altogether 1,132 licensed agreements were sampled out of all the Type A license agreements which were concluded during 1950–1964. The basis of selection was the questionnaire return of the 1966 _MITI Study,_ which solicited the nature of the technology improvements that the licensees had made on the basis of licensed technology. The sample size, 1,132, came to approximately 40% of all the Type A agreements concluded during 1950–1964. Thus, it was assumed that the nature of the improvements shown by these 1,132 items would give a general picture of the types of improvements that the Japanese manufacturing industries had made up to the time when the licensees answered the MITI questionnaire in 1966.

Manufactured Products and Export Markets: Dichotomy of Markets for Greek Manufactures

SOTIRIOS G. MOUSOURIS

Sotirios G. Mousouris

Sotirios Mousouris is Economic Affairs Officer at the Centre for Development Planning, Projections, and Policies of the United Nations Secretariat. He has been teaching economics, on a part-time basis, at the Bernard Baruch School of Business of the City University of New York and at other institutions in the area. He obtained Diplomas in Law and in Political and Economic Sciences from the University of Athens, practiced law, and worked in the Greek Ministry of Justice. He received an M.A. degree in Economics from Boston University and the D.B.A. degree from Harvard University.

Between 1964 and 1967 he published a series of articles in a Greek economic journal on "United States Direct Investment in Europe," "The Role of Exports of Manufactures in Economic Development," and "Greek Industrialists and Export Performance." He has also regularly contributed to the "World Economic Survey."

Manufactured Products and Export Markets: Dichotomy of Markets for Greek Manufactures

This paper will show that the *sui generis* pattern of Greek exports in manufacturing can be explained by a combination of modified versions of the Heckscher-Ohlin theory,[1] based on factor endowment, and Linder's theory,[2] based on trade intensity among countries of similar demand patterns.

The integration of these two theories provides the theoretical framework of the basic proposition: Greece, a country between the advanced and the less developed world, from the viewpoint of geography and level of economic development, faces a dichotomy of her export markets. She has two different sets of comparative advantages in manufactures, one for the advanced, another for the less developed countries. Greece therefore exports manufactured goods of different characteristics to these two areas.

According to Heckscher-Ohlin, Greece should export goods the production of which uses her relatively abundant factor intensively. Our contention is that Greece's relatively abundant factor vis-à-vis the advanced countries is labor and therefore she exports her labor-intensive goods to them; Greece's relatively abundant factor vis-à-vis the less developed world is capital and there she sells her capital-intensive commodities.

According to Linder, Greece should export her manufactures to countries of similar income per capita because of the similarity of demand patterns. It will be suggested here that Greece exports to both advanced and less developed countries goods for which there

---

EDITOR'S NOTE: This article was adapted from Chapter IV of Mousouris, "Export Horizons of Greek Industries," unpublished doctoral dissertation, Harvard Business School, 1967.

is a substantial demand both in Greece and the importing country. But because there is a difference in demand patterns between the advanced and the less developed world, Greece, having some overlapping demand with both areas, exports "higher quality" goods to the advanced and "lower quality" goods to the less developed countries. The Middle Eastern countries will be taken as representative of the less developed world and Western European countries will represent the advanced world.[3]

Dichotomy of Markets

The differences in factor endowment and demand patterns between Greece's two export markets are due to the level of economic development and, to a lesser degree, to geographical location. The difference in level of development is related to and, of course, influenced by demand and supply forces in each of these areas vis-à-vis Greece.[4]

The composition of demand, for instance, changes as the per capita income increases.[5] One of the most notable explanations of this phenomenon is provided by Engel's Law (i.e., the share of income spent for food declines as income rises). Generally, high-quality products are demanded at high-income levels.[6] An economically advanced country, such as the United States, would be first to demand high-income or labor-saving goods.[7] "In a country where the great bulk of population lives near subsistence level, the demand is naturally concentrated on simple necessities of life," a well-documented study by the League of Nations affirms.[8]

Hence, the level of economic development should create different *demand patterns* in Western Europe and the Middle East. Greece, being in the middle of these two areas in terms of economic development, has a demand pattern which overlaps with the demand pattern of both of them.[9] The proximity of Greece to Europe and the Middle East allows her businessmen to be aware of these different demand patterns.

The *supply* conditions change as per capita income rises. Increase in skill and education, overall increase in capital stock per worker, attainment of economies of scale resulting from enlargements of the market size—these are some changes in factor supplies which accompany increased income. "This change in factor supplies causes a systematic shift in comparative advantages as per capita income rises."[10]

Thus, the level of economic development is related to the supply of factors, or *factor endowment*.[11] Again, Greece, being in the middle, has two different sets of relatively abundant factors vis-à-vis Western Europe and the Middle East.

The dichotomy of markets indicates that for Greece to export manufactures either to the Middle East or to Europe, the following conditions should be fulfilled: (1) the manufactured product should lie inside the range of overlapping demand of Greece and either of those areas; (2) the manufacture of the product should use intensively factors that are relatively abundant in comparison to the market where the product is sold. Greece should have an export advantage for products which meet these two conditions.

Modified Versions of Two Trade Theories

Heckscher-Ohlin

The Heckscher-Ohlin theory emphasized primarily the supply side, in terms of factor endowments. From this aspect the theory is useful, but not sufficient to explain Greek trade patterns in manufactures.

Adapting the bilateral interpretation of this theory, used by Tatemoto and Ichimura,[12] Greece's factor endowments will be compared first with those of Western European countries and then with those of Middle Eastern countries, Since the objective of this research is to arrive at an explanation of Greek export patterns, Greek imports will be ignored.[13]

It will be shown that Heckscher-Ohlin's theory is useful in predicting the trade between Greece and the Middle East and Greece and Western Europe, although it does not suffice in predicting Greek exports in total. It will be shown specifically that Greek exports to the Middle East are intensive in capital, of which Greece has an abundance relative to the Middle East, and Greek exports to Western Europe are intensive in labor of which Greece has an abundance relative to Europe.

It should be pointed out, however, that as regards Greek exports to the Middle East, the fact that these exports are capital-intensive may be due in whole or in part to economies of scale.

Economies of Scale. Economies of scale, a complication which is here hesitantly introduced, relaxes the assumption of linearity in production functions and thus avoids one major limitation of the traditional Heckscher-Ohlin approach. In manufacturing industries decreasing unit costs at larger output derive from a number of sources. It should be noted that capital intensity and economies of scale, or labor intensity and economies of scale, are not mutually exclusive. They are, however, sufficiently different to warrant separate treatment in explaining the Greek trade pattern. Usually, capital-intensive technologies involve economies of scale. But at the same time, skilled labor or management, which are not considered to be capital, is frequently involved in large-scale production.[14]

Economies of scale may be achieved by external or internal economies (or external pecuniary and internal technological according to Kindleberger)[15] neither of which is directly and necessarily related to labor or capital.

Unfortunately, in the Greek case the available data are not of a sort which will make it possible to determine whether Greek exports to the Middle East would or would not have shown the capital intensity character predicted by the Heckscher-Ohlin theory in the absence of economies of scale.

Linder

Linder's hypothesis stresses the demand (consumption) side of trade. In its unmodified form it is inadequate to explain the Greek export pattern of manufactures. Linder's basic notion, however, somewhat modified, provides a necessary complement to the Heckscher-Ohlin theory in explaining the Greek trade pattern.

The Heckscher-Ohlin theory alone does not explain why Greece should be able to export capital-intensive goods to the Middle East in the face of the fact that Western Europe is better endowed with labor than Greece; or why Greece can export labor-intensive goods to Western Europe when the Middle East is better endowed with capital than Greece. The addition of Linder's hypothesis does offer a reasonable explanation of this phenomenon.

The basic idea underlying Linder's theory is that a country will not be skilled in manufacturing and selling abroad products for which there is no "representative" domestic demand. Our contention is that the capital-intensive goods that Greece exports to the Middle East are goods for which there is a substantial (although not necessarily "representative") demand in Greece but not in Western Europe, while the labor-intensive goods that Greece exports to Western Europe are goods for which there is a substantial (although not "representative") demand in Greece but not in the Middle East.

The existence of a limited range of overlapping demand between Western Europe and the Middle East enables Greece to penetrate these markets. Greece has a wider range of overlapping demand with either of these areas than these two have between them. This point is illustrated in Figure 1, using Linder's diagram where he summarizes his principle for trade in manufactures. The modification proposed here is illustrated in Figure 2.

In his diagram Linder illustrates the case of trade between two countries, country I and country II, which have different per capita incomes and therefore different demand patterns. On the horizontal axis he indicates income per capita; on the vertical axis he shows in ordinal numbers the degree of "quality" or "sophistication" of the demand structure.[16] "The higher the per capita income, the higher will be the degree of quality characterizing the demand structure as a whole. The line OP is intended to represent this relationship."[17] But the average quality of demand, according to Linder, will be composed of different qualitative degrees of the various products; therefore, a range of qualitative degrees of demand around the average degree on OP will be formed. Thus, for country I, in Figure 1, the various products demanded will lie

Figure 1. Linder's Trade
Diagram

Figure 2. Modified Trade
Diagram

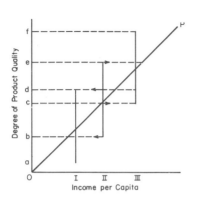

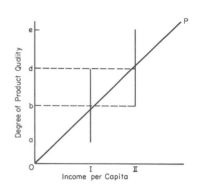

inside a qualitative range, a-d, and for country II the range will lie within b-e.

The modified diagram, Figure 2, presents three countries, or groups of countries. The Middle East is represented by country I, Greece by country II, and Europe by country III.

The qualitative range b-d is common for countries I and II; the range c-e is common for countries II and III and the range c-d is common for all three countries. The overlapping demands in these three "countries" relate to products whose quality falls within these ranges; it is in such products that trade may take place among these three countries.

Consequently, Greece ("country II") trades with—and in this case exports products within the quality range b-d to—the Middle East ("country I"), and products of a quality c-e to Europe ("country III"). Europe and the Middle East trade products in the range c-d which represents the overlapping demand of these two areas. Figure 2 shows that Greece has wider overlapping demands with either Europe or the Middle East than these two areas have between themselves. Hence, Greece has the opportunity to export "higher quality" products to Europe and "lower quality" products to the Middle East. The term "quality" or "sophistication" of a product is obviously vague. Linder has not attempted to define it further; neither will we. Using his tools in a modified form, one can, however, explain in combination with the neoclassical theory, the export pattern of Greek manufactures.

Both the Linder and the Heckscher-Ohlin theories are indeed necessary to explain the trade pattern. An exportable manufactured commodity must satisfy both the requirements that it uses the country's abundant factor intensively in relation to the importing country and that it lies inside the range of overlapping demands of the exporting and importing country. Similarity of demand patterns is not adequate to induce intensive trade in manufactures. A substantial—not necessarily "representative"—demand at home, overlapping with some demand for the same product in the importing country, is sufficient to turn the product to an exportable commodity.

The next two sections describe briefly the characteristics of the Middle Eastern and European markets and arrive at more precise hypotheses as to the nature of Greek exports to these areas. The last section tests these hypotheses against the data for Greek trade.

The Middle East

Factors of Production

The Middle East is generally less economically developed than Greece.[18] As is shown in Tables I and II, Greece has a higher income, a greater degree of industrialization, and higher literacy and urbanization rates than any Middle Eastern country.

The Middle East has a shortage of capital. This is also manifested by the level of per capita income which is in a way an index of the degree of capital abundance. Countries of relatively low income are notoriously capital-starved. At low stages of development poverty precludes the savings necessary to form capital.[19] The countries' few industries are predominantly labor-intensive; given the scarcity of capital this seems to be natural or even mandatory.[20] Grunwald and Ronall, participating in the theoretical controversy of whether the less-developed countries should

Table I. Standard of Living Indicators in the Middle East, 1957

Country	GNP per Capita (in $U.S.)	Illiteracy (per cent)	Urbanization (% of Total Population in Towns of over 10,000)
Egypt	$133	75–80%	33%
Iran	100	80–85	20
Iraq	195	85–90	20
Lebanon	270	50–55	40
Jordan	95	80	22
Syria	175	60–65	30
Libya	320[a]	80–85	21
Greece	330	25	50

[a] Approximately.

SOURCE: Kurt Grunwald and Joachim Ronall, *Industrialization in the Middle East* (New York: Council for Middle East Affairs Press, 1960), and author's calculations.

Table II. Industrialization in the Middle East, 1954-1958

Country	Number of Persons Employed in Industry (A)	Total Population (B)	Percent (A/B)	Share of Industry in GNP
Egypt	265,000	24,000,000	1.2%	12%
Iran	156,000	19,000,000	0.8	10
Iraq	80,000	6,000,000	1.3	12
Jordan	13,000	1,500,000	0.8	—
Libya	10,000	1,000,000	1.0	—
Lebanon	30,000	1,500,000	2.0	16
Syria	25,000	4,000,000	1.7	12
Greece	464,000	8,000,000	5.8	19

SOURCE: Calculations from Grunwald and Ronall, *op. cit.*, and Population Censuses of Greece, 1951, 1961, and United Nations, *Monthly Bulletin of Statistics*, January 1966.

adopt capital-intensive rather than labor-intensive industries, note: ". . . where capital is scarce and labor abundant, as in the Middle East, a proportionally higher employment of labor in relation to capital is advisable," and they provide empirical evidence that capital is indeed the scarce factor in the Middle East.[21]

The case of Jordan, as described by Grunwald and Ronall, is typical of the area:

> Several factors affect the pace of industrial development in Jordan. In addition to the limited market are the scarcity of managers and skilled labor, the high prices of fuel and power, difficulties in obtaining spare parts and having repairs adequately made, and last but not least, the lack of investment capital.[22]

Economies of Scale

Furthermore, Greece has a relatively larger domestic market than any individual Middle Eastern country. The Middle East comprises countries each of which constitutes a small national market, as there are not yet important free trade agreements in the area.[23]

The size of the market depends on the level of per capita income and population.[24] It is also influenced by income distribution and the existence of a nonmonetized sector. Generally the size of the market for manufactured goods—or the demand—increases proportionally with population but usually more than proportionally with an increase of income.

Chenery shows that there is a relationship between economies of scale and market size. The larger the market size, the greater the number of industrial sectors that attain economies of scale sufficient to make them competitive internationally. He further explains:

> When there are economies of scale in production, an increase in market size lowers costs and thus permits the substitution of domestic products for imports. An increase in size also affects output indirectly by increasing the intermediate demand from other industries which experience a substitution of domestic production for imports.[25]

It is reasonable, then, to assume that the individual Middle Eastern countries constitute markets of smaller size than that of Greece,[26] and that fewer industries could attain economies of scale than in Greece.

Demand Patterns

Although the level of development in Greece is higher than in the Middle East, historical data indicate that a few decades ago Greece was in the same economic situation that the Middle East is now. Since the level of economic development—or the level of per capita income—is a reasonable indication of the range of quality in the demand pattern of a country (according to Linder and others[27]), it follows that Greece in the very recent past must have demanded a range of product quality similar to that which the Middle East demands at present. Greece, through import substitution—which was the route that Greek industry followed—was first to develop industries satisfying the domestic demand for products of the aforementioned quality range. Demand for such products still exists, especially among lower income people.

This overlapping of demand patterns and the fact that Greece entered in the production of such goods before the Middle East give Greece an edge in the Middle Eastern markets. This prior entry has enabled Greek industry to develop skills, technological know-how, and managerial expertise, and to gain an advantage in exporting to the Middle East goods requiring these elements.

This advantage of Greek industry in the Middle East is reinforced by the proximity of the two areas. Geographical distance imposes barriers on trade through increased transportation costs and difficulty in communications. Linder considers distance a "trade-braking" factor which may distort trade patterns. In the case, especially, of underdeveloped countries distance becomes a serious factor because ". . . many domestic entrepreneurs have never raised their trade horizon very much above the local village market."[28]

Kindleberger[29] and Vernon[30] have repeatedly emphasized the role of distance in trade. Vernon recently wrote: "There is good reason to believe, however, that the entrepreneur's consciousness of and responsiveness to opportunity are a function of ease of communications; and further, that ease of communication is a function of geographical proximity."[31]

It is not only geographical distance, however, that hampers trade. Cultural and political relations, or cultural and political affinities or aversions, according to Linder,[32] play a very important role. Therefore, besides the factor of geographical distance, "cultural and political distance" should be also examined.

Distance

The Middle Eastern countries lie on the other side of the Mediterranean from Greece. This sea, a pool of great civilizations, has permitted the establishment of routes that have served as channels of cultural and commercial transactions since antiquity. Phoenicians, Egyptians, Greeks, Jews, Greek-Byzantines, Arabs, and Turks have dominated, fought and subjugated, or come in peaceful contacts with their neighbors. But these interactions always involved the exchange of customs, ideas, scientific knowledge, and institutions.

These communications were repeatedly disrupted in the course of history. In the last century the communication between the two sides of the Eastern Mediterranean was again disrupted after the extension of Western European (French and British) political and economic domination of the area. The discovery and exploitation of oil became an additional reason for the establishment of close ties between Western Europe and the Middle East. These ties, however, were severely weakened with the resurgence of Arab nationalism—frequently caught in the East-West confrontation— and the creation of Israel after the Second World War. The Suez crisis of 1956 strengthened further the anti-colonialist and even anti-foreign feelings in many countries of the Middle East. But where Western European goodwill was rapidly disappearing, relations with small nations, like Greece, were less seriously hurt. The Greeks in particular, who had been living for years in Middle Eastern cities, generally as successful entrepreneurs, were the last foreigners to leave. A number of them still live in Libya, Sudan, Egypt, Iran, and other Middle Eastern countries.

Communications and general cultural relations exist between Greece and the Middle East largely because of those Greeks of the diaspora. The Greek Government has done little in this field. The Cyprus problem had to appear—that put Greece on the side of the anti-colonialists—to impel Greece to search for new allies and improve her political relations with the Arab world. At present Greek political relations with the Middle Eastern countries—except Turkey—are warm. Greece assisted Egypt diplomatically during the Suez crisis and remained neutral in the Israel-Arab confrontation and the recent Egypt-Saudi Arabia rivalry.

Hence the facts, (1) that a large number of Greeks are still settled in the Middle East while there are very few Western Europeans, (2) that Middle Eastern political relations with Greece are generally better than those with Western Europe, and (3) that Greece is geographically closer to this area than Western Europe, allow Greece to enjoy advantages rendered by proximity, both cultural-political and geographical.

Characteristics of Exports to the Middle East

It is reasonable to expect that Greece would have an advantage toward the Middle East in manufactures where the production process uses capital intensively, where economies of scale are important, and where there is an overlapping demand for such goods in Greece and the Middle East. Capital goods and consumer durables especially seem to fulfill the above requirements. Such goods are in strong demand in the Middle East since an industrialization effort is under way.

The production of capital goods usually demands relatively high use of capital; this in turn could involve economies of scale. Naturally, Western Europe commands such factors in much greater abundance than Greece; however, as was previously mentioned, Europe's overlapping demand with the Middle East is much more limited than that of Greece. The advanced countries of the world produce capital or consumer durable goods which might not satisfy the needs of the Middle Eastern markets. As Linder suggests:

> A capital abundant country, i.e., a country which, with some likelihood, finds itself on a high level of per capita income, demands more sophisticated capital equipment than a capital-scarce country . . . . the reason for selecting relatively lower quality capital goods in a capital-scarce country is that it is a means of spreading the available capital more evenly.[33]

Dr. Ludwig Erhard, then Minister of Finance of West Germany, returning from a visit to Asian countries in 1958, emphasized that the supply of simple machines to small craftsmen was more important to the generation of purchasing power in underdeveloped countries than impressive looking projects remote from the people.

It seems very unlikely that manufacturers in an advanced country, like West Germany, would be interested in producing and selling abroad simple machines or equipment of outdated technology. There would be no "representative demand" for such products in Germany any more; and the German industries find more profitable uses for their capital.

On the contrary, Greece, whose level of development is closer to the Middle East than is Germany's, might still have a considerable home demand for simple machinery and generally for lower quality products. Such "lower quality" capital goods or consumer durables, although performing mainly the basic function of similar goods of higher qualities, are capital-saving rather than labor-saving; they use power which is more easily accessible in less-developed countries (oil instead of electricity); they are simple in design and have fewer automatic features and uncomplicated service and repair requirements. The production of such low-quality goods is quite standardized; Greece is in a technological position to produce them. And the Greek industrialist still produces them to satisfy domestic demand and could easily sell a part of his production to other countries.

Frankel offers empirical support to the above discussion in his analysis of Japanese exports. He shows that Japan's manufactured exports gained momentum during the crisis of 1929–32 which affected particularly the countries producing raw materials and foodstuff, most of which were underdeveloped. Japan managed to satisfy the world demand for cheap, low-quality manufactured products; the underdeveloped countries became the principal markets. Advancing the notion of "quality" in manufactures, Frankel notes:

> . . . A country with a large internal market for low-quality goods is more likely to compete successfully in countries with a demand for similar goods, than one whose internal markets are mainly in goods of higher quality, because less adaptation of production processes to export requirements will be needed in the former case. . . . The more a country is industrialized, the better it can produce goods of higher quality.[34]

This statement of Frankel provides a useful base for a discussion of the characteristics of the manufactured products that Western Europe is likely to import from Greece.

Western Europe

The position of Greece relative to Western Europe is analogous to the position of the Middle East relative to Greece. Thus, the above reasoning would apply if taken in reverse. Western Europe, in general, is more economically advanced than Greece. A much higher per capita income on the average, widely spread industrialization, higher urbanization and literacy, larger population in most cases, existence of customs unions or free trade agreements are some of the prevalent features in Western Europe. These traits result in relatively large market sizes—and consequently opportunities for scale economies—and a relative abundance of capital. The factor "distance" is not an obstacle in trade between Greece and Western Europe. Historically the culture and politico-economic ties have been almost always in the past—and still are—close and amicable.

Characteristics of Exports to Western Europe

The discussion in the previous section leads to the conclusion that Greece would not export capital goods or consumer durables to Western Europe. The production of such manufactures is, on the one hand, usually capital-intensive, involves economies of scale, and requires a high level of technology. Western Europe, on the other hand, would demand high quality in such goods; and for such high-quality goods there is not as yet substantial domestic demand in Greece. The same would be true, for instance, with new products which depend on research and development. Since research is a fixed cost component, it requires large-scale production. It is more likely that Western Europe will import such R&D-intensive goods from countries of higher per capita income. As Raymond Vernon suggests, the United States, a country of higher per capita income and higher cost of labor, would be the first country to produce and export labor-saving or high-income products.[35] It is probable, however, that certain "low-quality" capital goods or consumer durables would be able to penetrate Western European markets and exploit low-income sectors of the population. Those limited markets are sometimes ignored by the big European and American producers.

One category of manufactures that is likely to be sold to Western Europe from Greece is intermediate products. These commodities present certain peculiarities which will be briefly reviewed: first, on the demand side, in intermediate goods the market may be almost perfect, since the products are frequently standardized, the market knowledge adequate, and the process of industrial purchasing "rational." The existence of perfect markets means that an individual supplier faces a high price elasticity of demand. A small difference in price would be enough to bring the buyer to the producer.[36] This may explain why European customers would be interested in Greek intermediate goods. It does not explain, however, why Greece would produce such commodities. Examining the supply side, we find, however, a combination of a high domestic raw material content, a labor-intensive technology, and a high domestic demand for the final product manufactured in Greece. Those may have been the factors responsible for the undertaking of the production of intermediates.[37] This, in turn, may have enabled Greek industry to develop an "advantageous production function" in the Linder terminology. Those factors when reinforced by low-cost Greek labor allow for cost advantages in Greek intermediate products.

Consumer products in which Greece has a monopoly by virtue of high content of domestic raw materials, high product differentiation or traditional skills, may also be found in the list of exports to Western Europe.[38] These highly differentiated Greek products, sometimes luxurious consumer goods, are physically "unavailable" abroad and therefore can be sold in both areas, Western Europe and Middle East. Given its higher income levels, Western Europe may be the most important customer for such goods.

Hypotheses and Tests

The previous discussion leads to the following set of hypotheses:

1. Greek manufactures which are capital-intensive—relative to the average of the Greek manufacturing industry—are more intensively exported to the Middle East than to Western Europe.
2. Greek manufactures which are relatively labor-intensive are more intensively exported to Western Europe than to the Middle East.
3. Greek manufactures that involve high economies of scale—relative to the average of Greek manufacturing industry—are more intensively exported to the Middle East than to Western Europe.
4. Industrial (capital) goods are more intensively exported to the Middle East than to Western Europe.
5. Intermediate goods are more intensively exported to Western Europe than to the Middle East.[39]
6. Greek manufactures used as consumer durables are more intensively exported to the Middle East than to Western Europe.
7. Greek manufactures that enjoy monopolistic features are exported equally to both areas.

These seven hypotheses will be tested with empirical material below.

Tests and Conclusions

Chart 1* shows that the Middle Eastern countries import manufactures from Greece much more intensively than Western Europe.

---

* For the methodology employed in Charts 1–7, see the Appendix.

Only a small percentage of Greek commodities imported by Western Europe consists of manufactures. But as shown below, this small part is dominated by types of manufactures different from those bought by the Middle East.

Chart 2 indicates that Europe tends to buy relatively labor-intensive goods and the Middle East relatively capital-intensive goods. Chart 3 shows that the variable to total costs ratio of industries selling to the Middle East is lower than that of industries exporting to West Europe. The implication is that products coming from industries which enjoy high economies of scale seem to be more intensively sold to the Middle East. The findings illustrated in Chart 4 tend to support the hypothesis that the Middle East imports industrial (capital) goods from Greece more intensively than Western Europe. Chart 5 also tends to support the hypothesis that Western Europe buys intermediate goods in greater intensity than the Middle East. The hypothesis seems also to be supported by the empirical evidence in the case of consumer durables: The Middle Eastern countries import consumer durables more intensively than Western Europe (see Chart 6). On the other hand, the findings are inconclusive in the case of final consumer goods (see Chart 7).

The thesis that has been advanced in this paper is supported on the whole by empirical evidence. The two main export markets for Greece seem to buy different types of goods. The richer nations of Europe import primarily agricultural commodities, whereas the poorer countries of the Middle East look to Greece as a source of manufactured commodities. The relatively few manufactured products sold in Europe are distinctly different from those sold in developing countries. Europe buys from Greece in large proportion intermediate products or—to use another criterion—products which are labor-intensive. The Middle East prefers industrial and consumer durables. As far as final consumer products are concerned, a clear case cannot be made; they are bought in almost equal intensity by both areas. Since a large part of final consumer goods is made up of products in which Greece has a monopoly (as in the case of certain canned and processed fruits and vegetables, olive oil, records, motion pictures, and handicrafts) one could suggest that the last hypothesis has not been disproved by empirical evidence.

This evident dualism in comparative advantages of Greek manufactures provides several opportunities for Greek industry and poses a series of problems concerning the future direction of the country's industrialization.

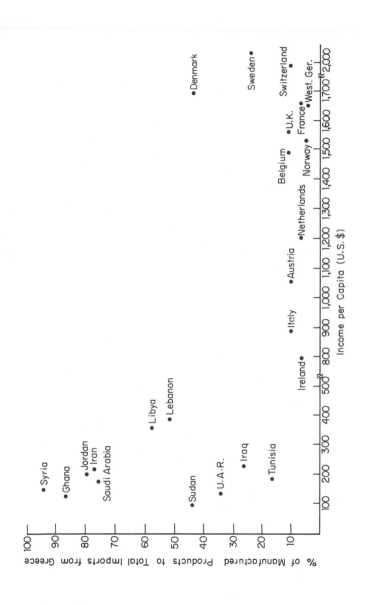

Chart 1. Manufactured Products: Percentage to Total Imports from Greece (Average Value 1961-1963)

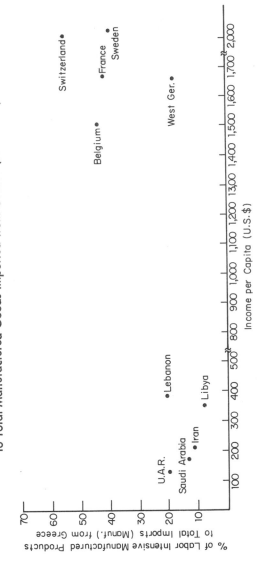

Chart 2. Labor-Intensive Manufactured Exports: Percentage of Labor-Intensive Manufactures to Total Manufactured Goods Imported from Greece (1961-1963)

SOURCE: G. Koutsoumaris, "The Morphology of the Greek Industry," Center of Economic Research, R.M.S., No. 6, Athens, 1963, p. 180, Table 5.9. A comparison of labor inputs to inputs of capital and management. The measurement is based on cost accounting data taken from 760 manufacturing firms for the year 1957. The contribution of *labor* is represented by the *total wage bill* (of labor and employees, fringe benefits included), the share of capital is made up of: (1) capital amortization charges (the rate of capital input needed to maintain the capacity of industry intact), and (2) interest and profits. An index number of labor intensity of more than 100 was considered to indicate a labor-intensive industry; of less than 100, a capital-intensive industry.

Chart 3. Economies of Scale: Composition of Manufactures Imported from Greece According to Economies of Scale (Variable Cost to Total Cost) of Greek Industries (Average 1961-1963)

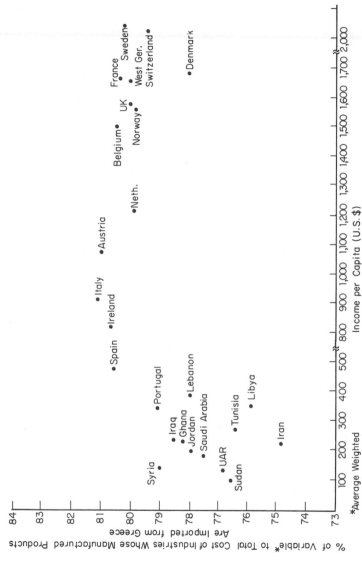

NOTE: Economies of scale are measured by the ratio of variables to total cost; a relatively low ratio indicates relatively high economies of scale.

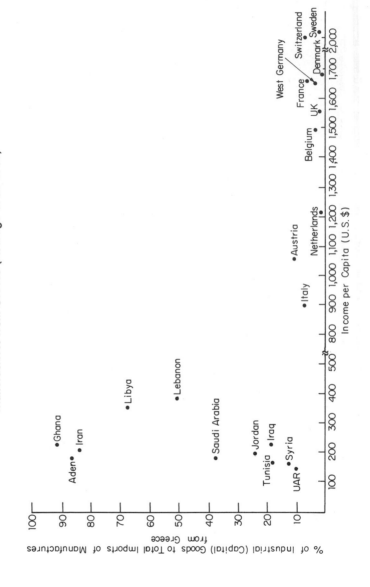

Chart 4. Industrial (Capital) Manufactured Products: Percentage to Total Imports of Manufactures from Greece (Average 1961-1963)

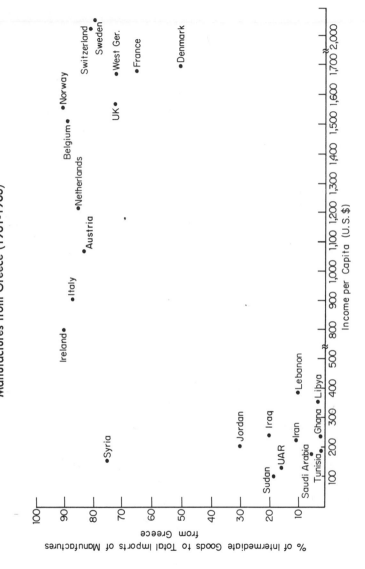

Chart 5. Intermediate Manufactured Products: Percentage to Total Imports of Manufactures from Greece (1961-1963)

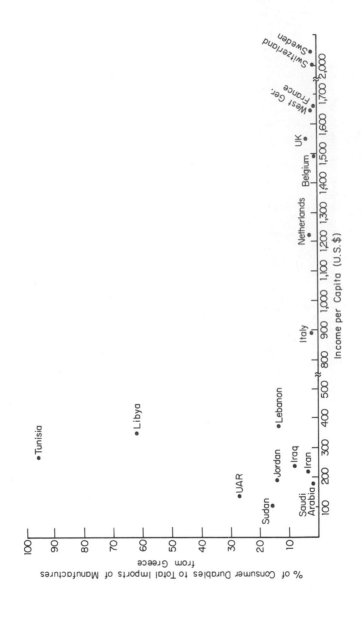

Chart 6. Consumer Durables: Percentage to Total Imports of Manufactures from Greece (1961-1963)

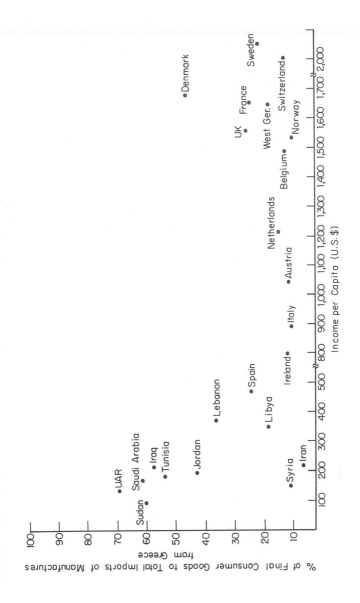

Chart 7. Final Consumer Products: Percentage to Total Imports of Manufactures from Greece (1961-1963)

FOOTNOTES

1 "Heckscher-Ohlin" will be used to refer to the simple factor endowment model of trade. See, for example, Preface to R. E. Caves and H. G. Johnson, *Readings in International Economics* (Homewood: Richard D. Irwin, Inc., 1968).

2 See Staffan Burenstam Linder, *An Essay on Trade and Transformation* (Stockholm: Almqvist & Wiksell, 1961).

3 The following countries are included under the head "Western Europe": United Kingdom, Ireland, Norway, Sweden, Finland, Denmark, Netherlands, Belgium and Luxembourg, West Germany, Austria, Switzerland, Italy, France, Spain, Portugal. The "Middle East" is defined here more freely to include countries beyond the conventional geographical frontiers of the area: Lebanon, Syria, Iraq, Iran, Saudi Arabia, Jordan, UAR, Libya, Tunisia, Sudan, Ethiopia, Ghana.

4 As W. A. Lewis points out, "The extent to which a country participates in international trade depends partly upon its resources, partly upon the barriers it places in the way of trade, and partly upon its stage of development." *The Theory of Economic Growth* (London: Allen and Unwin, 1955), p. 340.

5 The level of per capita income is a conventional measurement of economic development (it is used as a exogenous factor in our tests). See C. P. Kindleberger, *Economic Development* (New York: McGraw-Hill, 2d ed., 1965), pp. 4–7.

6 The "demonstration effect" has probably expanded the number of products demanded in both the advanced and the less-developed countries. This effect, though, pertaining mostly to upper income groups, is not able to create a "representative demand" in the Linder sense. See a discussion on "demonstration effect" in R. Nurkse, *Some Problems of Capital Formation in Underdeveloped Countries* (Oxford, 1953), p. 58.

7 Raymond Vernon, "International Investment and International Trade in the Product Cycle," *The Quarterly Journal of Economics*, Vol. 80, May 1966, pp. 190–207.

8 League of Nations, *Industrialization and Foreign Trade* (II. Economic and Financial, 1945. 11.A.10) 1945. F. Hilgerdt, the author of the above publication, further notes: "The expenditure on manufactured articles also changes in composition when income increases. In the U.S., for instance, expenditure on durable consumers' goods is relatively greater in the higher than in lower income groups. Also there can be no doubt that the demand for each kind of manufactures (furniture, clothing, etc.) is more varied and oriented towards finer qualities in the higher income groups" (pp. 24–25).

9 Differences in taste, based on cultural aspects, also influence demand patterns.

10 Hollis B. Chenery, "Patterns of Industrial Growth," *American Economic Review*, September 1960, Vol. 50, p. 625.

11 To define factor endowments we adopt here the conventional approach which emphasizes the exploitation of resources and not their mere physical existence.

12 M. Tatemoto and S. Ichimura, "Factor Proportions and Foreign Trade: The Case of Japan," *Review of Economics and Statistics*, Vol. 41, November 1959, pp. 442–446.

13 The usual interpretation of the Heckscher-Ohlin theory uses an index of "comparative capital-labor intensity"; that is, the capital-labor input ratio for competitive imports divided by the same ratio for exports. If this exceeds unity, then the country's exports are labor-intensive. This was the case of the United States according to Leontief.

Tatemoto and Ichimura computed the capital-labor ratio of Japanese exports going to the United States in 1951 and compared it with the ratio of Japan's total exports. (They also computed the same ratio of U.S. exports going to Japan and compared it with the ratio for U.S. total exports.) They found that the capital-labor ratio of Japanese exports to the United States is lower than her total exports. This seems to imply that Japan exported less capital-intensive goods to the United States and relatively capital-intensive goods to countries other than the United States.

The bilateral approach that we adopt differs in the following points from that of Tatemoto-Ichimura. First, we consider only manufactures and second, we do not limit the comparison of ratios of capital intensity between exports to one country and total exports. Instead we find the ratio of factor intensity for the Greek exports to all Western Europe and Middle Eastern countries. So the comparison is among countries in terms of their income per capita.

14 Increasing returns to scale do not necessarily imply capital-intensive process. Kindleberger remarks: "But, while high capital intensity and large scale enterprise are not identical, large-scale enterprises typically use capital abundantly, and very capital-intensive projects are generally large in scale." *Foreign Trade and the National Economy* (New Haven: Yale University Press, 1962), p. 70.

15 Kindleberger, *Economic Development*, pp. 150–154. He elaborates: "Internal technological economies are those resulting from the division of labor, the use of specialized machinery and other capital equipment with considerable capacity, the opportunity for using the insurance principle in massing inventories, and certain once-for-all contribution, such as a new design. . . . A minimum efficient scale of operation exists for every investment, and it is sometimes very large. One important external pecuniary economy in underdeveloped countries arises from the improved

organization of the market itself. When markets are fragmented and small, it is necessary to incur marketing costs to move production." p. 153.

16 Linder, *op. cit.*, p. 99.

17 *Ibid.*, p. 100.

18 See K. Grunwald and J. Ronall, *Industrialization in the Middle East* (New York: Council for Middle Eastern Affairs Press, 1960), Chapters II and IV; and A. Bonne, *The Economic Development of the Middle East* (New York: Oxford University Press, 1945).

19 See Kindleberger, *op. cit.*, Chapter 5. See also Simon Kuznets, "Quantitative Aspects of the Growth of Nations," *Economic Development and Cultural Change*, Vol. 8, Part 2, July 1960, pp. 1–96. He establishes the relationship between income per capita and household savings as a proportion of gross domestic capital formation.

20 There are, of course, islands of high capital-intensive industries in Middle Eastern countries, as results of natural resource exploitation (oil and colonization).

21 Grunwald and Ronall, *op. cit.*, p. 114.

22 *Ibid.*, p. 295.

23 The "Arab Common Market," including Jordan, Kuwait, Iraq, Syria, and the U.A.R., has only recently become operative; tariffs in industrial products have been reduced 10% and in primary products 20%. The economic unity of Syria and Lebanon, established in 1943 upon the termination of the French mandate, came to an end in 1950.

24 See Chenery, *op. cit.*, p. 645. He notes: "The use of national population as a measure of the market area must be qualified by the geographical location and trade policy of the country. In Western Europe both geography and trade liberalization favor an expansion of industrial markets beyond national borders. This is much less true in Latin America, Asia or Africa, where protection of new industry is the predominant policy and transport facilities are much less developed."

25 *Ibid.*, p. 645.

26 Large nonmonetized sectors, profound inequality in income distribution, and especially difference in per capita income neutralize the effect of larger populations.

27 Linder, *op. cit.*

28 Linder, *op. cit.*, p. 108.

29 Kindleberger, *Foreign Trade and the National Economy*, p. 15.

30 Vernon, "International Investment and International Trade in the Product Cycle."

31 *Ibid.*, p. 192.

32 Linder, *op. cit.*, p. 108.

33 Linder, *op. cit.*, p. 96.

34 H. Frankel, "Industrialisation of Agricultural Countries and the Possi-

bilities of a New International Division of Labour," *Economic Journal*, Vol. 53, June–September 1943, p. 195.

35 Vernon, *op. cit.*, p. 190.

36 See R. Vernon, "Problems and Prospects in the Export of Manufactured Goods from the Less Developed Countries," U.N. Conference on Trade and Development, Geneva, March–June 1964.

37 Chenery notes: "Intermediate demand in general grows more rapidly than final demand because import substitution requires increased production of intermediate goods." *op. cit.*, p. 644.

38 Handicrafts, records, canned olives or olive oil, for example, could be included in this category.

39 Intermediate goods are those used as inputs for further manufacturing process; usually standardized and they have a high price elasticity of demand. Chenery's distinction of manufacturing products has been adopted here.

APPENDIX

Methodological Note

Each exported product, based on ISIC classification at a five digit level, had to be classified according to factor intensity and scale economies and according to its consumption level; that is, final, intermediate, or reproductive. The first classification is derived from data which give average factor intensity and economies of scale for each industrial group producing the manufactured item under consideration. Thus, to measure economies of scale the ratio of variable cost over total cost is used. The higher this ratio, the lower the economies of scale. Admittedly, this measurement is only one among several used to evaluate economies of scale. Other methods are measurement of value added per establishment or the degree of concentration in each industrial group. The choice has been made here based on the belief that the measurement chosen is the most reasonable among those available in Greece. To measure labor and capital intensity, three measurements have been made: (a) average capital/output ratio, (b) labor/capital input ratio, and (c) wage bill/total cost ratio.[1]

The second classification, that of the level of consumption, is generally based on the broad framework suggested by Chenery.[2] Naturally, since objective criteria for deciding whether a product is intermediate or industrial exist only for a few products, judgment based on conjecture or personal experience often provided guidelines for the decision.

To measure export intensity, I decided to use the percentage value in drachmas of a particular type of manufacture from Greece in relation to total imports of manufactures from Greece by the country under consideration. Country X, for example, imports capital goods intensively from Greece if the value of the imported capital goods is 80% of the total imports of manufactures from Greece.

---

[1] To decide whether a product is labor-intensive, I used the average ratio for the Greek manufacturing industry as the dividing line. For instance, if the average capital input ratio is 1.5 and the same ratio for the pharmaceutical industry is 1.2, then according to this measurement the products of the pharmaceutical industry are considered capital-intensive.

[2] Chenery, *op. cit.*, p. 644.

The third problem is the selection of the appropriate statistical method for testing the hypotheses. The analysis attempts to show that the level of economic development of the importing country—which is usually approximated by income per capita—determines the composition of its manufactured imports from a country such as Greece. Hence, income per capita emerges as the independent variable.

A scatter diagram, where income per capita of importing countries is plotted against various percentages, is used to demonstrate the existence of two clusters of countries, one composed of low income and another of high income countries. The diagram may not necessarily show that as income per capita rises the percentage of intermediate goods, for example, imported from Greece increases. Thus, a correlation analysis does not seem to be the most appropriate method to illustrate the hypotheses. What the diagram will show is that almost all European countries buy Greek intermediate products in much higher proportion than the Middle Eastern countries.[3] The diagram shows income per capita on the horizontal axis.

The ratios for the vertical axis were calculated from data drawn from two sources: First from "The Morphology of Greek Industry" by G. Koutsoumaris which reproduces results of a survey of 760 manufacturing firms in Greece made by the National Statistical Service of Greece. This source provides information on a three-digit basis about labor-capital ratios and variables cost for each industrial group. Second, from the "Statistics of External Trade of Greece by Countries 1961, 1962, 1963," which offers a detailed account of manufactures exported to various countries. It was decided to use a three-year period (1961–1963) in order to even out random fluctuations in Greek exports.

To find the weighted average of labor-capital ratio of manufactures imported by a particular country, all manufactures included in the list over the three-year period were classified according to the capital intensity of the industrial group that produced them. This was done in the following stages: First, the total value (in drachmas) of all manufactured commodities imported by a particular country was found; second, the percentage that each commodity represents in the total value was determined; third, the sum of the percentages of goods produced by labor-intensive industrial groups was calculated. The same procedure was followed with products of capital-intensive industrial

---

[3] The Appendix of "Export Horizons of Greek Industries" shows the least square lines and coefficients of correlation.

groups. The two sums form a ratio. This ratio is the weighted average of the labor-capital ratio of Greek manufactures imported by a particular country.

The following example will illustrate the method of calculating the ratio of variable to total costs, to measure economies of scale: Egypt imported from Greece over the three-year period 1961–1963, "antibiotics and other drugs" of a value which represents 22% of the total value of manufactured goods imported from Greece. From the data which give the various ratios of the industrial groups it is found that the ratio of variable to total cost of the pharmaceutical industrial group is .61. Multiplying the two numbers ($.22 \times .61 = .1342$) and adding the sums of similar calculations for each item yielded a weighted average ratio for Egypt. In this case .78 is the weighted average ratio of variable to total cost incorporated in manufactured products that Egypt imported from Greece over a three-year period. This ratio is plotted against Egypt's income per capita. The same procedure is followed for every European and Middle Eastern country. The scatter diagram shows, in this case, the relationship between exports of products involving economies of scale and income per capita of importing countries.

In calculating percentages of industrial, intermediate, consumer durable, and final consumer goods the method used is simple. For each importing country a percentage (average over three years) of a category of manufactures is calculated and plotted against income per capita.

Marketing Factors in Manufactured Exports from Developing Countries

JOSE R. DE LA TORRE, JR.

Jose R. de la Torre, Jr.

Jose de la Torre is Assistant Professor and Member of the Institute of International Business at Georgia State University. He was formerly Research Associate at the Harvard University Graduate School of Business Administration and Assistant Professor of International Business at INCAE, Managua, Nicaragua. He was Visiting Professor at the School of Industrial Administration of the Universidad del Valle, Cali. He has also served as consultant to the Inter-American Development Bank and as editor for the United Nations Panel on Foreign Investment in Latin America. He holds the B.S. and M.B.A. degrees from the Pennsylvania State University and the D.B.A. degree from Harvard University.

His doctoral dissertation, "Exports of Manufactured Goods from Developing Countries: Marketing Factors and the Role of Foreign Enterprise," won the 1970 annual dissertation competition sponsored by the Association for Education in International Business. A summary was published in the Journal of International Business Studies, *Spring Issue, 1971. His other publications include "The Role of Multinational Firms in Promoting Manufactured Exports from Developing Countries," in Eliezer Ayal, editor,* Micro Aspects of Development *(forthcoming).*

Marketing Factors in Manufactured Exports from Developing Countries

It has been amply demonstrated that if the aspirations of the less developed countries of the world are to be fulfilled, relatively high priority must be given to the development of manufactured exports. The disadvantages of dependency upon primary products for export earnings, the limitations of reliance on import substitution as the main vehicle for industrialization, and, more generally, the constraints which insufficient foreign exchange earnings impose on promoting viable economic growth are most frequently cited as evidence of this need.

The factors which affect the feasibility of viable export industries in developing countries are numerous and varied. They range from the economic to the behavioral and will differ from country to country. However, some of these factors are common to many developing countries and the problems they pose justify efforts to search for common solutions.

This article examines the experience of three countries in exporting manufactured goods. Central to the paper is the proposition that the marketing characteristics of a product are a major determinant of its export potential for developing countries, particularly as these characteristics affect how, by whom, to what extent, and

NOTE: The author wishes to acknowledge the generous assistance of Professors Raymond Vernon, Dwight S. Brothers, and Louis T. Wells, Jr., at the Harvard Business School, under whose guidance this research was conducted. Also, the financial support of the Inter-American Development Bank and the Latin American Teaching Fellowship Program is gratefully acknowledged. The author is, however, fully responsible for any and all errors and shortcomings.

227

under what conditions successful export efforts are undertaken. What follows is an analysis of the relationships which appear to exist between a product's marketing characteristics—the independent variable—and various indices of export performance.

Marketing Factors in the Product Life Cycle

Classical and neoclassical economic theory supports the argument that developing nations enjoy a comparative advantage in goods whose manufacture makes extensive utilization of labor. Presumably, labor is an abundant and a relatively cheap resource in the less developed countries. If no factor reversals occur and production functions remain constant throughout the world, the larger the input of the cheaper resource (labor) in the manufacturing process of a given good, the greater the potential for a country that exhibits such factor proportions to specialize in that good's production and export.[1]

The relative factor-abundance theorem can also be brought to bear on the technological inputs to the manufacturing process. Less developed countries are generally poorly endowed with a research and development capability. Consequently, the theory would indicate that, barring any factor movement, those industries with low technological requirements will be better suited for export purposes.

More recently a new body of theory has emerged in the literature which attempts to explain trade patterns in manufactured goods on the basis of stages in a product's life—the product life cycle theory. The product life cycle (PLC) model states that as new products or processes are introduced, the consuming country is likely to be the producing country because of the close relationship between innovation and demand, the producer's concern with flexibility in changing his inputs and outputs, the low price elasticity of demand for the output of individual firms, and the desirability for swift and effective communications between producer and customers, suppliers, and even competitors at this stage. The model further indicates that as the product matures it becomes increasingly standardized; the number of producers increases since entry into the market is facilitated by the increasing availability of technology; mass production utilizing standard processes becomes the rule, lowering production costs; demand increases while becoming more price-elastic; prices tend to decrease as competition stiffens and a buyer's market develops; and profit margins are substantially reduced. In addition, product differentiation may gradually appear as producers strive to maintain their shares of the market. At this stage, if economies of scale are being fully utilized, the principal difference between production costs at any two locations is likely to be a result of differences in factor costs.

During the product's introductory stage, demand in other countries has been created and satisfied through exports from the first producing country. But a point is reached when transport and tariff costs offer an incentive to begin production in one or more of these other markets. When the possibility of lower labor costs is also considered, the aggregate cost incentive may more than offset the negative effects of producing at lower volumes. The original producer may then consider entering one or more of these second countries by investing in production facilities, especially if he is to maintain his share of the market in the face of the threat of local competition. If the cost savings are sufficient, the trade flows may even reverse themselves, with the original producing country now being an importer from the lower cost location.

A seemingly logical extension of the PLC model would suggest that mature products possess a series of characteristics which make them more suitable for export from developing countries—notably a lower requirement for technological inputs and/or higher degree of technological stability, an increase in the lower skilled labor content, and a higher degree of price consciousness on the part of the consumer at this later stage. However, one aspect of the product remains of critical importance to developing countries: the changes in marketing requirements which occur as products advance through different stages in their life.

As a product reaches maturity producers are faced with increasing competition. Let us assume, for the time being, that consumers are also likely to become more aware of their ability to substitute one manufacturer's product for that of another and will tend to search for the most economic one. Of course, if all producers accepted such uniformly rational behavior on the part of the consumer as given, a situation would exist where prices are determined by lowest cost. The producer's strategy would then be limited to an attempt to find a least-cost location for production. A likely production location for these mature products would be developing countries with low technological capabilities but large supplies of low-cost unskilled and semiskilled labor.

Certain textile products offer good examples of developments of this kind. Standardized textile products, such as yarn, thread, and raw cotton cloth, are produced cheaply in low-wage countries. Advanced nations have had to turn to high tariffs and import quotas in order to save certain elements of their national textile industries from competitive gains made by less developed country producers.

But manufacturers of mature products are well aware of the diverse behavioral patterns of most consumers, whether they be individual or industrial buyers. They realize that by appealing to a particular need in the buyer's emotional or intellectual make-up—through advertising, personalized promotion, slight design changes, service assurances, and a host of other methods—they are able to exert some influence over the consumer's buying decision. This is particularly true for those products exhibiting performance characteristics which are not readily perceived and are difficult to evaluate. The manufacturer thus attempts to create a loyal following among his prospective customers in order to extract a premium sufficient to cover his added promotional expenditures, attain a certain advantage over his competition, and gain an added profit. The case of common aspirins provides an example of a product where a few manufacturers have achieved a commanding lead over the cheaper unbranded item. This lead was obtained through extensive advertising, the establishment of brand images, the maintenance of better production quality control, and small, but consumer-significant, product improvements, such as buffering additives.

The basic PLC model does not deal explicitly with the effect that a product differentiation strategy could have on export potential. The analysis above indicates that the possibilities of such a strategy would imply that similarly mature products would exhibit substantial differences from a marketing viewpoint. How these differences affect export performance and potential from developing countries is the central question to be resolved.

Marketing Factors and Export Behavior

The research showed that a product's marketing characteristics affect not only its potential for export development, but the nature of the original export decision, the market to which it was originally exported, the various markets which have been reached at a later point in time, the channels through which it is exported and the degrees of control which are exercised over them, and, critically, the types of companies which are responsible for the export activity. In order to illustrate these relationships between marketing characteristics and export behavior, it is necessary to define what is meant by differences in marketing characteristics and to identify suitable measures of these differences.

Product Differentiation and Marketing Entry Barrier[2]

Firms engaged in manufacturing mature products may utilize different competitive strategies in the market place. The dominance of any one marketing strategy, or of particular elements within that strategy, will have an effect on the relative difficulty faced by prospective competitors. A newcomer wishing to enter the market, whether that newcomer be another domestic producer or an exporter from another country, must be prepared to overcome a "marketing entry barrier."

In order for a new firm (an exporter in a developing country, for example) to enter a market for a particular product where the existing firms are competing at a given level of product differentiation, the newcomer may have to accept a lower price than is commanded by the established firms. Or, on the other hand, it may have to incur extremely high marketing costs per unit of sales volume. Finally, the firm may have to contend with both forms of disadvantages. Moreover, the duration of the added disadvantages, and not only their absolute value, is also critically important.

For analytical purposes, all relatively labor-intensive, mature products which may be considered *a priori* as having export potential for developing countries may be divided into two broad categories: (1) those which are sold or traded in conditions basically determined by price considerations, e.g., gray cloth, and (2) those where product differentiation plays a significant role in the market place, e.g., standard mechanical typewriters.

The boundary areas encompassing both groups are described by Bain as follows. Products for which well-established and widely based markets generally exist constitute the undifferentiated category. Barriers to entry were classified by Bain as "negligible" when a new entrant suffered a product differentiation advantage which was between 0 and 5% of price and which lasted no longer than two years.[3] Many products in this category are considered industrial goods. Examples given by Bain are copper, rayon, cement, flour, most textiles, fountain pens, steel products, women's shoes, and men's lower priced shoes.

Differentiated products are further subdivided into two groups: (a) products with "moderate" entry barriers, where the extent of the disadvantages is estimated by Bain at 5% to 10% of price for two to five years; and (b) products with "great" entry barriers, upwards of 10% for more than five years in most cases.[4]

It should be noted that the disadvantage faced by the potential exporter when entering the market for any such products does not consist simply of a price differential that would be easily overcome. Instead, the percentage figure attached to each entry barrier level is merely intended to reflect, in quantitative terms, the total effect of factors such as brand loyalty, captive distribution channels, and advertising expenditures.

Bain's examples of products with moderate entry barriers include canned fruits and vegetables, men's higher priced shoes, metal containers, rubber tires, petroleum derivatives, and soap; those with great entry barriers include typewriters, cigarettes, liquor, and automobiles.[5]

Bain's classification of products into these three categories constitutes the independent variable employed in the study. This measure was correlated with various export parameters to determine whether a product's export behavior is related to its marketing characteristics.

The Effect of Marketing Characteristics on Exports

Products with a relatively higher marketing entry barrier require a more difficult or more costly marketing effort on the part of those attempting to initiate the export process than do products with a lower barrier. The exporting firm and its executives need to possess better knowledge of the market, of the competitive situation, and of the requirements for successful entry. Heavy demands are placed on their ability to plan, implement, and control marketing functions. Close contacts with market sources, capable of providing rapid feedback and information on market conditions, are essential.

Export Performance. The skills, knowledge, and contacts necessary to overcome the marketing barriers to entry are not abundant resources in developing countries. As a result, developing countries will experience relatively better performance in exporting those manufactured goods characterized by low marketing requirements.[6]

Export performance is, of course, a vague term. It has volume, growth, and profitability connotations. Ideally, data on profit margins, contributions, and the like would serve for comparing performance from a profitability viewpoint. But these data would be difficult if not impossible to obtain. Instead, it is necessary to rely on measures of export intensity and growth to determine the relative competitive ability of industries in sectors with differing marketing characteristics.

Any attempt to ascribe export performance to a single factor is bound to be unsuccessful. Obviously, many variables enter into determining why certain products perform better in export markets than others. What is intended here is to show that marketing characteristics are one of the important determinants of export behavior.

A useful measure of a country's *propensity to export* manufactured goods is the percentage of its total industrial production destined for export markets. Furthermore, a relative measure of any given sector's export performance can be obtained from *its* propensity factor normalized by the propensity factor for the total national manufacturing activity. Thus, an *export propensity index*[7] is obtained for comparative purposes.

A sample of 32 industrial sectors and subsectors in Colombia was analyzed for these purposes. The following formula was applied for computing the various export propensity indices.

$$e_i = \frac{X_i/P_i}{\sum\limits_{i=1}^{n} X_i \Big/ \sum\limits_{i=1}^{n} P_i}$$

where: e = export propensity index
           X = export volume in dollars
           P = total production volume in dollars
           i = a grouping signifying either an industrial sector (32 in our sample), or a group of sectors classified under a particular heading (e.g., according to marketing entry barrier)
           n = total number of manufacturing sectors in the country

Using as the normalizing factor (the denominator in the formula above) the export propensity of all Colombian industrial sectors, the resulting index for the 32 sectors in the sample was 2.10. This reflects the fact that while the sample sectors accounted for 60% of all manufactured exports from Colombia, they represented only 28.5% of total industrial production.[8]

After each of the 32 sectors was allocated to the appropriate group among Bain's three marketing entry barrier categories, the aggregate export propensity index for each group was computed.

For group I sectors, whose products were principally classified as having "negligible" marketing entry barriers, the index was 2.75. The aggregate indices for group II and III sectors ("moderate" and "great" entry barriers) were 1.12 and 1.45 respectively. If these two groups are combined, their index was 1.22. Table 1 summarizes these results.

All three indices were greater than unity since the 32 sample sectors included a large number of industries actively exporting, as evidenced by the aggregate sample index of 2.10. But it is evident that those firms manufacturing products classified in group I were more involved in export markets than the others. The comparison between groups II and III yields contradictory results. However, given the small size of the group III sample, and the fact that only those group III sectors which were exporting were included in the sample, the results may be biased in their favor. Also, foreign firms constituted a large proportion of this group, and their incidence, as discussed below, has a marked effect on exports.

Table 1. Export Propensity of 32 Manufacturing Sectors in Colombia

	Production[a] (A)	Exports[b] (B)	Percentage (B/A)	Export propensity index
All manufacturing sectors	$2,404.70	$58.14	2.42%	1.00
All sample sectors	686.22	34.81	5.07	2.10
Group I sectors	392.03	26.12	6.65	2.75
Group II sectors	203.34	5.48	2.71	1.12
Group III sectors	90.85	3.21	3.52	1.45

[a] Data relate to 1964, in millions of dollars.
[b] Data relate to 1968, in millions of dollars.

SOURCES: Departamento Administrativo Nacional de Estadisticas (DANE), *Anuario General de Estadisticas—1964*, Bogota, 1967.

Banco de la Republica, Fondo de Promocion de Exportaciones, *Informes No. 7 y 8,—1968*, Bogota, February, 1969.

Data were also obtained from a small sample of individual firms in which extensive in-depth interviews were conducted. The sample included 69 companies—38 in Colombia, 16 in Nicaragua, and 15 in Mexico—randomly selected, in the first two cases, from national exporters' directories. The sample firms were classified according to Bain's typology as applied to their respective product lines. The firms were also classified as "domestic" when management control was in the hands of nationals of the country, usually implying that ownership was also primarily national. Alternatively, they were classified as "foreign" when management control was vested in a foreign partner, regardless of the percentage of foreign ownership.

The data obtained from this sample also provide some supporting evidence as to the effect marketing characteristics have on export performance. Two measures of performance, export growth and export sales as a percentage of total sales ("export intensity"), are shown in Table 2 (A & B) for the domestic firms in the sample, classified according to their marketing entry barrier classification. The evidence indicates a slight tendency for firms in the lower marketing entry barrier group to perform better than the others.

Export Initiative.   Marketing characteristics also influence the nature of the original export decision. The higher the marketing entry barrier, the greater the need for or dependence on external agents or forces to initiate the firm along the export path, since products with higher marketing requirements demand a higher level of marketing skill on the part of the exporter. If the local manufacturer or potential exporter is unable or unwilling for any of a variety of reasons to supply such skills, the initiative will have to come from outside the firm.

The data provided by the sample indicate that the initiative for the first export attempt was located within the firm more frequently among group I companies (30%) than among group II (25%) or group III (none) firms. Thus, the higher the marketing entry barrier, the more domestic firms rely on elements external to their organization to initiate export activities.

Table 2. Marketing Factors and Export Behavior of Domestic Firms

Measures of Export Behavior	% of Firms in Each Marketing Behavior Category that Fell into the Particular Export Behavior Class[a]			
	I. Negligible	*II. Moderate*	*III. Great*	*All firms*
A. Export intensity[b]				
0%–10%	74%	77%	100% (2)	76%
10%–25%	7	15	—	10
25%–50%	11	8	—	10
More than 50%	7	—	—	5
	100%	100%	100%	100%
No. of firms responding	27	13	2	42
B. Export growth rate[c]				
Negative	14%	44%	50% (1)	28%
0%–20%	36	11	—	24
More than 20%	50	44	50% (1)	48
	100%	100%	100%	100%
No. of firms responding	14	9	2	25

(see footnotes on page 240)

Table 2 (Continued)

| Measures of Export Behavior | % of Firms in Each Marketing Behavior Category that Fell into the Particular Export Behavior Class[a] | | | |
	I. Negligible	II. Moderate	III. Great	All firms
C. *Source of initiative for export decision*				
Within the company	30%	25%	—%	28%
External	70	75	100% (1)	72
—foreign buyer	42%	38%	100% (1)	40%
—government	17	8	—	15
—licensor	4	17	—	8
—other	7	12	—	9
	100%	100%	100%	100%
No. of firms responding	24	12	1	37
D. *Proximity factor in first export market*[a]				
Bordering	54%	75%	100% (2)	61%
Intermediate	15	17	—	15
Distant	42	17	—	31
No. of firms responding	26	12	2	40

Table 2 (Continued)

% of Firms in Each Marketing Behavior
Category that Fell into the Particular
Export Behavior Class[a]

Measures of Export Behavior	I. Negligible	II. Moderate	III. Great	All firms
E. Export markets[d]				
Regional[e]	57%	57%	100% (2)	59%
Rest of L.A.	61	43	50 (1)	55
United States	39	50	—	41
Other developed	18	7	—	14
Other	4	—	—	2
No. of firms responding	28	14	2	44

(differentiating between domestic and export markets)

Measures of Export Behavior	I. Negligible Dom. mkt.	I. Negligible Exp. mkt.	II. Moderate Dom. mkt.	II. Moderate Exp. mkt.	III. Great Dom. mkt.	III. Great Exp. mkt.	All firms Dom. mkt.	All firms Exp. mkt.
F. Level of control over marketing channels[f]								
High	35%	8%	27%	8%	100% (2)	—%	30%	8%
Intermediate	22	28	27	25	—	50 (1)	22	28
Low	43	64	47	67	—	50 (1)	48	64
	100%	100%	100%	100%	100%	100%	100%	100%
No. of firms responding	23	25	15	12	2	2	40	39

Table 2 (Continued)

Measures of Export Behavior	% of Firms in Each Marketing Behavior Category that Fell into the Particular Export Behavior Class[a]			
	I. Negligible	*II. Moderate*	*III. Great*	*All firms*
G. *Change in level of control over channels*[f] (toward a:)				
Higher level	30%	15%	—%	24%
No change	22	46	—	29
Lower level	48	38	100% (2)	47
	100%	100%	100%	100%
No. of firms responding	23	13	2	38

[a] The absolute numbers are provided in parentheses for the group III firms, since there were only a small number.
[b] Export sales a percentage of total sales.
[c] Average yearly compounded rate of growth for 1965–1968 period.
[d] Percentages may add to more than 100 because of multiple answers.
[e] Represents exports to those countries formally associated with the exporting country through regional integration agreements.
[f] See text for explanation of control levels.

SOURCE: Interviews.

Export Destination. In addition to their effect on the nature of the original export decision, marketing characteristics are a determinant of the market to which the first export effort is directed. Market knowledge is an important element in determining the ability of a firm to introduce its products in a new environment successfully. And this factor becomes more critical the higher the marketing entry barrier of the product.

Let us assume that market knowledge can be represented by market proximity. It seems likely that people in any given country would tend to have a better knowledge about the markets, the people, and the opportunities available in neighboring countries than they would have about more distant nations. Familiarity would tend to diminish some of the fears and uncertainties generally associated with foreign markets. Therefore, a positive correlation should exist between market proximity, as measured in Table 3, and the firm's first export market.[9] The sample data show that initial export activity was more frequently aimed at bordering markets (65%) than at either intermediate (13%) or distant (28%) markets.[10] Of course, other factors such as lower transport costs and preferential duties through common market arrangements may account for part of this behavior. But insofar as the three sample countries are concerned, these cost and tariff advantages also exist with respect to certain market areas other than those classified as bordering.

Table 2-D presents the same data for domestic firms classified according to the marketing entry barrier. The evidence from the table is clear. Domestic firms show a tendency to limit themselves to neighboring markets in their first export attempts in direct proportion to the height of the marketing entry barrier.

A similar tendency exists when the extent of the firm's present commitment to various export markets is considered. The data in Table 2-E lend further support to the proposition that when complex product marketing requirements are superimposed on a situation involving a sophisticated market, the manufacturer in the developing country faces increasing difficulties in export marketing. The percentage of domestic firms in group I involved in nonregional markets is slightly higher than the percentage of group II domestic

Table 3. Classification of Market Areas According to
Market Knowledge and Proximity

Market Knowledge	*Market Proximity*	*Market Areas*		
		Colombia	*Nicaragua*	*Mexico*
Higher	Bordering	Panama Ecuador Venezuela	Honduras Costa Rica El Salvador	U.S. Guatemala
Medium	Intermediate	Caribbean Central America	Guatemala Panama Caribbean	Rest of C.A.
Lower	Distant	All others	All others	All others

firms similarly involved. If "other Latin American countries" are excluded, the performance of domestic firms falls drastically from group I to group III.

Distribution Channels. In order to export products that are characterized by the use of high differentiation strategies, producing firms have to rely to a great extent on their marketing skills and on their knowledge about market conditions in importing countries. The more sophisticated a product's marketing requirements, the greater the need that exists for the firm to have access to an organization closely related to the market to which exports are intended. As a result, exporting firms will have either to enter the market themselves or to hand over their export business to other firms that are capable of performing the necessary marketing functions.

Domestic firms in developing countries are generally unable or unwilling to take upon themselves the increased marketing requirements of differentiated products when dealing with export markets. These same firms, which for a variety of reasons exercise different degrees of control over their domestic marketing activities, will, when moving into export markets, surrender a significant portion of this control to foreign-based firms. Regardless of the level of control exerted over domestic channels of distribution, exporting firms exercise a lower level of control over distribution and other marketing functions as they move into export markets; and this decrease in control is more dramatic the higher the marketing entry barrier that characterizes the product.

From the standpoint of the domestic market, many factors influence the decision of whether to attempt to control distribution channels. Certainly, the firm's commitment to a differentiation strategy is one such factor. All other things being equal, many firms engaged in differentiating their products may attempt, as an element of that strategy, to control their domestic channels of distribution. But other factors will also influence the domestic behavior of firms. The lack of sophistication among domestic marketing institutions may force a manufacturer to take a more active role in the distribution of its products. Also, differences in industrial structure and consumer habits exist between advanced and developing countries. As a result, some products principally considered intermediate in advanced countries may be purchased to a larger extent by end users in a developing country, e.g., textiles. The choice of distribution channels may also be affected by differences in demographic structure and income distribution. Nonetheless, control of distribution channels constitutes an integral part of the firm's marketing strategy and, most importantly, it represents a critical variable in the export process.

The principal tendency observable among the domestic operations of the sample firms was the dominant use of controlled channels. The data show that company stores, exclusive distributors, and direct sales to consumers were the most commonly used channels in all groups.[11] In addition, there were few differences among the three marketing entry barrier groups. Control over export channels of distribution, however, shows more variance according to product characteristics and type of user.[12]

The interviews showed that domestic companies forfeit control of their marketing functions to some extent when they move into export markets. But the yielding of control was especially associated with those product lines that are more market-oriented. The decrease in control of export channels by the exporting firms, observed to be most prevalent for the highly differentiated products, was associated with a greater role of organizations outside of the producing country. These organizations usually consisted of independent foreign buyers and foreign affiliates of domestic firms.

This behavior is consistent with our previous findings. Domestic enterprises could easily cope with the problems of exporting relatively undifferentiated products, where price was the major purchase consideration. But their ability to compete successfully in foreign markets with highly differentiated manufactured goods was considerably lower. Evidence of the differences is presented in Tables 2-F and 2-G. The tables show the absolute levels and the frequency of differences in the level of control exerted by domestic firms over marketing channels when comparing domestic with export markets.

The Role of Foreign Enterprise[13]

The evidence presented thus far corroborates the claim that marketing characteristics are an important factor in the development of exports of manufactures from developing countries. The existence of this relationship between marketing characteristics and export behavior tends to support the hypothesis that market knowledge and marketing skills are necessary conditions for exploiting certain export markets. The lower performance of domestic firms in exporting highly differentiated products, as opposed to exporting products with negligible marketing entry barriers, has been attributed to the fact that the requisite marketing skills and knowledge seem to be relatively scarce resources in developing countries. However, it is the individual firm, and not the country, which is ultimately responsible for the performance of its products in export markets, and the degree of marketing skill available varies from firm to firm.

Foreign firms have greater access to market information, distribution channels, and marketing skills for export markets than do domestic firms. They generally form part of a multinational group or network of affiliates which has greater experience and broader exposure to worldwide competitive markets than do domestic enterprises. Since foreign firms are able to apply these skills to exports from developing countries, they export relatively more than domestic firms. Moreover, the higher the marketing entry barrier and the more distant or sophisticated the market of destination, the more pronounced is the advantage of the foreign firms.

Comprehensive data recently released by the U.S. Department of Commerce and reported in a study performed for The Council for Latin America[14] provide evidence of the impact foreign firms have had in developing manufactured exports from the region. Manufacturing affiliates of U.S. multinational firms accounted for almost two-thirds of the increase in exports of manufactured goods from Latin America in the decade between 1957 and 1966. Their exports increased 704.8%, from $83 million to $668 million, during this period, while domestic firms increased their exports by only 51.0%.

A better idea of the role played by foreign firms in the export process can be obtained from Table 4. In 1966 total value added by all U.S. affiliates in Latin America accounted for only 6.76% of the region's gross domestic product, while their share of total exports was 35.0%. A similar relationship exists for manufactured goods alone. U.S. affiliates accounted for 9.5% of Latin America's gross manufacturing value added, while their share of manufactured exports was 41.4%.

Further analysis of the data in Table 4 provides interesting insights into the activities of foreign subsidiaries in the region. A measurement of the relative importance of foreign firms in the export sector is provided in the comparison of the percentage participation of foreign firms in export markets with their participation in the economy as a whole.[15] This index (RXI) can be obtained at various levels of aggregation ranging from an overall index for all economic activities to that for any given industrial sector. The RXI index for all economic activities throughout Latin America (5.19) is somewhat larger than the index for the manufacturing sector (4.35). The key to this discrepancy must lie in the nature of foreign investment in Latin America.

Most foreign investment in nonmanufacturing activities is in either extractive industries or agricultural production.[16] These

Table 4. U.S. Affiliates' Participation in Latin America's Economic Activity, 1966
(millions of dollars)

	All Economic Activities	Manufacturing[a]	Nonmanufacturing
Gross domestic production	$94,203		
Gross industrial value added		$22,346	$6,019
Sales by U.S. affiliates: total	$12,567	$6,548	
Less: Current expenditures for material, supplies and services	6,202	4,424	1,778
Value added: wages and salaries, taxes, depreciation, and income (A)	$ 6,365	$ 2,124	$ 4,241
Percentage participation (A)	6.76%	9.50%	—
Total exports	$12,830	$ 1,613	$11,217
Total exports by U.S. affiliates (B)	4,497	668	3,829
Percentage participation (B)	35.05%	41.41%	34.14%
Relative export importance index (B/A)	5.19	4.35	—

(a) Includes only ISIC (International Standard Industrial Classification) classifications 2 and 3.

SOURCES: United Nations, *Statistical Yearbook*, 1968, and IMF, *International Financial Statistics*. U.S. Department of Commerce preliminary data. Taken from Herbert K. May, *The Effects of United States and Other Foreign Investment in Latin America*, a report for The Council for Latin America, New York, January 1970.

investments are often made with the intention of serving export markets, whether they be home or third country markets. This fact is demonstrated by the data in Table 4. Exports by nonmanufacturing U.S. subsidiaries represent 63.5% of their total sales. On the other hand, exports by manufacturing subsidiaries represent only 10.2% of their total sales. This difference reflects the fact that, in contrast with firms active in extractive industries and agricultural production, most foreign firms engaged in manufacturing activities in the countries under consideration entered originally for import-substitution.

Foreign manufacturing affiliates show a higher propensity to export than domestic firms, as evidenced by the RXI index. Since most foreign manufacturing subsidiaries in these countries were originally established primarily to substitute local production for imports, a situation that also applies to most domestic manufacturing firms, there is little reason to suspect that major differences exist between domestic and foreign firms regarding their principal commitment to domestic markets. The advantage of foreign firms in exporting manufactured goods seems to be the result of a greater ability in international markets, and not the result of differences in the original motivation for the investment.

But the higher the marketing entry barrier characterizing the product, the higher is the foreign firm's advantage in export markets. Data obtained from 32 industrial sectors and subsectors in Colombia (Table 5) provide strong corroboration of this view. While foreign firms are responsible for 49.8% of the exports of those industrial sectors included in group I, they account for 80.6% and 90.2%, respectively, of all exports among groups II and III.

However, such a comparison is not sufficient since it does not take into account the relative participation of foreign firms in the total production of each group of sectors. Column C in Table 5 gives a measure of the relative export importance index for all three groups. Group II sectors show a substantially higher index than group I. While foreign firms among group II sectors accounted for a slightly larger percentage of national production than group I foreign firms (31.2% vs. 30.0%) their contribution in the export sector was substantially higher (80.6% vs. 49.8%). The RXI

Jose R. de la Torre, Jr.

Table 5. Foreign Subsidiaries' Participation in Export Activity:
Colombia—32 Industrial Sectors, 1968

| Industrial Sectors Classified by Their Products' Marketing Entry Barrier | Production[a] | | Exports[b] | | | Relative Export Importance Index (C=B/A) |
	Total Volume (millions)	% Participation by Foreign Firms (A)	Total Volume (thousands)	Volume by Foreign Firms (thousands)	% Participation by Foreign Firms (B)	
I. Negligible	$392.0	30.0%	$26,126	$13,004	49.8%	1.66
II. Moderate	203.3	31.2	5,481	4,422	80.6	2.58
III. Great	90.8	71.3	3,207	2,893	90.2	1.27
Total	$686.2	35.8%	$34,813	$20,319	58.4%	1.63

[a] Production data relate to 1964, the most recent year for which detailed component data were available.
[b] Export data relate to 1968.

SOURCES: Banco de la Republica, Fondo de Promocion de Exportaciones, *Informes No. 7 y 8,—1968,* Bogota, Febrero 1969.

Estimates by Oficina de Planeacion Nacional, Office of the Presidency of the Republic.

Departamento Administrativo Nacional de Estadisticas, *Anuario General de Estadisticas—1964,* Bogota, 1967.

index for foreign firms in group III sectors, however, is lower than for the other two groups. This result appears to contradict the hypothesis that foreign firms perform increasingly better in the export field the higher the marketing entry barrier.

Various explanations can be offered for this apparent contradiction. Perhaps most fundamental is the fact that the percentage of foreign participation in any sector of economic activity is higher at the higher marketing entry barrier levels. When the original premises of the analytical model are considered, this should not come as a surprise. The conditions which require that superior market knowledge and marketing skills be brought to bear on the problems of exporting goods which are highly differentiated are also present in producing and marketing within the domestic market. As a result, those industrial sectors which are characterized by high marketing inputs will, in all likelihood, have a tendency toward domination by firms which possess considerable marketing experience.[17] Given this high foreign incidence among group III sectors (the denominator in the formula above), the RXI index will necessarily result in a low value.

But the model also indicates other reasons, not totally unrelated, for such dominance. Both the product life cycle model and the requirements of a product differentiation strategy imply that a certain degree of industrial concentration or oligopolistic behavior characterizes industries with high marketing barrier to entry. While no attempt is made here to determine causality or prove any such proposition, others have shown that some correlation exists between oligopolistic conditions and high product differentiation.[18] Accordingly, oligopolistic industries will have a tendency to extend their activities to world markets on the same basis that they compete in their domestic markets.[19]

The in-depth interviews provided further evidence of the differences in export behavior between domestic (Table 2) and foreign (Table 6) firms. The observed differences were consistent with the findings reported above and lend further support to the argument that foreign firms will have relatively higher indices of export performance with respect to domestic firms the higher the marketing entry barrier.

Table 6. Marketing Factors and Export Behavior of Foreign Subsidiaries

Measures of Export Behavior	% of Firms in Each Marketing Behavior Category that Fell into the Particular Export Behavior Class[a]			
	I. Negligible	*II. Moderate*	*III. Great*	*All Firms*
A. *Export intensity*[b]				
0%–10%	25%	40%	50% (1)	35%
10%–25%	38	20	—	25
25%–50%	12	—	—	5
More than 50%	25	40	50 (1)	35
	100%	100%	100%	100%
No. of firms responding	8	10	2	20
B. *Export growth*[c]				
Negative	20%	29	—%	23%
0%–20%	20	14	100 (1)	23
More than 20%	60	57	—	54
	100%	100%	100%	100%
No. of firms responding	5	7	1	13

(see footnotes on page 253)

Table 6 (Continued)

Measures of Export Behavior	% of Firms in Each Marketing Behavior Category that Fell into the Particular Export Behavior Class[a]			
	I. Negligible	*II. Moderate*	*III. Great*	*All Firms*
C. *Source of initiative for export decision*				
Within subsidiary	50%	35%	—%	36%
Parent company	33	35	33 (1)	34
External	17	30	67 (2)	30
—foreign buyer	12%	20%	—%	14%
—government	6	10	67 (2)	16
	100%	100%	100%	100%
No. of firms responding	9	10	3	22
D. *Proximity factors in first export market*				
Bordering	89%	60%	—%	64%
Intermediate	—	10	—	5
Distant	11	30	100 (3)	32
	100%	100%	100%	100%
No. of firms responding	9	10	3	22

Table 6 (Continued)

% of Firms in Each Marketing Behavior Category that Fell into the Particular Export Behavior Class[a]

Measures of Export Behavior	I. Negligible	II. Moderate	III. Great	All Firms
E. *Export markets*[d]				
Regional[e]	88%	70%	67% (2)	76%
Rest of Latin America	75	40	33 (1)	52
United States	75	40	100 (3)	62
Other developed	62	40	33 (1)	48
Other	50	10	33 (1)	29
No. of firms responding	8	10	3	21

F. *Level of control over marketing channels*[f]

(differentiating between domestic and export markets)

	I. Negligible Dom. mkt.	I. Negligible Exp. mkt.	II. Moderate Dom. mkt.	II. Moderate Exp. mkt.	III. Great Dom. mkt.	III. Great Exp. mkt.	All Firms Dom. mkt.	All Firms Exp. mkt.
High	22%	22%	50%	10%	100% (3)	—%	45%	14%
Intermediate	22	33	12	10	—	33 (1)	15	23
Low	56	45	38	80	—	67 (2)	40	64
	100%	100%	100%	100%	100%	100%	100%	100%
No. of firms responding	9	9	8	10	3	3	20	22

Table 6 (Continued)

Measures of Export Behavior	% of Firms in Each Marketing Behavior Category that Fell into the Particular Export Behavior Class[a]			
	I. Negligible	*II. Moderate*	*III. Great*	*All Firms*
G. *Changes in level of control over channels*[f] (toward a:)				
Higher level	44%	—%	—%	19%
No change	33	44	—	33
Lower level	22	56	100 (3)	48
	100%	100%	100%	100%
No. of firms responding	9	9	3	21

[a] The absolute numbers are provided in parentheses for the group III firms, since there were only a small number.

[b] Export sales as a percentage of total sales.

[c] Average yearly compounded rate of growth for 1965–1968 period.

[d] Percentages may add to more than 100 because of multiple answers.

[e] Represents exports to those countries formally associated with the exporting country through regional integration agreements.

[f] See text for explanation of control levels.

Source: Interviews.

Conclusions

The central theme of this paper has been that marketing factors play a critical role in establishing the conditions that determine suitability of a manufactured product for export from developing countries. Products characterized by a high degree of product differentiation require the application of more skills and knowledge in the export effort than is the case for those with low or no product differentiation. Since these marketing skills and knowledge are relatively scarce resources in developing countries, these countries perform less well in exporting highly differentiated products than in exporting products with negligible marketing entry barriers.

Individual firms are ultimately responsible for the performance of their products in export markets, and varying degrees of marketing skills are likely to prevail from firm to firm. As a result, export performance is bound to differ among different types of firms. Foreign firms, because of their membership in a multinational group or network of affiliates, have greater access to the required market information, distribution channels, and marketing skills for export markets than do domestic firms. Therefore, foreign subsidiaries export relatively more than domestic enterprises. And this higher level of export performance is more pronounced the higher the marketing entry barrier of the product and the more distant or sophisticated the market of destination.

Marketing factors clearly are not the only determinants of export performance. Neoclassical and product life cycle models provide other variables, such as product maturity and labor content, that significantly affect export performance. Data from the interviews also revealed the multivariate and complex nature of the problem.[20] What this research shows is that marketing factors need to be considered as important variables when policies are being evaluated to promote exports of manufactures from developing countries. Specifically, the findings of this research have direct relevance to two broad policy areas: strategy formulation in the multinational firm and economic planning in developing countries.

Recently, U.S. firms, faced with increasing competition at home from producers in other countries, have begun to search for lower cost locations for their manufacturing activities.[21] These so-called "off-shore" manufacturing facilities have been established in developing countries and could be the first real indication of the full closing of the product life cycle theory. Taiwan, Hong Kong, South Korea, and other Asian locations have thus far experienced most of this activity, but Latin American countries increasingly are being considered as possible "off-shore" locations.[22]

This research indicates that multinational firms are in a very favorable position to exploit some of the opportunities that are being created for exports from developing countries. Where marketing considerations play an important role, multinational firms have an advantage over domestic enterprises. They have the necessary marketing experience, market knowledge, and established marketing channels in their home markets, as well as in other countries in which they operate, to market manufactures made by any one of their subsidiaries on a world-wide basis. Where political, economic, and trade limitations are not prohibitive, these firms can follow a production location policy that reflects the maturity and marketing characteristics of their products. In the most advanced nations they would produce, for internal consumption and for export, high technology new products. As products mature and production costs become critical for survival, locations in developing countries would become ideally suited for world-wide production. For those products where differentiation is important a major role remains for the multinational enterprise.

The poorer performance of domestic firms in the export sector is not suggested as a sign of business incompetence on the part of the local entrepreneur. His behavior is entirely rational given the environmental and information constraints under which he is operating. A government, intent on promoting manufactured exports, may be able to assist local firms in overcoming these constraints by extending the argument for infant industry protection to the export sector. By providing subsidies to export activity (commensurate with import-substitution-industrialization benefits) and by designing programs to increase the amount of information available about export opportunities, the returns and risks of export business may be brought in line with those prevailing in the domestic sector.

If developing countries are to succeed in promoting exports of manufactures, they must be conscious of the role that foreign investment can play in the process. The evidence suggests that multinational firms can provide an important contribution to developing countries, not to mention their own profits, through their capacity for export development. Because of its access to export markets, a foreign subsidiary may continue to justify whatever cost it represents to the host country long after the benefits from the initial contributions of capital and technology have passed.

1 The theory is commonly known for the name of two of its early proponents: E. F. Heckscher, "The Effects of Foreign Trade on the Distribution of Income," American Economic Association, *Readings in the Theory of International Trade*, Blakiston Co., Philadelphia, 1949; and B. Ohlin, *Interregional and International Trade*, Harvard Economic Studies, Vol. XXXIX, Cambridge, Massachusetts, 1933.

2 Many of the issues raised in this section are derived from a study of twenty manufacturing industries in the U.S. reported by Joe S. Bain in *Barriers to New Competition*, Harvard University Press, Cambridge, 1956.

3 *Ibid.*, p. 127.

4 *Ibid.*, pp. 128–129.

5 Many firms in this last category which export to the U.S. market have capitalized on the foreign origin of their products in order to differentiate them from domestic competition. This is the case with typewriters (Olivetti), liquor (Scotch whiskey), and automobiles (Volkswagen).

6 Of course, the manufacturer could rely entirely on an importer to perform all the necessary marketing functions. In that case, the hypothesis could be modified to include exports of high marketing barrier products provided that foreign assistance takes place in the process. This alternative is explored in more detail in the next section.

7 The rationale for an index, while unnecessary in this example, derives from the possibility of comparing export propensity factors for similar sectors in various countries.

8 If agricultural industries are excluded from total industrial production the 32 sample sectors account for 39.5% of the balance.

9 Similar propositions linking the export markets to proximity have been repeatedly tested in the literature. See, for example, Hans Linnemann, *An Econometric Study of International Trade Flows*, Amsterdam, North Holland, 1966; and William H. Gruber and Raymond Vernon, "The R&D Factor in a World Trade Matrix," in Vernon (ed.) *The Technology Factor in International Trade*, National Bureau of Economic Research (New York: Columbia University Press, 1970).

10 Percentages add to more than 100 because of multiple answers in four cases.

11 The differentiation made between high-control and low-control channels was based on whether the manufacturer had any direct control over the final sale to the consumer. Obviously, company stores were highly con-

trolled channels where the manufacturer could directly influence the nature of the seller-buyer relationship. Private branding or the use of a manufacturer's agent would rank at the low-control end of the spectrum.

12 The criteria for determining control levels among export channels were similar to those utilized for domestic channels. Operating retail outlets or sales organizations in export markets were considered as the highest control level, the use of an export firm as the lowest level, and an active local distributor as the middle range.

13 A broader coverage of the issues raised in this section and of the strategic considerations affecting the export decision in the multinational firm can be found in Jose R. de la Torre, "The Role of the Multinational Firm in Promoting Manufactured Exports from Developing Countries," in Eliezer Ayal (ed.), *Micro Aspects of Development*, University of Illinois Press (forthcoming).

14 Herbert K. May, *The Effects of United States and Other Foreign Investment in Latin America*, a report for The Council for Latin America, New York, January 1970.

15 An index (RXI) was obtained according to the formula,

$$RXI = \frac{\% \text{ foreign participation in the export sector}}{\% \text{ foreign participation in total economic activity}}$$

16 For 1966, Department of Commerce data presented in the May report reveal that 61.4% of the outstanding investment at year end in Latin America by nonmanufacturing affiliates belongs to petroleum, mining, and smelting affiliates. These same firms accounted for 77.8% of estimated total sales of nonmanufacturing affiliates.

17 A good example is provided by the detergent industry. In most countries this industry is in the hands of the three international giants, Colgate-Palmolive, Procter & Gamble, and Unilever. This situation prevails in spite of the fact that the technology for detergent production is readily available and capital requirements are low ($200,000 will suffice for an optimal size plant). A Harvard Business School case series on the detergent industry in Central America (BP–817, 820, 822, and 825) illustrates the difficulties encountered by one domestic producer when faced with competition from the much more experienced international firms.

18 Verification of the existence of correlation between product differentiation and industry concentration is presented in William S. Comanor and Thomas S. Wilson, "Advertising Market Structure and Performance," *The Review of Economics and Statistics*, Vol. XLIX, November 1967.

In addition, most of Bain's examples of industries with high product differentiation appear also to be oligopolistic in nature, e.g., automobile, farm machinery, office equipment, cigarettes, etc. However, not all oligopolistic industries practice product differentiation, e.g., steel, copper, paper, synthetic fibers, etc.

19 Preliminary results obtained by Frederick T. Knickerbocker in connection with his dissertation research, "Oligopolistic Reaction and Multinational Enterprise," unpublished manuscript, Harvard Business School, April 1970, tend to support this view.

20 For example, capacity utilization, defined as the percentage of the firm's full-time productive capacity in use at the time, showed a strong negative correlation with export performance. These data suggested that a firm would not turn to export markets as long as its home market (usually more lucrative due to import-substitution benefits and protection) could absorb the firm's output.

In addition, Hal B. Lary, *Imports of Manufactures from Less Developed Countries*, National Bureau of Economic Research, Columbia University Press, 1968, shows the validity of the labor content argument.

21 The new trend in this direction, while quite meager at this point, is becoming noticeable. See Nathaniel H. Leff, "Investment in the LDCs: The Next Wave," *Columbia Journal of World Business*, November–December 1969.

22 Over 75% of all foreign subsidiaries in the sample were engaged in exports to their parent company market.